You Wake Me Each Morning

You Wake Me Each Morning

The Final Chapter

Connie Lawn

iUniverse®

YOU WAKE ME EACH MORNING
THE FINAL CHAPTER

iUniverse books may be ordered through booksellers or by contacting:

iUniverse
1663 Liberty Drive
Bloomington, IN 47403
www.iuniverse.com
1-800-Authors (1-800-288-4677)

ISBN: 978-1-4917-5327-9 (sc)
ISBN: 978-1-4917-5328-6 (e)

Printed in the United States of America.

iUniverse rev. date: 11/20/2014

Acknowledgements

I want to give special thanks to my parents and my boys, David and Daniel, and my husband Charles Sneiderman, who have given me love, patience, and something special to live for. Thanks also to Jack Farmer for the special assistance regarding Lebanon, and for making me realize I can strive much harder, and live life with greater intensity. Thank you to my lifetime friend, Marilyn Lowenberg-Goldstein, who helped me to finally appreciate my childhood days in New Jersey! Thanks to those who have given invaluable help in editing and publishing: Mark Bathurst, and Joyce McDowell. And thank all who have helped me in this glorious career.

Connie Lawn

Contents

The Mud of Washington

It was the summer of 1968, and I must have looked strange, even by sixties standards, in my gleaming white hard hat with a steel antenna swaying from its crown. I was the only field reporter covering Resurrection City. This huge demonstration, built by several thousand poor rural blacks who wanted to raise the consciousness of Americans to their poverty and lack of real job opportunities, was situated on the picturesque Mall in the heart of Washington, D.C. I was reporting from Resurrection City for WAVA, which was then the only all-news radio station in the D.C. area. In fact, it was probably the first all-news station in the world. In those days, to transmit live to the base station, I carried a mobile unit weighing 50 pounds; the hat and antenna were part of the outfit.

The huge tent city built by the poor had become a sea of mud, nestled between the Washington and Lincoln Monuments. So rubber hip boots were my wardrobe accessories, despite the fact that it gets pretty hot on a Washington summer day. The paraphernalia I carried became increasingly heavy as I sloshed around in the muck, so I asked some of the "brothers" to help me carry the equipment. I even promised them: "If you're nice to me, I'll let you fondle my antenna."

They weren't particularly tempted by the prospect of a lust-crazed antenna, but they were in fact extremely helpful to me. I was, incidentally, one of the few white reporters spared a dunking in the Reflecting Pool, which was in the center of their encampment.

The "city" of several thousand poor blacks was policed by the Tent City Rangers of Chicago and other militant gangs from across the country. In fact, the gangs were so tough that several branches of the local police (District Police, Park Police, Capital Police, and so on) were nervous about setting foot inside the crowded, muddy, bug-infested compound. But no one ever threatened me, or attempted to molest or harm me. That's more than I can say about a lot of politicians on Capitol Hill, or news directors I've known in nearly forty years in this business!

I did have a close call one night, however. I was scheduled to leave Resurrection City each night at 5:30, crossing Memorial Bridge to lily-white Rosslyn, Virginia, to deliver a "wrap-up" on the day's activities. One night, my "hosts" decided I'd learn more if I spent the night with them. I tried to convey this subtly to my news director, Pete Gamble.

ME: "This is Mobile Unit K I Y 549 calling Base Station."
HE: "Where the hell are you? You're late for your [expletive deleted] report."
ME: "I'm a guest of the bosses at Tent City."
HE: "You'll lose your job if you don't get your ass back here."
ME: "I'm having a great time and can't leave."
HE: (after a long pause, and in a voice the whole encampment could hear) "Are those goddamn holligans keeping you prisoner?"

At that point, one of the muscle-bound Tent City Rangers grabbed the microphone and gave Pete a tongue-lashing in words neither of us "honkies" had heard in our whole life.

The moment passed, and I spent what turned out to be a harmless if somewhat muddy night with thousands of impoverished demonstrators from across the country. My initial wariness became outright terror when one of the Rangers hurled me into a tent. I braced for the worst, but it never came. Most of the demonstrators treated me with respect, and were much more focused on talking to me about their grievances and the suffering in their lives than they were in harming me. We spent the night in conversation, and I learned more about black society in those few short hours than I ever had growing up in a racially mixed town and attending a rough, integrated school system.

The plight of the campers was indeed tragic, and I believe their demonstration did much to focus the country's attention on their problems. But little of that sympathy was evident when the local police forces managed to shut down Resurrection City a few weeks later.

That happened on the day the men and boys marched up to Capitol Hill to demonstrate and lobby their Congressmen. This gave the police an opportunity to move in and gather up the women and children. In some cases, billy clubs and tear gas were used with grim determination, in violent assaults rivaled only by the U.S. Cavalry against the Indians a century earlier.

I almost missed the bloody closing of Tent City. Earlier, I had parked my car in a motel parking lot across from the WAVA studios. When I went out to retrieve it, I discovered that the police had towed it away. In my frantic rush to get to the scene of the action, I flagged down a businessman commuting to work on a motorcycle and insisted he give me a ride. What a sight we were - he in his business suit, clutching an attache case, me looking like some avant-garde Martian in my hard hat with steel antenna, hip boots, and mobile unit. Nevertheless, the police - no doubt rendered temporarily stunned by our audacity - let us cross the lines at Tent City.

Two days later, after it was all over, I went back to Rosslyn Virginia, located my car and managed to steal it from the police lot. I had an extra set of keys, and simply drove my car over a log which served as a barrier. Surprisingly, I never heard from them again, and never paid a fine.

By that time, of course, the police had on their minds a lot more than my repossessed car. Washington and its suburbs again were erupting in racial warfare. In fact, the policemen's rage against Resurrection City was partially a reflection of the pent-up anger they harbored against many of the blacks. These incendiary elements had simmered since the aftermath of the April 1968 assassination of Dr. Martin Luther King,

Jr. It was a scary time, when major riots exploded in many American cities. Washington was among the hardest hit. Sporadically, over the seemingly endless summer, minor uprisings developed. I found myself in the midst of one - perhaps I was even the cause of it.

The trouble began at 14th and U Streets, an area in the center of the black ghetto, which was the wellspring of many local riots. The corner had become a gathering place because the offices of the Southern Christian Leadership Conference, or SCLC, were located there. When sparks started flying, and the simmer threatened to escalate to a boil, my news director sent me to 14th and U. I reported live from the location, noting that an angry cluster of people was milling about, eager to stir up some action. I was concerned the broadcast would exacerbate the situation, which it did.

Within minutes, the group had swelled to twenty, then thirty, and then into the hundreds. I definitely stood out, with my white skin, red hair, and antenna. About that time, the charismatic black civil rights leader, Jesse Jackson, arrived on the scene. This was years before he would become the first major black Presidential candidate, but even then he could mesmerize and control an audience. He stood up on a truck, and began his hypnotic chant: "I am ... a MAN ... I am SOMEBODY." Hundreds joined in and were broadcast live on our radio station, WAVA.

The crowd continued to boil, as did their sense of power and anger. Finally, Jackson realized my presence was making the crowd grow larger and madder. He glared down at me from the truck and announced, "You goddamn bitch, you're making it worse!" He then had me picked up and thrown bodily into the SCLC headquarters. From my vantage point inside the building, I had a clear view of the violence and rioting which ensued. Unfortunately, I made the situation worse by continuing the broadcasts; a consequence which is an inherent dilemma of my profession. In any case, by expelling me from the demonstration and banishing me to that building, Jesse saved my life - whether he meant to or not. For that, I will always be grateful to him, regardless of whether I agree with his philosophy, or with the scandals which later engulfed him, such as having a baby out of wedlock with a young assistant who was not his wife.

The Snows of New Hampshire: Where It All Began

A few weeks after the long summer of 1968, I left WAVA. The parting was not an amicable one, but I had to do it, after an editor pressured me to stay in Washington, and not finish my campaign on "the trial."

I had started in this business by camping out all over the country, and it was a source of pride to me to always be where my dateline said I was - Indianapolis; Eau Claire, Wisconsin; Grand Island, Nebraska; or Manchester, New Hampshire. After a summer at WAVA, some junior editors said they needed me in Washington, but directed me to cover the Republican National Convention in Florida and the Democratic National Convention in Chicago - all from the studios in Virginia. To make my reports sound authentic, I was to phone them in from the next room. I regarded this as unethical, but was too green at the broadcast game to protest. I did conclude one report that way, signing off, "Connie Lawn in Miami Beach." It would have been ethical had I done the same report and signed off, "Washington, D.C.," but the orders were to say Florida. I wish I had taken the matter to the owner, Art Arundel, at that point. But, I was scared and inexperienced, and did not know what to do. I sensed this was wrong, but did not know how to combat it. I am certain he would have vetoed the instructions.

Right after signing off from Miami Beach, I was sent to cover a Washington, D.C., City Council meeting. The president of the Council, John Hechinger, was surprised to see me. He exclaimed, "I thought you were in Florida!" When I explained what had happened, he insisted it was illegal, and threatened to investigate the status of the station's license. That confirmed my own feelings and vindicated my reluctance to mislead my audience as to my location.

Moreover, I had covered every primary in the '68 campaign and was standing next to Robert F. Kennedy when he was shot in Los Angeles. I also conducted one of the last interviews with him. My three days and nights of non-stop coverage were broadcast on WAVA, and gave us some of the widest exposure in Washington. I was very emotionally involved in this presidential race and did not want to miss the Democratic Convention. So I went back to our studio at night and prerecorded some women's features, which were due at the end of each day (that format was ethical, since it was clear I was not doing the show live). Next, I bought some plane tickets and flew off to the infamous Chicago convention, claiming the WAVA credentials when I arrived. The station had never paid me for my long hours of overtime, or for my coverage of the Bobby Kennedy assassination, so I considered us even.

My career as a journalist actually began in the snows of New Hampshire in January 1968. Fresh out of college, I had worked very hard landing a job on Capitol Hill, the site of the U.S. Congress. I finally wrangled a job, after spending months walking down endless corridors, past countless heavy wooden doors marked with signs like "Senator from Alaska", "Congressman from Florida," and so on.

Even today, many young people, dewy-eyed with ambition and idealism, set out as I did for Capitol Hill in search of a job from which they expect glamour, excitement, and lots of elbow-rubbing with the mighty and powerful, whose names - casually injected into cocktail conversation - are fodder for impressing friends. The reality, however, is that for the inexperienced - as I was then - Hill jobs can entail stupefying hours of menial tasks like typing and filing. Those jobs are essential, of course, and are an important part of running the legislative machinery; but they are not my forte, and definitely not what I had in mind. At the same time, I realized that several of my girlfriends, who had graduated from Radcliff (now Harvard) and Harvard Law

School, had congressional jobs not much better than mine. Clearly, Capitol Hill was not where my future lay, and I decided to direct my ambitions elsewhere.

My departure from the Hill came somewhat sooner than expected when, one Friday morning, I walked in on one of my bosses, a congressman, in the private bathroom of our offices. He hadn't locked the door and was sitting on the toilet, reading a newspaper. The impressions that stick in my mind are the look of shock on his face and the cute garters he wore on his socks. Two days following the incident, on a Sunday, his secretary phoned me long distance from Rhode Island to tell me not to show up for work the next day!

At least the timing was good. I had attended a Capitol Hill party the night before, and had seen a sign-up sheet for volunteers to go to New Hampshire to help Senator Eugene McCarthy campaign for President. That state's contest was the first in a long string of Presidential primaries. I knew little about the man, and my own anti-Vietnam War views were just beginning to take shape. It seemed to me a reasonable idea to campaign for a man whose platform included getting American troops out of Vietnam. So on Monday, newly fired from my short-lived Hill job, I signed up for the campaign. Instead of typing bottomless stacks of letters to constituents, I found myself on a filthy, overcrowded bus bound for New Hampshire.

It was bitterly cold when we arrived the next day. We were assigned to go from door to door, asking residents to sign petitions and urging them to vote for McCarthy in the primary. I saw myself as a crusader on a noble mission, and I had the battle wounds to prove it. My fingers became frostbitten from hours of traipsing about in the frozen neighborhoods, and for years afterward, residual pain on extremely cold days evoked memories of the experience.

At night, we slept on the floors of local churches. I became adept at snatching pillows from the church pews. Enduring the rigors of campaigning in a New Hampshire winter made for a very strange experience for a girl like me with a fairly traditional upbringing, who had expected to be married and starting a family at the ripe old age of 22 (an age which I now believe is far too young for marriage).

The McCarthy people did not go out of their way to make life any easier for the volunteers. The campaign was run by a very ill-tempered press secretary, Seymour Hersh, later a best-selling author who is perhaps best known as the nemesis of Henry Kissinger. He was flanked by a tough and ruthless assistant, Mary Lou Oakes, who was only a tad nicer than Ghengis Khan. Their hardline pragmatism was probably a necessary counter to the gentle mysticism of Gene McCarthy, but it also did little to endear the Senator and his mission to his volunteers, the public, or the media.

One glaring example of their stand-offish style stands out in my mind. A blind, talented young student from Harvard Law School named Hal Krents drove up to New Hampshire to offer his services. Hal, a man of wit and courage who later inspired the play, "Butterflies Are Free," was a superb musician who wrote such songs as "There Aren't Any Dirty Books in Braille. He made the three-hour drive from Boston to New Hampshire, equipped to sing and play on his guitar songs he had written especially for the campaign. According to Hal's friends, he compounded his sacrifice by allegedly driving part of the way himself, through the snowy mountain roads of New Hampshire. His fellow law students swore, deadpan, that even though Hal was blind, he'd had to drive because they were all ill, suffering from high fevers. They said they'd told him which way to twist the wheel and when to brake the car.

Hal's musical creations were a morale-booster, and did much to relax and inspire the overworked volunteers who heard them. But they went unappreciated by the Senator's staff, who gave Hal and his friends the cold shoulder and never even considered using the songs. That kind of attitude was a marked contrast to the way the Kennedy people treated their friends and reporters, and helped Bobby Kennedy overtake Gene McCarthy's campaign a few months later.

Nevertheless, my experiences in the campaign proved invaluable. After three weeks working in the McCarthy camp, I wrote a detailed newspaper article about the zealous young army of volunteers and their efforts to win the hearts and minds of the New Hampshire populace. I sent the article out to several newspapers across the country, and weeks later I was told by friends familiar with the piece that it had been published in a few places. But local reporters in those towns had changed my name to theirs. They had even used the New Hampshire dateline, although they were nowhere near New England! That experience soured me on newspapers for good, and I turned my attention to radio and television

A friendly network radio engineer helped me select a cheap tape recorder and showed me how to use "alligator clips." The clips are actually a wire which is slipped into an outlet from your tape recorder. The other end has two jacks, which clip onto the metal jacks inside the mouthpiece of the phone. Of course, you first have to dismantle that mouthpiece to get to them. Only then can you transmit the sound from your tape recorder to an audio engineer in a studio anywhere in the world. There it is recorded for later use on the air.

This method cuts out any excess noise behind you, when you are transmitting a voice or "actuality." You can also broadcast from your microphone the same way, and the sound is enhanced by the amplification device in your tape recorder. In those early days of the cheap, portable cassette tape recorders, Sony had perfected the equipment so that broadcasts could be delivered smoothly. For this reason Sony soon overtook its competitors, and drove many of them out of the radio news business. The company's technological breakthrough also enabled many new journalists like me to break into broadcasting. Before, it would have been much too expensive, and the equipment too cumbersome.

I found it very easy to write short, colorful radio reports, because I had heard them all my life. In addition, I listened very carefully to the style of other reporters whom I admired, and imitated their techniques. My first piece was sold to Westinghouse Broadcasting in New York. Later, the editor of the all-news radio station there got fired for using my story without authorization.

I soon convinced all the networks to let me sell them "actuality" or the voice of Senator McCarthy. In those early days, his campaign was not well covered. A reporter assigned to him usually placed top priority on television, and radio was merely an afterthought. Soon, I was selling actuality and, in some cases, reports to Westinghouse, Metromedia, ABC, NBC, CBS, UPI-Audio, and the Canadian Broadcasting Company. NBC even allowed me to do features for their "Monitor" radio series. Most of these organizations were honest, and eventually paid me. However, I did have the misfortune of hooking up with one called "Radio News Overseas," or a variation of that name. Other freelancers who knew I was working for them warned me I would never get paid, but I was too ambitious - and perhaps too naive - to believe them. Alas, they were right, and RNO got several thousand dollars' worth of my work from all over the country free of charge. This experience gave whole new meaning - for me, at least - of the term "freelance."

I was crushed when I realized the news director - a guy I thought was such a nice, honest boy from New York - had lied to me and had never intended to pay me. At one point, I approached New York Attorney General Louis Lefkowitz about the situation. He told me there were several complaints about the organization and suggested we all get together and sue. Unfortunately, none of us had the time or money to wage a lawsuit, and RNO got away with their duplicity. This was to be the first of several times I would be cheated by radio organizations - all of them, it so happens, headquartered in New York. These occasions left a bad taste in my mouth for New York-based stations. I never took any of them to court, although I believe I would have won a lawsuit. Part of the reason is that other reporters advised me not to, saying, "Don't do it. You'll become known as a troublemaker and will never be hired." I now think their advice was wrong, but at the time it was difficult to know what path to take.

All in all, however, radio turned out to be far better for me than newspapers. Radio stations, I found, were voracious and could take much more material. They could not steal your piece (or your voice), but they could still misuse you, not pay you, or take advantage of a cub reporter desperately trying to gain experience and exposure.

Of course, it is the high points of radio that have kept me in the business for over forty years. It is a marvelous thing to create audio pictures. As an internationalist, it is a thrill to pick up the phone and instantly speak to people in Israel, New Zealand, or other far-off countries. And it was exciting to run into a store or a strange house, when you were rushing from a story, and frantically ask, "Do you have a phone I can unscrew?" Then you must rush to finish before the men in white coats come for you! It was less amusing when you have to make a mad dash for the press plane and leave the phone dismantled. In 1968, I became known as the "Black Tornado" who left phone parts dangling in homes from New Hampshire to California!

Now, technology has changed dramatically. The phone companies have outsmarted us, and we can no longer unscrew their phones. There are two ways to go – hi tech and expensive, or low tech. You can spend big money for a satellite phone, Skype, or an ISDN line, which are meant to give in-studio quality. On the other hand, most phones are now so good, you can broadcast directly into the receiver. If you have actuality, you can hold the phone over the tape recorder, and just transmit, if there is not too much noise around you. Or, you can just talk. Most of the pieces I now do are talk back, unless I am anchoring a news cast. I can phone from anywhere. Some of my best analysis and talk back pieces for the BBC, Australia, or New Zealand were transmitted from my favorite phone booth on the top of the Kennedy Center. I could look down at the Washington monuments at my feet; feel inspired, and convey a sense of history. Then, I could return to the play or concert I was attending. I think I like the good new days! In fact, I liked that location so much, I married my second husband, Charles Sneiderman. on the Kennedy Center Terrace, outside the phone booth, in May, 2000.

Go West

Radio reporting led me from New Hampshire to the other presidential primaries in Wisconsin, Indiana, Nebraska, Oregon, and California. I stayed with McCarthy for the first two primaries, but my heart was always with the Kennedys. (In fact, during my early liberal days, my goal had been to work with Bobby Kennedy on Capitol Hill, but all I was able to get was a bit of volunteer research work in his office.)

When Bobby Kennedy jumped into the race after McCarthy's spectacular success winning the New Hampshire primary, I hesitated for a time. His decision to join the fray reinforced his reputation as "ruthless," and did little to cement his friendship with Gene McCarthy. But Kennedy also looked like a man who could win on the "dump Lyndon Johnson - end the war" ticket.

Thus, for the next few months, I zigzagged between the political races of Kennedy and McCarthy and even spent some time covering the campaigns of Hubert Humphrey and Richard Nixon. Humphrey was very courteous and often invited me to fly on his Vice Presidential Lear jet, free of charge. (Traditionally, reporters pay one and a half times first class rates, when traveling with any candidate or official.) The only problem with Humphrey, who entered the contest after Lyndon Johnson was forced out by the antiwar sentiment, was his verbosity. One British reporter traveling with us said he was like a candy machine gone awry. You put in a nickel to get one candy bar. Instead, the candy kept coming, expelled from the machine.

Nixon, though interesting to cover, was cold and formal. In those days, before Bobby Kennedy was shot, most reporters thought Nixon didn't have a prayer of winning, and he was not the choice candidate to cover.

My decision to leave McCarthy for good came during the Wisconsin primary, after his evident disdain for the press corps was graphically demonstrated. We usually had trouble keeping up with the Senator, and were often intentionally directed to the wrong locations, so that we missed his appearances. One day, in Grand Island, Nebraska, he invited us to cover a cattle auction. The Senator paraded to the middle of the dirt arena, where he waved to the crowd of tough Westerners, and then fled in a hurry. We tailed behind him, but were forced by the Secret Service to stay several feet back.

Suddenly, we heard the proverbial thunder of hooves, and a herd of cows rushed into the arena. We ran for our lives, with the stampede a scant few paces behind us. McCarthy was in no danger, but we had a very close call. It's all right for politicians to hate the press, or to resent their ubiquitous press entourage. But it's an undeniable fact of life that they have to work with us if they want good media coverage. And wiping out one's press contingent is not an effective way to ensure a spot - much less sympathetic coverage - on nightly network news!

This episode was all I needed to act. I switched candidates in the next state, Indiana. Having little money, I rented a small broom closet (literally!) in a hotel on a main street in Indianapolis. All the candidates' headquarters were on this street, and it was an excellent way to gain an overview of their campaigns. My little closet overlooked the Kennedy headquarters, which was located above a movie theater; ironically, the film that month was "Camelot."

The hotel's charge for the broom closet was outright usury, and it became an extravagant luxury for me. I spent practically all the money I earned paying for airfare, and usually considered hotels an unnecessary expense. When I couldn't find a handy church floor, I was sometimes able to persuade the network engineers to let me stay in their "battery room." Often, they had rented some rooms in the hotel as a recharging area for their batteries. My companions in sleep were dozens of red and green lights blinking around me! Of course, I was offered many rooms to share with some of the lonely male correspondents, who ached for female companionship. But, that was a price I was not willing to pay.

Switching candidates provided me with some very poignant insights. On one occasion, Vice President Humphrey was visiting his family drugstore in Huron, South Dakota, with Bobby Kennedy scheduled to arrive a few hours later. I accompanied Humphrey and was moved to watch him standing at the old soda fountain counter, recounting how the men used to bat the breeze and talk politics in the old days. From those down-home gatherings, it was a natural progression for Humphrey to move into local and later national politics. Many of us listening to him opposed Humphrey, because his intense loyalty to Lyndon Johnson prevented him from criticizing the Vietnam War. But that experience at the drugstore, and a walk with him down Main Street, softened many of us and deepened our understanding of him as a man. Unfortunately, the general public never saw that side of him, and he lost the election because of his loyalty to his President, as well as the increasingly hysterical tone he adopted in the last weeks of the campaign.

I have another poignant memory of that visit, and it shows how disruptive a reporting career is to family life. Two of America's top political reporters, Richard Valeriani and Lee Hall, had their wedding anniversary that day. He was covering Humphrey, she, Kennedy. Richard learned I would be staying behind in Huron. He bought a present at Humphrey's pharmacy and asked me to give it to his wife when she arrived with Kennedy. I did so, happy to serve as a go-between Cupid on their anniversary. That type of separation, however, may have contributed to their divorce years later, as is too often the case in a mobile profession like reporting.

When Bobby Kennedy arrived in Humphrey's hometown, he was received less enthusiastically than Humphrey, the favorite son. Moreover, Kennedy had his own problems conveying a sense of warmth and humanity. The fact is that Kennedy was an extremely nervous man.

As my coverage of him became more frequent, I always managed to sit at his feet, near my tape recorder. My machine sat on the floor of the stage, with my cheap microphone attached to his mike. Most of the time, Kennedy's legs and feet shook so hard he caused my tape recorder to rattle. Bobby, sensitive to his diminutive stature, also preferred to have most of his body sheltered by a podium when he spoke. One time, he leaped onto a stage at Concordia College in Fort Wayne, Indiana, aghast to discover there was no podium. His face blanched. He turned desperately to the reporters and his staff, pleading, "Where's my podium? I can't work without a podium." We all felt an instant, overwhelming desire to help him. Finally, someone from the college staff managed to come up with a podium, and the show went on as usual.

Kennedy's orations were usually the same, as were those of most of the candidates. The only variations were the locations and reactions of the crowd. He would give about ten speeches a day, always ending with a quotation from George Bernard Shaw, who said, "Some men see things as they are and ask 'why'; others see things as they should be, and ask, 'Why not?'" The phrase was a signal for us to turn off our tapes and run like hell for the press bus or plane. The last-minute, mad scramble was particularly hard on Kennedy advisor and resident prankster Dick Tuck. He was in charge of rounding up Kennedy's black-and-white springer spaniel, Freckles. Someone once asked Tuck how a man with his distinguished background could stand it, baby-sitting for a dog in the midst of a grueling presidential campaign. He shot back, "It may be just a mutt to you, but he's an ambassadorship to me."

The Kennedy campaigns were really no joke for a dog, and poor Freckles - like the reporters and Kennedy supporters - often risked his life in the undertaking. One of the most obvious risks was the plane itself. Sometimes we took off and landed thirteen times a day. A giddy sigh of relief and a burst of applause accompanied each safe landing. Some of the planes - such as the old Purdue planes in the Midwest, which slanted sharply back toward the tail - were so dilapidated that there was serious concern about their airworthiness. It was small wonder the reporters made a beeline for the on-board bars the moment they climbed the ramp.

The crush of the crowds on the ground was often overwhelming. The Kennedys always attracted large, frenzied crowds, and covering them reminded one of being surrounded by fans waiting for Elvis Presley or the Beatles during their heyday. Even the toughest and most experienced reporters in the Kennedy press corps had trouble fighting their way to the front so they could hear and record the speeches. In those days, I became the crowd breaker for the pack. I had to get there and record the speech, because I had to sell it to make the money I needed to keep traveling with them. Unlike the others, I was the only reporter in the group who had no company to foot my bills. I fought so hard that no policeman or guard was able to keep me from my candidate. And about 20 other reporters would pour after me through the path I managed to break. Once, a male colleague said he had intended to help me bulldoze my way through the guards, but added, "You were so damn mean, I figured you'd do all right without our help!"

At the end of Bobby's speech, the crowd often surged forward to touch him, an experience that must have been painful for such a shy person. Many were the times I threw my body on top of my $28 tape recorder, to protect the valuable recording within from the surging masses. Once, in the Midwest, the enormous crowd could not be controlled. Panic ensued. Senator Kennedy, his wife and staff, reporters, and former astronaut and Senator John Glenn and his wife (who were campaigning for Kennedy) were crushed against a fence. The pressure was intense, and some of us were on the verge of suffocating. Fortunately, at the last minute, the fence collapsed, allowing us to flee and run for the cover of the airplane. We barely made it back alive, and the press bar was emptied faster than usual that afternoon.

Life With Bobby

I was not always a welcome figure on Bobby Kennedy's campaign plane or bus, and was by no means universally regarded as "one of the guys." I was, after all, the only free-lance reporter covering the Senator, and I didn't even have press credentials from anyone except Bobby himself. (We all wore badges around our necks proclaiming us members of the "Kennedy Press." Once, a top Kennedy staffer gave me one of the coveted "PT 109" gold pins to add to my press tag. These insignias were replicas of the patrol boat John F. Kennedy had commanded in the Pacific, and had special cachet among Kennedy followers.)

One morning, I got up especially early to cover Kennedy pressing the flesh at a factory. I had to awaken two hours earlier than my colleagues, to get my stories on the air before the press bus left. As I was about to board, Kennedy's press secretary, Frank Mankiewicz, tried to keep me off. He claimed there was no room, although I could see several empty seats. As I argued with him, Dave Breasted from the New York Daily News came to my defense. He pointed out that I was working my tail off and sending out more stories than many of the other reporters combined. Others jumped off the bus and concurred with Dave. So, despite Frank's short-lived power play, I was allowed to rejoin the "boys on the bus." But Frank and I had bitter relations after that, and the tensions between us were exacerbated by a favor the Senator began to grant me after each primary victory.

The television anchor man on Channel 9 in Washington, D.C., Tony Sylvester, asked me if I could manage to score a phone interview with Kennedy in time for the 11 p.m. news. I was flattered and excited by this chance to have my voice on television in Washington, - one of the country's top markets - and worked like hell on the assignment (for which I was never to be paid). Kennedy may have been aware of my quarrels with Frank, or perhaps he admired my independent spirit. Whatever the reason, he always gave me those interviews, even before he went downstairs to hold a press conference for the rest of the international and national media. Obviously, that increased the resentment some harbored against me.

This sympathetic and preferential treatment of me was the reason I was one of the many with Bobby Kennedy in his hotel suite in California, moments before Sirhan Sirhan shot him. So my phone interview with him, which was transmitted back to Washington (via radio this time), was one of the last exclusive ones done with him before his tragic assassination. It was nearly 3 a.m. in Washington when we did that interview, but the public's interest in this, the last primary, was so intense that most of the East Coast stations continued to broadcast live. Thus, most of the country saw the shooting on television, or heard it on radio, as it actually occurred.

A few days before Kennedy's death, we all visited Disneyland. Spirits were high, and they were drifting along on the Mississippi Paddleboat floating down a manmade river. Some of the cameramen were feeling uptight, however, and itching to get the Senator alone, with the paddle wheel behind him, for a good photo of the candidate in a relaxed setting. The reporters standing near him, conducting interviews and blocking "their" shot frustrated them. One threatened to throw me into the drink. I assured him that if I went in, I'd take him with me - and reminded him that his necklace of cameras was much more expensive than my cheap tape recorder. Before we knew it, several of the reporters and staff were flipped overboard into the river, but it was all in good fun, and not until the equipment was safely stashed! This incident typified the work-hard-play-hard atmosphere in the Kennedy camp, and was a reflection of his joie de vivre.

After the paddleboat docked, Bobby and Ethel Kennedy gamely braved the most daring rides at Disneyland. Ethel even went on a particularly harrowing roller coaster, although she was pregnant with her last child. She sat in the front, and as the ride slammed to a halt, her swollen stomach struck the chair hard. Fortunately, she had no difficulties with the birth later on.

Soon afterward, the Kennedys strode arm-in-arm to the plane. An especially touching photo of the two of them appeared in many of the nation's newspapers. It showed them from the back, their arms around each other's waist. They looked like a carefree young couple, very much in love. The scene acquired even greater poignancy a few days later, when Bobby lay on the floor of a Los Angeles hotel, his brain destroyed by a bullet, as his brother John's had been only a few years earlier.

Death Claims Another Kennedy

The shooting of Robert F. Kennedy was especially traumatic for us because most of the newsmen, even those who began the campaign as rabid Kennedy-haters, had been totally won over by his charm and enthusiasm. Touch football games and sharing drinks with the family helped us feel closer to them. After the shooting, we were doubly shocked to realize that many of us had spoken with the assassin, Sirhan Sirhan, only moments before in the press room of the hotel. He had wandered freely from the kitchen to the press room next door, asking us when the Senator would come downstairs and which elevator he would take. I remember noticing that he carried what appeared to be a paper tube wrapped around one arm, but never thought to ask what was in it. The hotel lobby, kitchen, and press area were mobbed. As you might imagine, campaign supporters and hangers-on are a mixed bag of people. Many political groupies are unconventional in speech or appearance, and Sirhan by no means stood out in the crowd.

Senator Kennedy had just concluded his victory speech as Sirhan struck. After proclaiming, "onto Chicago," he left the platform (where I had been standing with other reporters and supporters). Kennedy was walking towards the kitchen and the press area. The bullets sprayed wildly, and at least seven people were wounded, some quite severely. From my vantage point, there was little evidence that Bobby Kennedy realized the long-feared attack had come. But some of my colleagues insist he silently signaled his rage and anguish moments before lapsing into unconsciousness. By some accounts, he asked his wife Ethel whether anyone else was hurt. If he did, I was not close enough to hear him. The wounded Senator Kennedy was laid out on the floor near the kitchen, where he had fallen.

The heat in the area was intense - nearly 100 degrees - and it was worsened by the hot lights of the television cameras beaming down on the bleeding candidate. Ethel cradled her husband's shattered head in her arms and turned furiously toward the technicians. "For God's sake," she snapped, "turn off the lights - *turn off the lights.* Let him breathe!" The engineers - who had shared many happy private moments with her and her husband, nonetheless could only respond, "Sorry, lady, this is history."

A few feet from the Kennedys, a skirmish was in progress. Several of the Senator's supporters had cornered Sirhan. Football player Rosie Greer, standing nearby, wasted no time in wrestling the gun from the slightly-built assassin and then wedged his hands behind him in a hammerlock. Sirhan was then flung onto a long, mobile kitchen serving table. The massive Greer jumped onto Sirhan's back, nearly crushing the life from him. Sportswriter George Plimpton grasped the assailant's hair and methodically pounded his head against the edge of the table. Sirhan probably would have been killed, and those of us watching saw no reason to interfere. But Plimpton's new wife, Freddie, rushed up to her husband, pleading, "Don't, George, don't! He's sick - he's sick!" Thus it was she who saved the life of the killer of the man who, having just won the final Democratic primary, would have been well on his way toward winning the Democratic presidential nomination.

The scene at the Ambassador Hotel was one of total chaos. It was nearly impossible to phone in our stories in the ensuing confusion. Ironically, I now controlled one phone, because I had just placed a call to a boyfriend in San Diego before Senator Kennedy came out. I'd called Allen - a young doctor I had met on a trip to Vermont - to tell him the campaign was nearly over, and that I planned to visit him the next day. Then, as the Senator approached the platform, I laid down the phone, assuring Allen that I would be right back. When I did return several minutes later, Allen was as shaken as I. He had heard the shooting and screaming over the phone, and turned on his television to see what was happening.

Because I'd made the call, I had one of the few phones available for my own use, possession being nine tenths of the law. We hung up quickly, and I managed to get a line so I could phone a story to Washington. Frustrated reporters all around me were unable to get a line out, so I beat most of them with a live report to Washington. Even though most of the country knew about the shooting, since it was carried live on television, there is always something special about the immediacy of an eyewitness report from someone on the scene.

Afterward, I knew ambulances would be coming, and that I'd better make arrangements to get to the hospital. Unlike my colleagues, I had to provide my own transportation, so I scrambled out the door ahead of them. Senator Kennedy and his wife were rushed into the first ambulance. Pierre Salinger and his French wife, Nicole, commandeered a motorcycle and sped off, following them. Pierre had been press secretary to John Kennedy, and now had to witness the horror of history repeating itself.

A second ambulance pulled up, and a newsman shot in the stomach was loaded into it. Barely thinking, I jumped into the back with him. By the time we reached Central Receiving Hospital, I was covered with blood that had seeped from his stomach wounds. I hopped out of the ambulance and walked, unchallenged, through the hospital's emergency treatment area. There, I watched Ethel's sad, desperate conferences with the doctors who were struggling valiantly to keep her husband alive. There was such turmoil at the scene that I was all but invisible, able to observe as events unfolded. Eventually, the decision was made to move Kennedy up the street to the Good Samaritan Hospital, which was better equipped to deal with the emergency. I ran up a steep hill but found myself locked out on the lawn in front of the hospital with my colleagues.

As the night wore on, we found one pay phone nearby and all of us went on automatic pilot, filing our stories and performing our duties as dispassionate individuals. The Kennedy press corps waited on the grass all night, leaving only to phone in our reports. No one seemed to need to eat, sleep, or even go to the toilet. Twenty-four hours after the shooting, however, our veneer began to crack. By that time we were installed in a press room which had been set up in the lounge of a rest home across the street from Good Samaritan. At seven o'clock that evening, we watched Walter Cronkite anchor the CBS evening news. It was only when we saw the films of the shooting for the first time that several of us began to cry. It was as if we needed the electronic box to certify that the event was real, that it had actually happened.

The shooting of the Senator was tragic and horrible by any measure. At the same time, in a perverse way, it was a vindication of the constant coverage of him and a payback for the millions of dollars the news organizations had spent to track his every waking moment. It's no secret that a candidate or public figure cannot be ignored on even the most routine mission. We ghouls of the media know we must be there to cover unforeseen disasters like shootings, plane crashes or car accidents. For that reason, when a President leaves the White House in his helicopter, the cameras and tape recorders keep rolling until it is well out of sight. If it crashes after that, it's up to the "pool" reporters on board the vehicle to cover the event … if they survive.

Despite the suddenness of the Kennedy shooting, few of the regular reporters were caught off guard. After all, they had waited all night to cover the final victory speech in the last presidential primary of 1968. But one poor British journalist, thinking he had outsmarted us all, learned a costly lesson. He wrote a glowing story about Kennedy's speech, complete with quotes gleaned from Kennedy's earlier victory speeches. He phoned his story in to his newspaper, which was one of the major publications in England. Then he went to sleep a half-hour before the shooting. He awakened at 6:30 the next morning, rushed to the airport, and flew 3,000 miles to New York. During a stopover, before returning to London, he phoned his editors overseas to check on his story. Only then did he learn, to his horror, that the man he had followed meticulously for the past four months had been shot! Fortunately for him, however, his editors didn't fire him for his last-minute lapse. Rather, they allowed him to return to Los Angeles and pick up the story from there.

Once back in Los Angeles, he found an exhausted press corps ensconced in the nursing home-cum-press room. By that time, I had firmly hitched onto WAVA and gave them reports every 20 minutes, day and night, for two nights and three days until Senator Kennedy officially was pronounced dead. Again, there was little time for emotion here; there was simply too much work to do. My coverage of the unfolding story became a blur. I slept, sitting up, for 15-minute intervals until the phone rang and it was time to broadcast again. I was still very much a free-lancer, and did not have the luxury of my own phone. The networks, efficiently rising to the occasion, had installed their own as soon as the press room was opened. Ever resourceful, I peeled a network label off one phone and wrote my own name on it. In addition, whenever we went outside to be briefed by Frank Mankiewicz, I unscrewed the mouthpiece off the phone and kept it with me. I did put the network label back on, before we left the press center for good. Then, I reasoned, anyone who wanted the phone could have it!

When I returned to Washington a few days later I found, much to my surprise, that my broadcasts had been followed by nearly the whole city. Friends said they had listened to WAVA constantly at the swimming pool, while hooked up to their portable radios during their daily jogs, and at work. WAVA put me on their full-time staff, making me their first and only "street reporter." Before that, all their material was "rip and read" from the wire copy. This demonstrates the advanced status of all-news radio in Washington in 1968. WAVA never did compensate me for my Kennedy coverage; nor did the station pay any of my overtime during the next three months of arduous work. But for a young reporter, exposure is so important that it is easy for a news organization to take advantage. Moreover, the owner of WAVA at the time pointed out - with some justification - that his station gave cub reporters the chance to get a jump-start in the business, without having to go out to the boondocks. It was true that the sky-high rates paid by the other stations in the area actually did prevent a new reporter from working in them.

With my return to the East Coast came one of the most bitter periods of the campaign. I wanted desperately to be included on the funeral train that took the Senator and his family the 270 miles from New

York to Washington. By all accounts, it was an extremely emotional, heart-wrenching experience. Enormous crowds lined the sidewalks. All of the Kennedys and their longtime supporters were on that train. Even the toughest reporters said they were deeply moved as the oldest of the Kennedy sons walked the length of the train to personally thank everyone who had covered Bobby.

I was not allowed to get on that train. Without the Senator alive to take me under his wing, the sentiment of my antagonists on the staff prevailed. Even amid the intense grief that characterized that time, petty political infighting asserted itself. My adversaries in the Kennedy camp could now repay what they had seen as the preferential treatment I had received during the campaign.

At least I was somewhat comforted by the memory of a campaign train ride we all had shared through Indiana early in the Senator's campaign. In those days, while thousands lined the rails, some of the sharpest reporters had written a ribald song to the tune of "The Wabash Cannonball." It mocked Kennedy's ruthlessness and efficiency. After it was sung, Bobby looked up at the group and, with a wide grin, shot back, "Up yours - sideways." I have the only tape recording immortalizing that episode, having started my machine when the song began. At one point, the Senator came over and said, "Nobody's recording this, are they?" I was too embarrassed to admit I was, not knowing that the session was supposed to be a private one, "on background." So, looking as innocent as possible, I slid a newspaper over my machine and kept it running. I still have the tape, but never have broadcast the intimate sounds of the laughter, the camaraderie, or the spontaneous, most non politically correct remarks.

Bobby Kennedy's last train ride ended in Washington, where he was buried at Arlington National Cemetery in a grave near the eternal flame of his brother's tomb. The funeral was conducted with the great style the Kennedys were capable of achieving. I was deeply moved by the ceremony, as were most of my countrymen, regardless of their politics. I still believe the writing and broadcasting I did that night were the best of my career. One of the sickest things about our business is the fact that tragedy often produces the best reports, and inspires our finest efforts.

WAVA: Was This the Real World?

After the Kennedy funeral in June 1968, I began my first full time job with WAVA. I had received several job offers that summer, including one with WTOP Radio (the CBS affiliate), which was to become Washington's second - and most professional - all-news station. It's said that hindsight is 20/20, and later I was sorry in a way that I didn't accept the job offer. But WTOP was not all-news at the time, and I was quite dedicated to that format. In any case, there was soon to be a change in personnel at WTOP that was followed by the typical "bloodbath" that ensues in the early days of a new regime. At such times, many of the old reporters are swept away and replaced by new ones. With my luck, I consoled myself, I would have been identified with the old guard and fired anyway!

At WAVA, I sharpened my skills, learning to report "live" on a variety of topics. It was much more confusing than covering a political campaign, which is a "one-issue" experience. At WAVA, I might start the morning by heading for the White House or Capitol Hill; then rushing down to the District Building (to cover a local political issue); then dashing off to cover a demonstration in front of the Department of Agriculture or the Pentagon; and finally staggering off to an economic press conference. The first such conference I went to related to the Federal National Mortgage Association, more commonly known as "Fannie Mae." Quite frankly, I first thought the term referred to a candy company. This is no doubt disillusioning to one who might assume that reporters always have a firm grasp of all the facts!

The situation became so confusing that I learned one important trick: forget the story you have done as soon as you broadcast it. Go on to something new. If you don't, you will have a hard time separating your stories, and you can easily get the names and issues all jumbled together in your mind. To be sure, it's an odd technique of "unlearning," totally different from the process used by a politician, who must try to retain as many names or facts as possible. I felt it was better to forget about - or at least compartmentalize - my learning.

That summer, the stories which had the most meaning to me by far dealt with the Poor People's Campaign, and the long, hot march of the Mule Train up from the Deep South. I picked up the marchers outside Washington and visited their campsite in nearby Bailey's Crossroads. Today the area is a densely populated tract of homes and shopping centers in Falls Church, Virginia. At the time, however, it was surrounded by 40 acres of scrub forest, and was situated at the end of a dirt road. Years ago, during the Civil War, many Confederate soldiers hid in those woods. From their vantage point, they staged guerrilla attacks against the Union forces of the North. Ten years after the Poor People's March, I moved to a home in the woods in Bailey's Crossroads. I often wonder whether my home in the woods was once the temporary shelter of the 300 marchers who formed the poor people's Mule Train.

Although the WAVA chapter was a short one, lasting only three months, I was remembered for years afterward as the strange red-haired girl with the antenna on her head. It was my ticket into a number of exotic places. Once, during a demonstration on Capitol Hill, I was searching frantically for a toilet. I was almost desperate enough to squat and void in front of the 10,000 demonstrators and 1,000 cops - antenna and all - when I remembered that the Botanical Gardens (sometimes called the "hothouse for the Legislators," as if they needed one) was at the foot of the Hill. I trotted over to it and made a beeline for the ladies room. As I sat on the toilet, my editor's booming voice came through: "Base Station calling Mobile Unit K I Y 549." The women in the other booths started to scream, and panic erupted. My editor, oblivious to the chaos he had caused, said, "I can't hear you; change the location of your transmission." I retorted that I would go to the men's room, if he preferred.

Soon after that, I flushed the toilet on him and on my first full-time job with a radio station. The parting was not what I would have chosen, and I would like to have made a career at the all-news station. But, events moved on. There were a series of orders given to me which I considered to be unethical, and I did not want to compromise my professionalism in any way by following them. I had no indication that the owners or top management knew about these orders, but I could not get to them. I had to either obey or quit; I chose the latter.

In later years, WAVA also changed their ownership and format, which happens frequently in radio. But, it was a noble experiment. And, I believe it was an inspiration to Ted Turner, in later years, when he made his noble move to all-news television.

Chicago: The World's Friendliest Convention

Chicago was my next destination, and the 1968 Democratic Presidential Convention in that city was one of the bloodiest ever held in this country. Antiwar sentiment was becoming rabid. In the days before the convention, huge crowds had gathered in the shadows of the Chicago Hilton, the convention headquarters which called itself the "World's Friendliest Hotel." Thousands of antiwar, pro-McCarthy demonstrators from every walk of life gathered in the park across from the hotel. But the ones receiving the most attention - and generating the most rage from the police - were the hippies, the yippies, and the other anti - establishment groups. The Chicago police simply did not know how to handle this eclectic and volatile bunch, and fierce battles erupted each night. As many acknowledged later, the scenario was essentially a police riot, not a civilian one.

The police plowed through the demonstrators, wildly flinging billy clubs and tear gas. At one point, as I walked through the crowds with press tags hanging clearly from my chest, I was the victim of an attack, and thus temporarily became an unwilling participant in the news, as well as a reporter. The police charged, and one heavy officer slammed his billy club down on my head. His eyes widened with shock and disbelief when the club bounced back at him. Those were the days of the stiff, teased hairstyles and wigs. My own waist-length hair was rolled up under such a wig, and it probably was the only thing standing between the billy club and a skull fracture.

One of my colleagues, Winston Churchill III, wasn't so fortunate. As he and his fellow British journalist, Stephen Barber, strolled through the park that night, Churchill also found himself on the receiving end of the billy-club treatment. Barber, desperately trying to rescue his friend from the battering, yelled at the cops, "You can't hit him - he's Winston Churchill!"

"Right, Buddy," one of the cops sneered, "and we're the tooth fairy." They began hitting him even harder, breaking his wrist in the process. I've often wondered: Were the police unaware that Churchill was a journalist, trying to cover a story? Or were they all *too* aware, and attempting to stem the flow of news from his typewriter?

The bloody scenes continued. Coincidentally, that week the Soviets had invaded Czechoslovakia. On Chicago streets there began to appear signs with pointed messages such as "Welcome to Prague." Even on the last night of the convention, when Hubert Humphrey won the Democratic presidential nomination that probably would have gone to Bobby Kennedy, the police couldn't leave the situation alone. I attended a farewell party in one of the suites of the Gene McCarthy headquarters. It was a rather quiet, melancholy affair. Most of the guests were drinking beer, but there may have been some pot-smokers as well. Suddenly, the police burst in. They started to beat people up and kick them out of the room. One of the cops kicked me brutally in the groin, damaging my bladder for years to come. The pain was so intense, that I lashed back and kicked him in the same area. My fondest hope is that he experienced at least as many complications in later years as I did … and that he remembered me every time he had to use that part of his anatomy!

The next morning, I had an extremely moving chance encounter with Senator McCarthy. I went down for an early breakfast in the Hilton coffee shop and saw him sitting all alone, but encircled by the ubiquitous Secret Service entourage a few feet away. They started to chase me away, but he motioned me to join him. We ate together as we sadly discussed the campaign and its bloody finale. Some critics later charged he was unfocused and mystical, that he lacked the drive of one who really wanted to be President. They accused him of trying to use the antiwar movement as a vehicle for generating personal publicity. But when I told him that it had looked for a while as though he might make it, his eyes glowed with a look of fierce ambition and determination. Clearly, this was a man who had indeed wanted to be President, and he certainly had come closer to that goal than many ever would. In the process of seeking the brass ring, he also played a major role in forcing Lyndon Johnson from office.

World of the Casting Couch

With the Chicago Convention over, thousands of campaigners and political groupies of various stripes picked up the pieces and staggered back to their homes across the country to take up their everyday lives - if only temporarily. They enjoyed a brief respite from the campaigning, as the two nominees - Richard M. Nixon and Hubert Humphrey - and their staffs regrouped for the final four-month onslaught.

I was back in Washington, getting medical attention for the injuries I had incurred in Chicago. At the same time, when it really sank in that I was no longer working for WAVA, I descended into a depression. For a few days I continued to go to press conferences at the District Building (the seat of the Washington, D.C. government) and to the local black churches, but of course I had nowhere to file my stories. For a reporter, being unable to report is the ultimate deprivation. After that experience, I vowed to keep some "free-lance" clients if at all possible. If you have several stations to report to, you are never really out of a job. It is always painful to lose a client; but that is mitigated by having others to fall back on. It also keeps me more independent and less anxious to please. I find I am so grateful for a job, I do all I can to make the boss or the news director happy. Many of them dislike that, much preferring a tougher reporter who will stand up for himself or herself, and who will give them some fight. While it's natural for me to fight for a story, I often have had trouble summoning the wherewithal to "sell" myself.

I really admire and respect reporters who can convince the network bosses they are special and should be hired - and then hang on to their jobs (although most of them exist in a climate of uncertainty entailing frequent hirings and firings). Somehow, this is a survival skill I never really acquired.

I also became entangled in the ruthless internal politics of whatever station I worked for. In addition, the "casting couch" pressure became very rough wherever I went. That's where the news director, or some other power figure, threatens, "You can't have [or keep] your job unless you go to bed with me." Later, if one is foolish enough to succumb to this pressure, he will often lash back with, "You don't expect preferential treatment just because you slept with me, do you? That would simply be unprofessional." It's the old "damned if you do, and damned if you don't" syndrome. Now, the tables have been turned. With so many men "out of the closet," the pressure is sometimes just as intense on male reporters as it traditionally has been on women. When my male friends come crying to me that their would-be bosses have propositioned them, I feel pangs of empathy, but frankly not much sympathy.

In any case, the situation is now much improved. Both men and women can sue for sexual harassment, as well as racial and age discrimination. Sometimes the atmosphere becomes a bit too acrimonious. But, it is a far cry from the days of rampant abuse and lack of protection. The younger generation of employees, in all fields, do not realize how truly fortunate they are.

The Invasion of Czechoslovakia

As I was licking my wounds and contemplating the future, a boyfriend, Larry, suggested we go to Czechoslovakia. We were an odd pair - some no doubt would call us unbalanced - embarking on a journey to a strange country, 4,000 miles away, a scant two weeks after it had been invaded by Soviet tanks and thousands of Russian soldiers. But both of us were of Eastern European origin and we were deeply moved by the tragedies often endured by the peoples of those regions.

Intrigued by the prospect of being in the middle of a breaking story, I agreed to go, although it was a "pay my own way" arrangement. Before we left, I visited the networks in New York to see if I could report to them. Some thought it could be an interesting experiment. At that time, the well-known reporters were not being granted visas to enter Czechoslovakia. Moreover, the resident foreign correspondents were losing their visas and being forced, one by one, to leave the country.

A gamble on an unknown correspondent seemed like a good idea. ABC and NBC news were not very generous, and offered merely to process any television film I could ship to them. But CBS gave me the names of cameramen they employed in Czechoslovakia, as well as in Poland, Hungary and Yugoslavia. (Early on, my plan was to later work my way through all of the Eastern European countries; but I ended up becoming so involved in Czechoslovakia that I spent most of the next six months there.) I was able to use the photographer, Jiri Pollack, as I wished, and CBS would take care of any expenses surrounding the filming. Everything else was my responsibility, and I would be paid only if a story was used. Armed with my list of cameramen, Larry and I flew across the Atlantic.

En route to the troubled area, we stopped in Paris and found rooms in a dingy student hotel on the Left Bank. I had spent nearly two years in Paris as a political science student, and had a lot of friends to look up in a short time. One of them was David de Rothschild, son of the banker, Baron Guy. I had originally contacted the Rothschilds many years before, after John F. Kennedy was assassinated. I had been moved to write a long poem about "dynasties, their tragedies and their destinies," and sent it to David, who was my age. We became pen pals, and ended up going to the same university in Paris, L'Institute d'etudes politiques, or "Science Pol."

I spent an enjoyable evening reminiscing with David in his elegant apartment on the exclusive Avenue de Foch. Reluctantly, I left, not wanting to desert my traveling companion in a strange city. The next day, I read in the afternoon papers that a gunman had briefly kidnapped Baron Guy. A shot had rung out in the same apartment I had vacated just hours before, and the Baron was taken on a wild, terrifying car ride through the city before he was ultimately rescued. My sense of timing was incredible. Of course I was lucky to have left the scene in the nick of time; but as a reporter, how I wished I'd spent a few more hours in that apartment!

I reflected that there is something about me that seems to bring bad luck to people, and the Rothschild incident was just one example. Years before, during my student days in Paris, I had hitchhiked my way across Europe and the Mediterranean. Too often, violence wasn't far behind. In Paris, for instance, there were student riots. (Of course, the students in Paris are always protesting something or other and taking their grievances to the streets, sometimes with explosives.)

Then there was Cyprus, where civil war erupted between the Greeks and Turks. I spent three days and nights pinned down at the airport in Nicosea. What a pity I had no one to report to in those days! The pattern of fights and riots continued throughout the Middle East and other areas I visited. Year's later, four people I interviewed as a working reporter died within the year. Three were major politicians, but one was simply a tourist from St. Louis I had interviewed for my radio station there. That same night he was mugged and shot to death in his hotel parking lot. So I guess the Rothschilds got off lucky.

It was time to reach Prague, and resume my adventures. My friend Larry and I managed to get a flight on a Czech airline, and we flew into the maelstrom. Never had I seen such an ancient airplane, and I worried that it was held together with paper clips, rubber bands, and a prayer. The pressure must have been defective in the cabin, for our ears nearly exploded upon landing. Interestingly, however, the bathroom of the plane somewhat compensated for any other discomfort. It had an ornate, antiquated bathtub and old-fashioned gas lamps on the walls. I doubt that either of them functioned, but it gave one the impression of an "Orient Express" of the air.

Prague brought us back to reality. There, the scene was total chaos. Russian troops and tanks were everywhere. The amount of armor was formidable, but many of the soldiers looked like confused kids, playing with their first toy machine guns. The Soviets had not quite solidified their hold over the populace, and the people had a limited time to make some painful decisions about their future. Word had it that they would have six months to leave the country legally and still retain the right to return. After that, however, the borders would be sealed, and any attempt to escape would be at the risk of their lives.

Now, thousands were preparing to leave. But first they had to convert their "soft" Czech currency (which could not be used outside the Soviet Bloc nations) into hard currency, preferably American dollars. On every street corner there were dozens of fast-talking entrepreneurs - ranging from students to businessmen - offering to turn Czech currency into dollars at exorbitant exchange rates.

When we arrived, the legal rate was 16 Czech kronen for one dollar. On the black market, it was 100 to one. For the first three days, I refused to exchange, knowing I could spend the rest of my life in a Czech prison if I happened to swap money with a plainclothes Czech policeman. But after a while, the temptation was too great. Besides, I needed a great deal of money to free-lance there, because, as is often the case, the time-honored currency used in getting information was the bribe. I was fortunate in that the people I changed with were merely citizens trying to make a buck, but I was keenly aware that my own luck bore a sharp contrast to their own worsening state of affairs.

Larry and I got rooms in a third class Czech hotel near the railroad station. It was a very folksy arrangement, with no locks on the door and one bathroom shared by everybody at our end of the hall. I was amazed by the honesty of the Czech staff in that hotel. I often left my passport, as well as American cash, in the room for hours on end. More often than not, desperate people in a country under occupation would have jumped on it as a means of escape. But during my entire stay there, not one penny was taken. I lost only a hairbrush, probably spirited away by a hotel maid who couldn't resist that small bit of Western luxury.

I was also very touched by the humanity of the Czech people. After only two days in Prague, Larry decided the overall atmosphere was much too depressing for him. He fled the country to spend the rest of his vacation in sun-drenched Greece. I went down to breakfast and the *zaftig (hefty)* Czech waitress started to set two places at the table, as she had done for the past two days. I motioned to her, "only one," and explained that my friend had left. Sorrowfully, she lowered her large frame down onto the chair opposite me, put her head on her arms, and cried for me.

Alone in Prague, I made my way up a main boulevard to the City Hall. As I approached it, the number of Soviet tanks and soldiers increased. Some of the soldiers were so young they had never shaved before. This was probably their first time away from home. Some holiday for them! Occasionally I would spot flowers resting on a tank, placed there by brazen Czech students in fits of bravado. The armed and armored soldiers proved a stark contrast to their antagonists. The Czech girls wore miniskirts up to their crotches. Some of the boys had the long, shoulder-length hair that typified the original "Bohemians," named for a province of Czechoslovakia.

At the tanks, I made my first contacts with the few remaining American reporters from the Associated Press, the *New York Times, the Washington Post*, and the *Christian Science Monitor.* Most of the electronic reporters could not get into the country and had not been pre-positioned there before the invasion. They were astonished that I'd made it in on a tourist visa, two weeks after the invasion. I asked them how to protect myself, and they referred me to the Czech official in charge of foreign reporters. When I went to see him, I discovered he was a striking, distinguished-looking man, with an elegant mane of white hair and a well-trimmed mustache and beard. His English was flawless, and after several minutes of conversation I confided to him my intentions. He assured me that I would not be thrown into a Czech jail simply because I was reporting illegally while on a tourist visa. He said I would have to renew it every three weeks, but warned me I could be deported from the country if I were caught.

My new friend was the perfect example of "The Good Soldier Zweig," the Czech literary character, an official who bowed openly to authority but privately resisted any way he could. I was later to meet many Czechs who epitomized this philosophy. Some brave parents, for example, had no choice but to allow their children to attend the schools which indoctrinated them with the heavy-handed policies of the Soviet occupiers. At night, these parents secretly met with their children and other families, to "un-teach" the propaganda they had been spoon-fed by their teachers. These parents took a tremendous risk, for discovery by the authorities would have meant jail. They also risked being turned in by their own children, in retaliation for grudges they might harbor against their parents. Over the ensuing years, nearly all of my Czech friends did end up in jail, but I never did learn the exact charges on which they were held.

In Prague, I had my debut - my first experience as a television reporter. I failed abysmally. With no producer, director, or editor there to guide me, my work did not measure up to network standards, and it probably was never used. (In any case, I was never paid for it.) But it was one heck of a learning experience! The Czech cameraman, Jiri, was young, sharp, and as willing to take risks as I. We narrowly escaped being jailed the first day of filming, when I asked him to take some shots of the government building where a Central Committee meeting was in progress. The camera-shy Soviet guards sent us away at gunpoint. We did manage to take several photos of buildings and events on the forbidden list, but these had little meaning to our stateside audiences, who did not realize the risks involved in obtaining the pictures.

A few days later, I began to explore Prague's ageless Jewish quarter, once the home of Freud and Kafka. The old Synagogue - the most ancient in Eastern Europe - still stands as a museum and graveyard. The cemetery is so tiny that bodies were often buried on top of each other. It is now a sea of tombstones, with very little open space. Hitler systematically destroyed most of the Jewish community, and very few older Jews remain. I did a feature story on "The Dying Jewish Community of Prague," which I prepared for the Hebrew High Holy Days. After numerous interviews, the cameraman and I stood in front of the old Synagogue to do the "stand-up piece," or the reporter's closing comments. As I was speaking into the camera with my eyes riveted to the lens, a teenage Soviet soldier across the street raised his machine gun and aimed it directly at my head. I kept talking, afraid to stop and reluctant to waste the expensive film. I assumed - hoped - he was only kidding anyway. Later, I began to tremble when I realized how easy it would have been for him to blow off my head. That may have made for good footage, but it wasn't the way I planned to make my name in this business.

That night, still shaken by the encounter, I went to a Czech bar to unwind. I decided to forgo my usual coffee; it was an occasion that demanded something stronger than caffeine. After a few moments, a handsome, blond, curly-headed Czech youth came over to talk. Ladislav, as he introduced himself, was one of the intelligentsia. Lede's (his nickname) English and French were fluent, so we communicated easily. He was also one of the few Czechs willing to chat with me without the protection of his buddies. Ladislav was charming and very persistent; after a few days, he persuaded me to move out of my third-class hotel and share his apartment in the exclusive suburbs of

Prague. It was there, a stone's throw from dangerous tanks and artillery and enemy soldiers, that our romance thrived.

There was one major glitch in my new living arrangements. Ladislav's father, currently the Czech Ambassador to North Korea, had been a solid supporter of the old hardline leader, Novotny, and never approved of the more enlightened policies of the liberal Alexander Dubcek. Lede took a tremendous risk associating with me, but it also was a convenient expression of his youthful rebellion.

The highrise apartment was beautiful and as modern as any in the West. It overlooked the Moldeau (Vltava) River, which wound in sinuous curves far below us. The beautiful music of Smetana's "The Moldeau" filled the apartment day after day. Tiny Russian-style dachas, surrounded by pine trees, were not destroyed when the apartments were built. We could look down at them and escape into time. At night, I read from Solzhenitsyn's The Cancer Ward and other anti-Soviet books I had naively brought with me for instructional reading when I came to Czechoslovakia. Later, Czech friends of mine were imprisoned for reading just such material.

My months in Prague were a marvelous emotional and learning experience for me. Through Lede, I met many Czech law and medical students from Charles (Carlova) University - one of the oldest in Europe. They often engaged in intense debates about their future. They were tied irrevocably to the region where their families had lived for hundreds of years, and didn't want to leave. Nor did they want to surrender their material possessions or the elitist lifestyle (compared with most Czechs) they enjoyed. A few of the students saw pictures of Czech refugees in *Time* and *Newsweek* magazines (which, strangely enough, could still be purchased in the top hotels of Prague). The condition of the refugees was really not so bad, but they were living in bunk beds in dormitories in Vienna. Still, this was enough to deter most of my friends from leaving. In the end, when the borders were sealed, the majority had decided to stay. Several years later, most of them - the lawyers, doctors, professors and the cameramen - were jailed by the Soviet and Czech authorities whose power had firmly solidified.

Those lively debates gave me an enormous appreciation for countries like the United States, Australia, and New Zealand, which were settled primarily by refugees who - whether by intent or design - had made long, arduous ocean crossings to reach their new lands. Sitting in those apartments in Prague, I learned it takes a special breed of people to become refugees by choice. Regardless of one's reasons for leaving, it takes a high degree of foresight, courage, and determination to do so. The majority of the people in this world have remained in their place of birth, accepting a known suffering rather than venturing toward an unknown fate.

As my new friends pondered their futures, I briefly returned home to Washington as a means of trying to help Ladislav legally leave his country. To accomplish this, we would try to get married, but first I had to get a set of papers from my "village mayor," stating I had never been married before. Fortunately, I knew Washington, D.C.'s "village mayor," Walter Washington, from my days at WAVA and persuaded him to sign the papers. He thought it was an utterly ridiculous exercise, and pointed out that I could have been married anywhere in America and he'd never know it. However, he played the game, and executed some beautiful documents for me.

Clutching my papers, emblazoned with the impressive official seal of Washington, D.C., I hurried to the Czech Embassy, where I was treated with a great deal of suspicion. I was just as chary of them, and convinced I saw "Cheka" Secret Service agents lurking around every corner. After grilling me for two days on my experiences in Czechoslovakia (most of which I censored), the Czech officials reluctantly cosigned my documents, sealing them with wax and bright red ribbons. I was now free to return to Prague, but the problem was money: there was none.

To finance the return trip, I turned to the time-honored way for a reporter to make money quickly: public relations. I called a firm I'd once done some writing for and they subcontracted me out to a black revolutionary newspaper in the heart of Washington's ghetto. Within a few days, I was penning rabidly anti-white editorials. I had few problems with the other staff members, but one day the big, black office German shepherd rushed me. Terrified, all I could blurt out to him was, "Do you like whites?" Fortunately, he was color-blind.

The publication's boss, however, did have his problems with colors, especially red and black. His newspaper was losing money, and he turned to other means of raising revenue. The office became a thriving black market for stolen clothes, televisions and radios. If you didn't see what you liked, another item could be "custom stolen" for you, in any size, style, or model you requested. The boss did eventually pay the employees, but in checks from a Kansas City bank. When, after working for him for two months, I finally got one and tried to cash it, I was dismayed to find the check had bounced. About that time, the paper folded, and the owners quickly decamped to some other location or city, never to be heard from again. The word was out in the ghetto they were really a front for a major heroin ring, but I never saw any evidence of that. I think they were just small-time con artists, and I was one of their many victims.

As hard as it was for me to lose that money, it was tragic for one of my coworkers. The girl had become pregnant and planned to have a legal abortion at a local hospital. When her check bounced, she could not pay the hospital rates and had to settle for a gruesome back-alley abortion. The poor girl bled to death on a Washington side street. Regardless of one's sentiments on abortion, no one deserves that fate.

Revolted and heartsick, I wanted only to return to Czechoslovakia. My parents had been terrified the whole time I was there, but they also bowed to the intensity of my emotions. They advanced me the funds to return, and soon I was on my way back to Prague, bearing my documents and Christmas gifts for my friends. Shopping in the American department stores for those gifts was a wrenching experience. My Czech friends had few possessions, but treated what they had with the greatest care and respect. Their stores were nearly empty, and even the meat or duck they ordered in restaurants was measured and listed on the menus by grams. When I contrasted their lifestyle with the surfeit of goods in American food and department stores, I was suddenly overwhelmed with a profound sadness.

Returning to Czechoslovakia in December, I found the entire country transformed. Snow and bitter cold had replaced the summer's warmth. The new Czech authorities were now entrenched, and ruling with a firmer hand. But there was still a great deal of turmoil, and it was possible to get away with a lot of illegal activities. I continued my free-lancing, but concentrated on radio. Getting phone lines out was difficult. One had to sit for more than ten hours in the lobby of the Hotel Alcron to get an international line. Telexes were all right for the print reporters, but their material was heavily censored. I finally resorted to feature material and airmailed my radio cassettes to networks in the United States and Canada. The system worked well; for some reason, the airport authorities apparently never bothered to listen to - or censor - my tapes.

I moved back into Ladislav's apartment, since his parents were still posted in North Korea. This time, the American Embassy in Prague was well aware of my situation and just as concerned about it as my parents were. They warned me that the apartment complex was reserved for the families of high-ranking Czech and Soviet officials, and they could do little to help me if I got into trouble. Just to be safe, I did check in with them each week and was profoundly touched and gratified by their concern for me. After all, I was just one American citizen, but the whole embassy seemed genuinely worried about my welfare. The embassy staff also remembered the trouble my family caused them during my earlier visit. I had sent my parents in New York a postcard with a few sentences on it. They were convinced it was in code, and nearly turned the whole State Department upside down until they learned I was safe and in good health.

This time in Prague, I assumed the role of a Czech housewife. I walked across frozen, snow-covered fields in my long black coat and fur hat, feeling like some romantic character in a Russian novel. Grocery shopping was a daily chore, and the lines were long - but not as tortuous as those in Russia. There was actually a modern supermarket attached to the apartment complex, and the shelves were much fuller than I would have expected, although there was certainly a shortage of fresh food. Everyone knew I was a foreigner, but they were very helpful. I managed by pointing a lot. Trudging back to the apartment across the expanse of dark snow was a frigid but safe experience. Although I was a stranger in a strange land, I had no fear of getting mugged or robbed, as I often had in Washington, where on three occasions gangs of tough young kids had unsuccessfully tried to rob me near my home.

Christmas season was a time for private parties in my apartment complex near Prague. The intensity of the Czechs' religious spirit surprised me. In all homes, Christmas carols and religious songs were sung, often in English. One of the cruelest blows of the Soviet invaders was the crushing of religion, but that really had not asserted itself by the end of 1968. My Czech friends expressed a sense of personal hurt and bewilderment at what the Soviets were doing to their country. Several of them told me, "We loved Russia. It was a great Slavic power that made it. We were all so proud of them. There was no reason to be so heavy handed with us."

New Year's also was a time for a public show of spirit. As midnight approached, I was surprised to see firecrackers tossed from many apartment windows. In some flats, anti-Soviet songs were sung, even though the housing complex was now home to an increasing number of somber Soviet officials.

In early January, the senior law students of Carlova University went skiing in the Krkonose Mountains. That was Leda's class, and I was pleased to be invited. As usual, I stood out like a sore thumb. I had only one ski jacket, a black one with an Indian on the back, emblazoned with the words, "Fagowees, Washington, D.C." This was a ski club I belonged to back home. The "Fagowees" are the lost Indian tribe who constantly asked, "Where the F--- are we?" (Just try translating that into Czech or Russian!)

The Czech ski area was extremely primitive at the time. Ski conditions were similar to those I had learned on in the Eastern United States - ice, punctuated by bits of snow. But in America, the skiers had fancy skis with sharp edges to grip the ice. In Czechoslovakia, many skied on homemade wooden skis with no edges whatsoever. The poles were also homemade- big, thick affairs. Some looked like they were carrying tree branches, rather than poles. The boots they wore were meant for cross-country skiing and lifted up from the skis at the heel. Despite these handicaps, many of the Czech skiers were superb and negotiated the ice and steep, narrow paths with tremendous skill that they had developed early in the game. There was only one way to get up that mountain - on a long "t-bar" that cut straight up through a narrow trail sliced through the pine trees. If you fell off that lift, you had to ski straight down, dodging the t-bar, skiers, and trees. That was one ski lift I made certain to stay on.

Toilet facilities were a problem in the Krkonose, which is to say that there were none where we skied. Anyone who had to go simply stood or squatted in place. No one seemed embarrassed but me. And, thanks to a painful bladder resulting from my encounter with the Chicago cop, I had to go often. The first time I squatted in public, I laughed so hard I started to ski down the mountain in that position. Fortunately, a handy tree stopped me. The second time, I leaned back and rested my arm in the snow. It was deeper than I thought, and half my body got buried in the drift. My pants were down, and my lower cheeks were in peril of developing a bad case of frostbite. I did a lot of yelling and cursing in several languages before some kindhearted Czechs came to my rescue - but not before they brought a large crowd around to witness my plight. All this in my Fagowee jacket!

Still the ski experience was a memorable one, and the people couldn't have been nicer. The food at the hotel was quite spicy, and one night I asked the waitress whether there was any ice cream for dessert. She was shocked, for there was no refrigeration in the mountain village. Thus even in their snowy location they had not developed a habit - or means - of keeping frozen items. But the next day, they made a point of serving me ice cream for dessert. The owner had walked 15 miles to a nearby town to buy some and dragged it back on a sled. They wouldn't even let me pay them for their trouble.

It was very sad to leave such a splendid environment. Indeed, I had so much Czech money I could have stayed for months if I wished. By this time, the black market exchange rates had gone through the roof. I didn't want to change any more money, but some of my friends were now quite desperate to get out so I exchanged every dollar I could with them. I paid for the ski vacation in Czech money. The entire two weeks for Ladislav and me, including rooms, food, and ski expenses, cost the equivalent of 15 American dollars. The Czechs' misfortune was a tourist's bounty.

We left the ski village by bus for the two-hour trip to Prague. En route, the Czech toilet habits asserted themselves again. We stopped on the road and ran for a young pine forest. Everyone on the bus sought trees to afford them some modicum of privacy. The problem was that the trees were skinny, and no one was completely hidden. It was like a scene from a Monty Python comedy, watching 50 people squat behind 50 scrawny trees. Behind each one, bits of steam rose up from the snow.

We returned to a radically different Prague. It was as if the winter's ski vacation marked the final end of the "Prague Spring," that brief period of liberation and creative revival. Even though Russian tanks had been in the streets since August, it was still possible to find some merriment, and a few remnants of the sophisticated, cosmopolitan Czech culture. Now, however, the clampdown was for real.

At about that time, a young Czech student, Jan Palach, burned himself to death to protest the invasion. There was a massive turnout at his funeral; it was one of the last major acts of defiance on the part of the liberal Czech intellectuals, many of whom had once participated in those demonstrations.

Some in my circle of friends who had procrastinated about leaving now tried to escape across the borders. Those who were caught were sent directly to jail. For others, who had been active under the earlier Dubcek liberalization, the knock on the door came in the darkness of night. A few remaining reporter colleagues were also terrified. The Associated Press correspondent lived in a constant state of dread and tension. He was sure he was being followed by the Czech Secret Police, and remembered an earlier AP reporter who had been charged with spying and spent many years in a Czech jail.

I sent back a few more final reports and some features on the ski trip. Then, my old white-haired friend in the Ministry of Foreign Affairs could no longer protect me. When my tourist visa expired, it couldn't be renewed. Nor did the Czech authorities allow me to marry Ladislav, even though my papers were in order. I bribed nearly every official I could find, since that was by now the well-established means of getting anything done. They were delighted to take the money and continued to ask for more; but in the final analysis, they could not or would not help.

Ladislav took me to the airport, where we said a tearful goodbye - although I refused to believe it was a final farewell. I returned to my small apartment in Washington, which I had sublet before leaving. Even in the freedom and sunshine of that glorious Washington spring, my heart remained in Czechoslovakia. Lede continued to write and request presents. I even promised I would buy him a car, if he got to America. Then, one day I got a letter from one of the girls who had been on the ski trip with us. In the middle of her note, she asked how I felt now that my Czech bridegroom was married. It seemed that he had married his old girlfriend (also the child of a hardline Czech diplomat) and hadn't bothered to tell me about it. I sat there on a cement bench in the sunshine, heartbroken and sobbing like a baby, but that was not the first time - or the last - I was to be "used" by a man.

The "Token Honky"

Back in Washington in 1969, it was once again time to look for a job. I found it terribly depressing to be home alone in my apartment and see thousands of my neighbors walk off to work each morning while I had nowhere to go. In those days, I thought that to work in Washington, you had to be employed in Washington. It was to be another two years before I realized the importance of the Washington dateline in broadcasting to other cities and countries around the world. Earlier, I'd done all my free-lance reporting from other cities and nations, sending the reports back to networks in New York or to individual stations in Washington.

I was doing some free-lance broadcasting for the Canadian Broadcasting Corporation, but that had not yet grown into a full-time job. Thus I began the task of systematically visiting local radio and television stations in the D.C. area. Around and around I went, exhausted by the oppressive heat and humidity that are an inescapable part of summers in the Nation's Capital.

Many of the news directors shrugged me off, saying that I had both too much and too little experience. Although they conceded I had two college degrees and had acquired some exceptional experience over the past year, they said I didn't have enough steady, on-air experience to be hired for a full-time job in the Washington market.

The accepted wage scales also hurt me. In the D.C. area, a reporter was paid $20,000 a year to start, except at the small, non-union stations like WAVA. But without solid experience in a small, "boondocks" market, an entry-level reporter could not expect to be hired by a major station in Washington. I pleaded with them to give me a job as a "gofer" (one who runs errands and does occasional research) or a production assistant, but they rejected the idea, fearing I would rapidly tire of such mundane tasks.

Other factors also contributed to the dearth of available jobs. The television stations had lost millions of dollars in revenues, having been forced to take cigarette advertising off the air. This regulation necessitated drastic cuts in news budgets, at least for a time. In addition, television was feeling the increasing social pressure to hire minority reporters. This decision was justified, as minorities had long been denied equal opportunities in all facets of American business. In a city like Washington, which was nearly eighty percent black, this was even more important. News executives were scrambling for black women reporters so they could satisfy two quotas at once. I knew I couldn't change my color, but I did consider giving myself some long Spanish, Italian, or Greek last name. One of my friends actually did that, and was hired for $100,000 a year in New York. They even gave her speech lessons and changed her makeup, hair, and wardrobe. But I knew I couldn't carry off - much less sustain - such a charade.

So I turned the tables. Unwilling to leave Washington for the "boondocks," I applied for a job with WFAN, the only black and minority television and radio station in the area. They were pleased to hire me immediately, as their token white, or "honky."

WFAN - Channel 14 was a shoddy affair. The station was located in one of the worst sections of Washington. To make matters worse, its radio affiliate, WOOK, was running an illegal numbers racket among the black community, which caused a scandal a few months after I arrived. The numbers game was played in a unique way. During a gospel hour broadcast, the preacher would read scripture from the Bible. The number of the chapter and verse were a tip-off on which numbers to play. The racket had an enormous number of listeners and did much to boost the ratings of an otherwise third-rate station. Since then, a Washington lottery, an immensely popular offshoot of the numbers game run by the government, has become legal - as well as immensely popular.

The other problem at the station was the management. The owner was white, and he blatantly took advantage of minority or oppressed workers. The two station engineers, for example, were Cuban refugees. They were highly skilled and educated, but didn't have the necessary licenses to work for a better station. The father-and-son team was paid a total of $90 every other week.

I was assigned each week to do three television shows, which I both produced and hosted. The programs were about politics, the theater, and sports. I even provided transportation for most of my guests, since few people knew where the station was located. For my efforts, I was paid the princely sum of $25 a show. Some weeks, however, the station conveniently forgot to pay me. Nevertheless, the shows gave me the opportunity to meet a wide variety of people. They also provided the all-important exposure and experience so anxiously sought by everyone in the entertainment and broadcasting business. To do my theater show, I had to go to stage or movie openings every night for a year, in either Washington or New York. At first, it was exciting, but the excitement soon paled and I found it exhausting and tedious. I understood in short order how drama critics could become so cynical. The three shows I hosted were totally different, but I was fascinated by the similarity among actors, sports figures, and politicians - traits which have allowed several actors to turn their sights on politics or diplomatic service.

During that year, I managed to persuade many top Washington politicians to be interviewed as my guests. All of them, of course, were appalled when they saw the condition of the studios. I could almost hear them thinking, "How did I ever get talked into coming to this dump?" Most of them, however, kept their reservations to themselves, and some even came back for return engagements.

Despite - or maybe because of - the challenging conditions where I worked, I did produce some memorable shows. I had become very involved with the "dissenting priests" movement, which involved

Catholic clerics who believed in marriage for the clergy, birth control, and abortion (not necessarily in that order). For one show, my guests were two such priests and one senior Father from the Archdiocese of Washington. They were sitting in the waiting room, where I was about to chat with them before the show. At that moment, one of the big "stars" of the station called me into his office. I told him I was rushed - with ten minutes to go before airtime. But he insisted, and I didn't want to offend the star. I went into his office, and he promptly closed and locked the door behind me. What ensued was something out of a '40s movie, as Mr. Bigshot then proceeded to chase me around his huge desk. His huge, drooling St. Bernard even joined in, no doubt thinking we were playing some kind of game. The star chased me from one side, and the dog from the other. This scene created so much noise it attracted outside attention. There was a knock on the door, and when he opened it I was relieved to see his wife standing there. I looked at her, shouted, "You deal with him, lady!," grabbed my three confused priests, and ran downstairs to the studio. We made it with thirty seconds to spare. No time to comb my teased wig, or put on makeup. I must have looked as though I'd just had a tussle with the good Fathers.

The interview began with a ten-minute discussion of celibacy versus sex and birth control. Suddenly, the thunder of paws was heard in the distance. I don't know what became of Mr. Bigshot, but his St. Bernard apparently had escaped from the office and was making a beeline for the studio. There was a loud crash as the mutt knocked down a television camera and two lights. The sole director-cameraman cursed in Spanish, switched cameras, and the show continued without missing a beat. I asked the senior Father a question. Then, as he prepared to answer, I looked into the television monitor. To my horror, the drooling visage of the St. Bernard appeared on the screen where the priest's face should have been. I leave it to others to make the moral judgments; but our small audience will never forget the experience.

Another memorable show involved a visiting South Vietnamese politician. His embassy had contacted me to request that he come on my program to explain to the Washington audience - especially to the black viewers, whose sons bore the brunt of the fighting in Southeast

Asia - why it was necessary for them to fight and die for his country. I'd been assured that he spoke fluent English and would be a most articulate guest. When he arrived in his chauffeur-driven diplomatic car, I greeted him in English. He smiled, bowed, and hadn't the slightest comprehension of what I was saying. After fumbling for a few minutes, I realized he spoke French. It turned out to be a very uncomfortable show. I would ask my questions in American-accented French; he responded in Vietnamese-accented French, and I tried to translate for the audience. He was very short, so the cameraman had put his chair on a podium, so he wouldn't be dwarfed by me. As he was talking, he inexplicably kept moving his chair backward. Suddenly, in the middle of a sentence, with the camera trained on him, the chair toppled over the edge of the podium. He flipped over backward, a look of utter horror on his face. It was as if a bomb had been placed under the chair. We quickly cut to commercials, and the show ended abruptly, several minutes early.

It wasn't only my political programs that made good television. On the drama show, entitled "Theater Week," one guest was producer Otto Preminger. He had done some great movies in his day, but was in a slump when I interviewed him. I actually got him to admit that his most recent movies paled in comparison to his earlier ones. It turned out to be an exceptionally lively half-hour, and we argued spiritedly throughout the interview.

After Preminger's appearance, I brought in the cast of the musical "Cabaret," which was then playing at Washington's National Theater. I had enjoyed the show enormously, and had become quite close to the stars before inviting them to the station. Fortunately for me, they were good sports.

When we arrived at the station, we saw a fire truck and an ambulance outside. I naturally assumed one of the neighborhood boys had overdosed on drugs - unfortunately, that sort of thing was common. Then, a colleague pointed to our transmitter tower, where a small black figure could be seen slowly scaling toward the top. He was halfway up, and in alarm I shouted to the engineers, "For God's sake, shut off the power! He'll fry at the top!" They did manage to turn off the juice, moments before he reached the high-powered electrical terminal at the pinnacle of the tower.

The young man was a Vietnam veteran; no doubt scarred by the action he'd seen over there. Nowadays, his condition would be called "Post-Vietnam Stress Syndrome." At that time, it wasn't a medically recognized illness, and the victims bore their suffering and confusion all alone. Many were not marked on the outside, as were the double amputees I'd seen in the veteran's hospitals. (I shall never forget standing vigil at Walter Reed Army Hospital, waiting for former President Dwight Eisenhower to die. Our press room was in an auditorium, where hundreds of the wounded were wheeled in for their daily entertainment. At one point, a singer urged them all to clap their hands and stamp their feet. He was too callous to notice that most of them were missing hands or feet).

The veteran on the radio tower didn't have the same handicaps, but he was at least temporarily insane. About fifteen minutes before his ascent, he'd walked into the lobby of the studio and announced, "I want to be on television." After ranting and cursing for a while because he had no takers, he left in frustration, with a parting obscene finger-and-forearm salute. Outside, he started climbing. He was going to be "on television," one way or another.

Finally, atop the five-story tower, he balanced himself on a huge light bulb and slowly began to peel off his clothes. Piece by piece, his clothing dropped to the ground- socks, shoes, pants, shirt, and shorts. He was stark naked, clad only in sunglasses to show "the brothers" how cool he was. Ultimately he began to defecate on the crowd several hundred feet below.

Even though we couldn't get the story on the air, I knew it was newsworthy. I dashed inside and started working the phones, calling up all the local news directors in the area. At first, few believed me, and accused me of drinking. But they all agreed to send reporters and news trucks, and the incident became the lead local news story of the night. One of the news directors didn't have a clue where we were. "Connie," he said, "how are we going to spot your transmitter?" I replied, "Ed, It's the only one in Washington with a naked black man on the top!"

The poor man stayed on the tower for several more hours. After a time, an Army helicopter was sent to rescue him. It had a rope and a tire sling hanging from it, and perhaps it reminded him of some of his Vietnam experiences. When the chopper approached, the vet grabbed the tire and started to loop it around the top of the transmitter. The pilot realized what was happening at the last minute and managed to pull away before the tire could be affixed to the tower. But the structure shook violently, nearly dislodging the veteran. He managed to hold on, but his shades toppled to the tarmac, thus rendering him totally naked.

A few more hours elapsed. My befuddled casts from "Cabaret" had long since returned to their theater, muttering that the others would never believe this. At last, the man shouted he was ready to descend but was afraid to climb down. (Doctors later theorized he'd quite literally been "high" on a drug, and its effects had now worn off.) The helicopter was called back. This time, the man put the tire around himself and flew off into space, his arms and legs outstretched and a broad smile on his face. By this time, some of us were viewing him through a high-powered telescope borrowed from a factory next door to the studio. We could also see that he had a huge erection. As we watched him soaring through the night sky, I thought he looked like a black Christ in some surreal Fellini movie.

On to the Boondocks

I think I learned a lesson from my friend on the transmitter tower. Maybe he was right: there *was* more than one way to get "on television." Clearly, remaining on Channel 14 was not helping to clear my way to the better stations in Washington. So I made my next career decision: "Boondocks," here I come!

I went to New York to visit friends at the various network headquarters. After contacting every executive I had met during the hectic 1968 campaign, I finally found somebody at ABC who liked me. That pleased me, since ABC had always been my favorite network, even in the days when they were number three. They were innovative, willing to try new things, and specialized in international stories, even when a war or revolution in some faraway country might not be the clear lead story.

An ABC Vice President, Bill Sheehan, decided I should have a network audition, which was not the easiest thing in the world to get. After taking the screen test, I was told I had potential but needed a lot more work. It would also help if I lost weight, which I could never quite do. I traveled around the country, visiting ABC-owned and -operated stations. I had some good offers, including one high-paying job as a writer at their station in San Francisco. However, none of the offers were for on-air work. I didn't want to live in San Francisco anyway; there were too many other people like me there, and I thrive on variety.

A different tack was called for. *Broadcasting* magazine - a bible for the industry - listed a number of on-air openings in small stations around the country. I tried one in Huntington, West Virginia, on the theory it was really not that far from Washington. They invited me down, and the journey entailed a rough airplane flight over the rugged West Virginia mountains. The airport was a killer at the best of times, wedged between the steep hills. But this flight was complicated by a sudden blizzard, and we were forced to land miles away. A bus fought its way through the mountain storm and got us to Huntington, a tough coal and steel town in the heart of Appalachia. I checked into the only hotel around and staggered into bed, leaving a wake-up call for six-thirty a.m. before my interview the next morning. For some reason, when I got the call from an operator with a strong hillbilly accent, my still sleeping mind thought I was back in Czechoslovakia. When the woman shouted, "Good morning! It's time to wake up," I blurted out, "How did you learn to speak English so well?" Understandably, the poor woman was insulted, but I never could convince her that it was unintentional.

My audition at the station was a debacle as well. They didn't like me, and I didn't like them. It was a clear example of a failure to communicate - and disastrous interpersonal chemistry. I returned to Washington and began to seek out other ABC affiliates. WTEV-Channel 6, in New Bedford, Massachusetts, was expanding rapidly and needed new talent. At least they were in New England, where I had attended Simmons College in Boston (as well as summer classes at Harvard). And, though New Bedford was on the southern coast of Massachusetts, one could drive from there north to the ski areas of New Hampshire and Vermont in just three hours - a decided advantage for this frustrated ski bum.

WTEV flew me up and treated me like visiting royalty, putting me up in a well-appointed motel on the ocean, and paying for expensive fresh seafood meals. The General Manager and I got on famously. I was offered a job as a reporter and part-time "anchor" woman. Although the pay was low - $140 a week - it was also a lot less expensive to live in New Bedford than in Washington. I signed the contract without benefit of legal advice, which turned out to be a big mistake.

I whipped back to Washington, sublet my apartment to a bachelor, and moved to New Bedford. When my motel expenses ran out, I found a boarding house on Main Street. Mine was a small room with one hot plate for cooking, but no private toilet. I had to share the bathroom down the hall with the rest of the boarders, many of whom were retired Portuguese fishermen. One, who said he had been a captain, looked and acted like Ahab, straight out of Moby Dick. The whaling ships in the Herman Melville novel had sailed from New Bedford, and my captain was a perfect caricature, even down to his wooden leg. My neighbor monopolized the bathroom for hours at a time. What was he doing, I wondered - waxing his leg? In any case, I could never get into it when I needed to, and often was forced to improvise, by using the wastebasket in my room as a chamber pot.

My public life on air was nearly as glamorous as my private one. My boss was as good as his word, regarding the reporting and anchor position. I got a lot of good "street" experience, running around on location with a camera crew, but they always mistrusted my "big city" news judgment. I was not the only one who suffered from their myopic and provincial view of the world. Shortly before I arrived, a Lithuanian sailor had jumped from a Soviet ship to an American Coast Guard vessel and asked for asylum. The station bosses, not realizing it was a major story with international implications, downplayed the event. As a result, a reporter and crew were sent down from ABC News in Boston to cover the unfolding drama for the national news.

Usually, I wasn't assigned to cover the big juicy stories, but was relegated to "women's news." That was about a century after Lizzie Borden in nearby Fall River "took an ax and gave her parents forty whacks," and years before the New Bedford rape trial also became an international story. Women's news in 1969 consisted of comparison price shopping at local grocery stores, and an occasional story about the Pope's continued opposition to abortion and birth control. The effect on the local region of the Pope's encyclical on abortion was one of the sadder stories I covered there. Most of the Portuguese women of the area were devout Catholics, and wanted to obey the dictates of their Church. At the same time, many were normal, hot-blooded women who wanted to enjoy open relationships with their "old men," as they called their boyfriends. Their compliance with the Pope's dictates against contraception and abortion led to many unwanted pregnancies - and gruesome, illegal abortions. Sadly, that situation has changed little in the intervening quarter century.

While I was working some real flesh-and-blood stories of the street, my boss also gave me another assignment. When I wasn't scurrying about outside in search of news, or anchoring newscasts (before an audience in the dozens at one a.m., five-thirty a.m., and seven-thirty a.m.), I was the Weather Girl (not to be confused with the sexy Exercise Lady who was on-air after me and did her routines in a black negligee). Now, I have the greatest respect for trained meteorologists, but harbor the utmost contempt for women who are selected for their anatomy to read the weather.

In fact, a sex symbol was precisely what I was supposed to be. I was provided a wardrobe that included a dress that stopped at the top of my thighs. One such dress was even spotted, making me look like a two-legged leopard. I was supplied a red wig, with straight hair that fell down to meet the hemline of my dress. It was beautiful, but if I swung my head around to point at the weather map, it would fall off, right in front of the audience.

The short skirt was hardly a hit with the audience. Our first weather show came at five-thirty in the afternoon, on the heels of "Gilligan's Island," which had an audience of children. One irate-mom wrote in that her child had been watching "Gilligan" and then our newscast. He called to his mother, shouting, "Look, Ma - that lady forgot to put her pants on!"

Of course, my mail was not nearly as interesting as the Exercise Lady's, although I did get a mixed bag of letters from viewers in Southern Massachusetts, Rhode Island, and Northern Connecticut. The gym gal, however, performed her gyrations in a see-through wardrobe, just after midnight. She actually kept score of the number of women who wrote in saying they had become pregnant while watching her moves.

I stubbornly refused to become proficient in weather reporting, and to this day I don't know the difference between a high-pressure and a low-pressure system. We had a wire copy machine which provided the forecasts. I would copy the predictions by writing them in big letters on a chart, which was then suspended from the camera. That way, I could look right into the camera, read the notes at the same time and act as though I knew what I was talking about. I was really in trouble, however, when the cameraman moved the camera back for a wide shot and I couldn't read my notes. At those times, I just made up the rest. We were always wrong anyway, and the good people of New England - who could better predict the weather with their bunions and bad backs - knew never to believe a weatherman.

Often, my forecasts were dramatically off base. One day I confidently predicted azure-blue skies, an excellent day to visit the many beaches on nearby Cape Cod. But there were no windows in our studio, and I hadn't noticed the torrential downpour outside. After the newscast, I received over a hundred calls from people advising me - with some heat - to stick my stupid head out the window and open my eyes.

I had even less luck with nautical terms. Once I said the wind was 50 knots per hour. Dozens of native sailors called in to inform me: "It's knots, not knots per hour!" Another time, a huge naval frigate docked into New Bedford Harbor. Knowing the word "frigate" had sexual connotations for the gutter-minded, I also knew I couldn't say the word on the air without cracking up. So I decided to change the word "frigate" to "sloop." My viewers educated me instantly that there is a many ton difference between the two vessels.

One of my hottest forecasts occurred on New Year's Eve. I made the mistake of going to a dinner party with some of my few friends on staff. I had one glass of wine, which was enough to make me drunk. When we returned to the studio for the eleven p.m. newscast, I was quite tipsy. I couldn't read the words on my chart, even when they were close. The technicians decided to make it even harder for me, by setting fire to the bottom of the chart. I read as fast as I could before flames consumed the whole chart. The whole episode made me double over with laughter - short skirt and all - helpless to go on. Fortunately, most of our viewers were either too drunken themselves or too busy partying to notice anything was amiss.

Then there was the "Bozo Caper." Bozo the Clown as an actor, dressed in the traditional funny suit - frizzy red wig, big red nose, polka dots, and floppy shoes. Many t.v. stations in the nation had a Bozo franchise. When Bozo was not performing his kiddy show, he was fond of walking around the studio - in full costume - and reading aloud from the most risque books on the market. They were often hard to find in Puritanical New England.

Late one night, as I was anchoring the news and destroying the weather forecast, Bozo walked toward me, stopping just out of camera range. There, he proceeded to read passages from *Lady Chatterly's Lover*, make sucking noises, and employ obscene hand gestures - all this as I was about to tell my audience about the latest victims of car crashes and the death of Gamal Nasser in Egypt.

Only a few nights later, on a Monday night, ABC broadcast the football games. When they ended, Dick Cavett's variety show was supposed to come on for ninety minutes. After that, I was to anchor the final newscast, which usually aired at one o'clock in the morning, later if the football game was long. On the first night of this format, the football game ended at ten minutes to one. ABC cut to Cavett. Affiliated stations all over the country assumed they had ninety minutes to go before the final newscast. But precisely at one a.m., Cavett signed off - after only ten minutes on the air. Panic erupted; we had to be on the air in thirty seconds, and nothing was written! Frantically, I ripped out a long chunk of wire copy from the tape machine and picked up the script from the eleven p.m. show. Then, with wire copy streaming behind me, I ran down the steep metal stairs to the studio.

I got behind the podium and breathlessly tried to read the first story. I called for the film clip to follow it. I reported somberly, "Chaos has broken out in Egypt, following the sudden death and tumultuous funeral of Nasser. Here's a report from our ABC correspondent in Cairo." Up came a tape of girls in shorts - huffing and puffing. It was a film story about a girl's gym class in Providence, Rhode Island, which ran for three minutes. I muttered something about technical difficulties and then moved on to a White House story. Up came the film of problems in the ski fields of Vermont. Now I was into my third story. I thought I'd be safe if I introduced a local, rather than a national report, since it seemed clear to me that the technicians had the local tapes lined up. I talked about the superintendent of schools in Providence, who was threatening to quit. Then I said, "Here's the superintendent with his side of the story." Instead, a picture came up of a man slicing open a dead, glassy-eyed fish. We had queued to the fourth story, about pollution in the New England rivers. It also ran for three minutes. When it finished, I looked straight at the monitor and said, "If you think you're confused, so is Superintendent So-and-so." Then I burst into uncontrolled laughter. There was no stopping me. Finally, I just put my head down on the podium and laughed hysterically for the next four minutes. Surely, an award-winning newscast …

Strangely, those events were not enough to get me fired. I was finally done in by old-fashioned office politics, which are probably no less ruthless in a television studio than they are in any other business, anywhere in the world.

Along with some friends of mine from Harvard, I had rented a share in a magnificent ski cabin up an isolated mountain road near the ski fields of Sugarbush, Vermont. I've always been generous and enjoy sharing possessions with friends. So I put up a note on our office bulletin board, inviting anyone who wanted to share the cabin.

Two of my coworkers used the cabin, but not as I'd planned. One was the publicity director of the station. For months, Paul had written business notes to me. On the bottom they were signed, "With love." To me, there was nothing strange about that; I sign notes the same way when I care about people. He was married, but had always behaved in a business-like manner toward me. I never realized he had subtly been making a play for me. But we had a very ambitious young secretary who realized he was "on the make," and she went after him, tooth and nail. Peggy was also married, but she wasn't fanatical about it by any means. As time went on, Peggy and Paul fell into an affair. Peggy began to move very quickly up the office ladder. In a span of three months, she became a cameraman, then a film editor, and ultimately a reporter. She soon posed a real threat to my job and to that of Sue Schiffer, who spent three days a week serving as the Washington correspondent and two days reporting from Boston. She was a brilliant, quality person, who later went on to win a coveted White House Fellowship (one of the most prestigious and hard-won in the United States). In time, she even worked for Vice President Rockefeller and Secretary of State Kissinger. But even her job at WTEV was in serious peril because of the utterly ruthless Peggy and an unprincipled boss.

One night as I was preparing the eleven o'clock news, I received an irate call from Peggy's husband, a fine young man who was a student at Brown University in Rhode Island. He demanded to know why I had let his wife go off with Paul to my ski cabin and where that cabin was. I was totally shocked. Cut off from the office gossip, I had no idea of their affair, much less that I was an accessory to it. I was only too happy to give him directions to my cabin.

Relations were never quite the same in the station after that. Little by little, I was squeezed out of important projects. I knew my time was limited when life-size publicity pictures immortalizing the station's "personalities" were hung on the wall. No such pictures of me were displayed, even though my photo was still in the regional *Television Guide* each day. A large photo of our "secretary," Peggy, won a spot on the wall, however.

I did receive a promotion of sorts. Instead of working the night shift, I was to report to work at four-thirty a.m. and anchor the three morning newscasts (viewed by the fishermen and factory workers, who were probably a far more serious audience than we had at night). Afterward, I was allowed on the street with a camera crew to report news stories. Best of all, I no longer had to do the weather!

Waking up at three-thirty in the morning was an excruciating trial for me. Like a vampire, I have a nocturnal metabolism. In addition, I had now moved to a small house on an island just outside New Bedford. When I woke and walked my dog, I was astonished by what I saw on the beach. It was so cold the waves had actually frozen into huge slabs on the shore. Sometimes, the slabs were heavy enough to crush my neighbors' small rowboats. I knew the oceans froze in the polar climes, but had never expected to witness it in Massachusetts.

Aside from having to awaken at an uncivilized hour, the new assignment went well for me. I learned a lot and received complimentary phone calls from my small but loyal audience. The Navy "Seabees" at a nearby Rhode Island Naval base even had a luncheon for me, at which I was "roasted" for my lack of nautical experience. I told them I had once been "Miss Safe Boating Queen" as a teenager in New Jersey, but that didn't deter them from telling dozens of jokes at my expense. They thought "Miss Barge" or "Miss Bilge-Pump" was more apropos. After listening to them for two hours, I could almost agree with them.

It's said that all good things must come to an end, but even the bad things fizzle out. I had managed to survive a year at the station, and my contract was nearly up. One day, infused with a false sense of confidence since everything had been going so well, I bounced into the newsroom after my anchor shifts. The news director, Jack Delany, called me aside. He was a tough, experienced Boston newspaperman, but the alcohol on his breath, even at seven in the morning, betrayed the fortification he needed to fire me. So it had happened: the promotion posters (minus one for yours truly) had foreshadowed the inevitable. For whatever reason, the station had determined that I was expendable.

I was dazed for a few days, but slowly began to pack. I gave notice to my Polish landlord, whose face reflected the dismay in my own heart. His family and I had become close friends during the few months I'd rented his home. Often, he would contrive to be visiting me when my dates showed up. My special boyfriend at the time was a dashing Portuguese man named Les. My landlord had been vastly amused at my status as the Weather Girl, and always greeted Les or my other dates with a cheery, "Hi, buddy. Been under the weather lately?" Then he would offer a sample of his strong home-brewed whisky. Sometimes he and my date would get so drunk that the two of them would wind up the evening vomiting in the bathroom. Such was the glamorous social whirl in which I was caught up in New Bedford.

But the landlord and my other neighbors on the island were as sad to see me go as I was to leave them. Most of my neighbors were Cape Veredians, mixtures of Portuguese and African, from the Cape Verde Islands off the coast of Senegal and Mauritania. They were some of the warmest, most open, most generous people I had ever known. Although they were held in contempt by some of the New England Yankees, they were better read and more articulate than most of their detractors. At the end of a very small street on my island, there was only one store - and it was a bookstore.

I was truly sorry to leave these good people, even though the year had been hard for me. I packed up a rented U-Haul truck, hooked it up to my rusting Chevrolet convertible, and left New Bedford at sunrise. Other New Englanders unkindly referred to the region as the "armpit" of Massachusetts, but it was hard for me to say good-bye. There was nothing else I could do - WTEV was the only television station in the town, and I couldn't see any other work there for me.

As I pulled away from the first house I'd ever lived in on my own, and my first real television news job, I began to sob. I cried most of the way during the six-hour drive to my parents' apartment in New York City. In fact, so deep in the doldrums was I that I couldn't find a way to get off the superhighway and wound up circling Manhattan twice. Finally, I found the right road off the expressway and descended into the jungles of New York.

An East Coast Odyssey

I arrived at my parents' New York apartment, looking like a time-battered hobo. For a few days, I could do nothing but lie around. I was so completely shattered by my experiences of the past year; I was receptive to pressure from my father to leave reporting - and Washington. He had a long-standing hatred of reporters, dating back from the days when unscrupulous "yellow journalists" had hurt him. Dad also had a similar regard for the politicians in Washington. He was fond of saying: "The best thing you could do to most of them is flush them down the toilet." My father had long wanted me to go into business with him, and I began to see things his way - at least for a while. So once again, I hooked up a U-Haul to my car and drove the 250 miles to Washington. There, I sadly reclaimed my apartment and told the landlord I was leaving for good, sealing my decision by selling or giving away the furniture I'd accumulated.

To further complicate the chaos in my life, my German shepherd, Tracy, climbed into the bathtub one morning and began to give birth to a dozen mixed-breed puppies. The garage mechanics behind my former house near New Bedford had tried to tell me she was being romanced by a mongrel, but I'd foolishly dismissed their warnings out of hand.

Dogs were forbidden in my sterile Washington apartment, and I had enough trouble concealing Tracy from the strict landlord, who also happened to be a former CIA agent. Twelve squealing, yipping puppies proved no challenge to his acutely honed spying skills. I promised him I would be out in three days, rather than the two weeks remaining on my lease. Meanwhile, the puppies were the talk of the apartment complex.

Several of my big shot neighbors - including Senators, Congressmen and Hill staffers - spent endless hours around my bathtub. It was amusing and touching to see the high and mighty reduced to putty by squirming bundles of fur.

My apartment empty, I loaded up my thirteen dogs and my crates of memorabilia, and left Washington. Strangely, it was less traumatic than I'd expected; leaving the city I had aspired to and planned to make my home since my politically active high school years. Perhaps I subconsciously knew I would soon return to the beautiful monuments, the long stretches of green grass and sinuous curves of Rock Creek Parkway. Besides, it's hard to be too despondent in the company of twelve curious puppies snuggling on your lap, or crawling around under the pedals of the car.

It is easy to get lost, though. Distracted by my furry family, I took two wrong turns, and added hours to my trip. My plans were to return to Vermont and spend a month in my ski cabin before embarking on my new life in New York. En route, I stopped again in New Bedford to say good-bye to my handsome Portuguese boyfriend. That made the situation much worse and deepened the sense of loneliness I felt during my month of self-imposed isolation in the Vermont ski chalet.

Vermont offered a setting conducive to reflection and introspection. I spent the days in near solitude, skiing in the cold, magnificent New England mountains. At night, no one ventured up the winding snow-covered mountain road to visit. The splendid isolation was a terrifying experience for a city girl, for the woods surrounding the cabin were inhabited by bears and myriad less-threatening forest creatures. With the spring thaw now underway, the bears were just beginning to stir. All night long, my dog Tracy would bark at the animals outside. The shepherd was a frightening sight with her fangs bared and her hackles raised. But I knew these displays were unlikely to fool anyone, and that she could do little in the event of a real emergency. Her puppies offered no protection, either. I'd given them all away to fellow skiers at the Sugarbush ski area. It broke my heart to part with them, but I hope they gave joy and comfort to many families. Back at the ski lodge, my only defense was a towering, stuffed brown bear - ten feet high - which stood in the living room of the cabin. I moved it in front of the enormous glass wall of the A-frame cabin, hoping it would scare away any smaller live bears seeking entry.

The bears didn't drive me away, but the mud did. As the snows melted, the mountain trails became rivers of mud. Spring rain replaced the winter snows, and the downpour was incessant. This was the season when some who had endured the harsh Vermont winter became so depressed they committed suicide. Others chose a fate nearly as bad - they left for more accommodating climes, like Miami. This was no place for me, either, since I was depressed and, by this time, physically ill. I got into my car and started the journey to New York. But I had the type of Chevrolet that could be started without the key in the ignition. By mistake, I'd left the keys dangling from the trunk, not realizing my mistake for two hundred miles. By then, they were a part of the New England landscape. The only extra keys to my parents' apartment were on that key chain and my folks would be out of the country for two weeks. I had no choice but to return to Vermont. I broke into my ski cabin - stuffed bear and all - and spent another two weeks with the rain, the animals, and the mud my only companions. By the time I started the trip a second time, even I was ready for New York City!

Good-bye Washington - Hello Washington

I spent six months in New York, living in my parents' luxury apartment overlooking Central Park. I never really did get involved in my father's diverse business ventures; he was undergoing one crisis after another and had no time to train me to work with him. So, for lack of anything more pressing to do, I began to make the rounds of the television network headquarters and the local television and radio stations, but it was an exercise in ambivalence. I didn't really try too hard to sell myself. Every time I sat through an interview and was then escorted through the offices to meet the other employees, I detected undercurrents of intense political struggles among them. But at least they were treating me with respect this time. Memories of the insults I'd endured over the years burned into my consciousness, as I walked through the studios. I remembered how hard I'd worked to get temporary jobs with the NBC election units at the end of each primary campaign in 1968, to get enough money to finance me through the next state. I'd done what it took, and was proud of my contributions. But during one stop in Chicago, the NBC unit manager blew up at me, for reasons I still cannot fathom, other than his disdain for opportunistic free-lancers. He tore my NBC badge off my coat and accused me of being a "camp follower." I was reinstated a few moments later by other bosses, but the hurt and humiliation stayed with me.

This time, in New York, I was treated as a professional. Even the brush-offs were handled in ways befitting a member of the club, and not an outsider. Still, if I couldn't even survive the office politics and sexual pressures of a minor station in Massachusetts, how could I ever expect to stomach them in New York City, where they were multiplied exponentially? For one thing, it was a buyer's market; there was a surfeit of talent around. News directors and talent agencies were saturated with us. It was pathetic and demeaning to go into a local talent agent and see so many bright young singers, performers, and "on-air personalities" sitting around in a crowded room, hoping to be noticed by someone with the power to give them a job. These people had struggled for years to perfect their skills, but were often cast rudely aside by the brusque New Yorkers. It was then I realized that I'd be better off in an area where I felt more at home, where I could be of use to someone.

Besides, it's often noted that you either love New York or you hate it; there's nothing in between. And I really disliked New York. My only joyful moments had been the times I'd walked my dog Tracy through the area of Central Park known as Dog Hill. My only friends in the city were fellow dog walkers I met there. It was a magical place filled with the most unimaginable combinations of dogs and people. One Broadway playwright had two large Irish wolfhounds and a small Pekinese. The two large ones often voided on the small one, who returned to his Fifth Avenue apartment a soaked, stinking mass of tangled fur. Another time, a huge Great Dane put his massive paws on my shoulders and tried to mate with me. He was so heavy I couldn't push him off. He reminded me of some of my old bosses! A large crowd stood around, laughing at us, but no one made a move to get the hound off. Finally, he descended of his own volition. A few moments later, a handsome man in an expensive leather jacket came up to me. He extended his hand, saying in elegantly accented English, "Good morning. My name is Niels Larsen, and I'm a great Dane too." He was no relation to the other Dane, but he was a suave gynecologist with a successful practice on Fifth Avenue. We became good friends. In fact, the following year he was a guest in my apartment at the Watergate complex on the very night the notorious Watergate break-in occurred.

Dog Hill notwithstanding, I had by now become quite homesick for Washington, and when some thug pulled a gun on me one afternoon in Central Park and another exposed himself to me, I resolved to call it quits in the Big Apple.

I had a bit of luck with two of the New York stations when I proposed doing free-lance work for them from Washington. In addition, the importance of the Washington dateline was constantly reinforced in my mind. Although New Yorkers deem their city the center of the universe and most of numerous big corporations are headquartered there, I noted that every hourly newscast is dominated by the stories from Washington. I knew that if I returned to D.C., I could work for New York stations from there, as well as for other stations across the country and around the world.

And so I repacked my rusty old Chevrolet, which by this time had accumulated several hundred dollars worth of New York parking tickets. I'd long overstayed my welcome at my parents' apartment, and they tried not to seem too overjoyed to see me and my dog leave. Many were the times we'd embarrassed my father's business guests. There were times they would walk into the elegant, mirrored bathroom of my folks' apartment, make themselves comfortable on the commode, and heard a low, rumbling growl. Tracy was fond of sleeping in the shower, and didn't take kindly to intruders in her "kennel." It was comical to see my father's $100-an-hour lawyer run screaming, half-naked from the bathroom and almost collapse with fright outside the door.

Relieved to be back in Washington, I rented a townhouse in the same complex near Capitol Hill where I'd previously lived. It was gratifying to renew my old friendships. I began to do free-lance work for WNBC radio, a major outlet in New York City. It was great fun covering the New York Congressional delegation, but it was also very hard work. The New Yorkers were the largest and most politically active delegation on Capitol Hill. The Congressmen were smart, stimulating, and great fun to be with. One Congressman, Charles Rangel, always wanted to mate my dog Tracy with his own German shepherd, but I tried to tell him I'd had quite enough puppies, thank you very much. Another charming Congressman, Hugh Carey, occasionally took me to dinner. He went on to become Governor of New York. The rest of the delegation tried to arrange a marriage between Congressman Ed Koch, and me. It was his driving ambition to become Mayor of New York City. But Koch, a fine man who went onto serve as Mayor for several years, was not the kind to let marriage interfere with his devotion to duty. Another Congressman, Joe Addabbo, was a friendly, robust Italian. I affected the habit of kissing his ring and calling him "Godfather" before we began our interviews. I'm sure that caused some talk among the investigative journalists who watched us carrying on in the hallways of the House of Representatives.

Working on a per-story basis didn't bring me great riches, but I was self-supporting and able to pay the rent. I spent little money for food. Since I was very much onboard the "Washington merry-go-round," I was invited to an endless round of luncheons, cocktail parties, and dinners. They were exhausting, but as a single and ambitious careerist, I knew it was essential to attend as many functions as possible to meet the people who kept the wheels of Washington turning. How I yearned for the chance to spend a quite night at home, watching television. But I didn't dare step off the merry-go-round to do so.

As a free-lancer, I offered many advantages to the stations I worked for. It cost them much less than it would have to send out their own correspondent, for whom they would incur overhead costs like benefits and insurance. I received no benefits whatsoever from the stations; they could fire me at will, without having to pay unemployment compensation. As my career progressed, my client stations were in constant flux. I quit many because they failed to pay me; others fired me because they didn't like me, my style, or my approach to the problems of their jurisdictions. But I managed to keep a nucleus of about five stations over the years, and they've been my mainstay ever since.

To start out, I had run ads in *Broadcasting* magazine, offering to cover congressional delegations and other local news events for stations around the country. In those years - the early 1970s - there were very few reporters on Capitol Hill offering this kind of service. I believe there were only three active free-lancers in the electronic media, all of them women. News directors had also made advances at my two colleagues in their time, and disgusted, we set off on our own. We all went in different directions, but each of us became quite successful. I branched out to as many stations as I could handle on my own. My friend Carol expanded as far as she could, investing enormous sums in television and radio equipment, and hiring a large staff of reporters. Sue (my colleague from New Bedford days) became the television reporter for a major chain of stations, but maintained her independence by being her own boss in Washington.

My ads brought a large number of responses. I also continued to promote myself by attending media conventions across the nation. The best was RTNDA – or the Radio-Television News Directors Association. The other good one was the NAB, or National Association of Broadcasters. These are often referred to as "meat markets," and it is quite demeaning to put yourself on display to thousands of news executives. However, it's also an excellent way to be seen, become known, and distribute your literature. Unfortunately, most of the real job hunting is conducted during noisy cocktail parties - the journalistic equivalent of the "smoke-filled room." But the executives let their hair down and friendships are easily established. I typically got more job offers from the parties than I did from pounding on doors. The trick was to stay sober, pass out my card, and follow up the offer the next day. It was quite a successful strategy.

Soon I had a string of stations stretching from Canada to New York, south to Florida, and west to St. Louis and California. It meant an enormous amount of effort. I was constantly on the go, working eighteen-hour days, six days a week, with a few hours on Sunday. There was no time for any meaningful private life, and I couldn't have combined such a schedule with the responsibilities of family life. I incorporated myself under the name "Audio-Video News Bureau," a name I used just for my advertising and my credentials. I "tagged out," or ended my stories with the name of my station.

The main drawback to the type of news I did was its public relations aspect. I sometimes had the uncomfortable feeling I was "flacking" for the legislators I covered. To balance this somewhat, I instituted a weekly feature entitled, "The Most Ineffective Congressman of Your District." This didn't endear me to them, but it helped keep them on their toes.

For the first time in my life, I was making real money in the business. That isn't to say that everything went smoothly. I persisted in trying to get a "real" job in the local Washington market. This was becoming harder, because I was now pegged as a "free-lance personality." The news executives could see that I had an independent spirit and might not be keen on the blind obedience they expected. This underscores one of the many dilemmas of this business: They want you to be a "self-starter," one who can initiate stories on your own, and let nothing get in the way of covering them. Yet if you become too independent, they see you as a "hot dog" - they don't like you, don't trust you, and don't want you!

Another paradox is the age issue. If you're too young and inexperienced, they don't want you. But it is precisely when you are young, eager and desperate that you are at your most ruthless and willing to do practically anything to get the job and cover the story. Once you have some years under your belt, you are less prone to take chances than hungry cub reporters. Also, women especially age very quickly in this business, and can be considered over the hill by thirty. (Now, thank God that has changed, due to the magic of plastic surgery! It has become a fountain of youth for those in the media, and in public life in general). Thus it's vital to hit the ground running - while you're young. There is another fine distinction worth mentioning: The executives want to hire you when you have some experience but are still fresh enough to be trained for the special style of their particular network. Somehow, I had crossed over the line between no experience and too much experience, without hitting the middle period in which networks felt they could mold me to their image.

By and large, I get on well with most of my colleagues, even my fellow free-lancers. We understand the unwritten rules of the game and usually don't try to steal each other's jobs or clients. In fact, the system works so well that I've made only five or six real enemies among the thousands of reporters I've worked with over the years. All things considered, the news business on the whole tends to be a fairly honorable profession. It's also one of the most fun and most fulfilling ones to be in. As the saying goes, "It beats working any day!"

I did have one promising opportunity that was ruined for me by one of my female colleagues, one of the proverbial ones ruthless enough to sell her own grandmother for a story. During the 1968 primaries, I encountered this nameless woman reporter, who had been sent out by one of the networks to cover a candidate. At that time, she was one of the biggest and bitchiest female reporters at the network, but within just a few years she became relatively obscure and lost several jobs. Her colleagues on the campaign trail roundly despised her. Once, while she was doing a stand-up interview, a technician came along and sliced off her microphone cable. She stood there, totally oblivious, talking into the wind.

This woman resented the fact that I was sending radio reports back to her network, although none of her male predecessors had objected. In fact, they had even encouraged me and thrown a lot of stories my way. She wanted to do both radio and TV; but television consumed so much of her time that it took her hours longer than me to get the radio spots off to network headquarters in New York. Finally, she phoned the news desk with an ultimatum: I would continue working for them, she said, only over her dead body. While some of the editors no doubt found the notion tantalizing, they realized she had a year to go before her contract ran out.

She even went one step further. She heard I was being considered for a one-year internship on her network, a training program that could have opened the way for a reporter's job there. In a way, I suppose it was flattering that she obviously regarded me as a threat to her career, but I was heartbroken at the way she single-mindedly set out to ruin me. She phoned all the top executives at the network and spouted off many reasons (mostly false) why I should not have that internship. I was dropped from consideration.

It is often said that you have to "know" somebody to make it in this business. In my case, I might have advanced a lot further by now if I hadn't known this particular reporter. Thus, with my most solid chance at network training squelched, I resigned myself to picking up what piecemeal work I could in Washington, in addition to the free-lancing, which by now was really going well. I constantly circulated my resume and got a phone call one morning from WPGC radio in the Maryland suburbs. It was a rock station, one of the bigger ones in the Washington market. The program director was obviously a real nut. He hadn't the slightest interest in another boring reporter, but wondered if I wanted a three-hour spot on their morning show. The money was poor - only $75 a week - but the exposure in the Washington area was good. I agreed to give it a try.

My job was to be an assistant disc jockey for the morning "drive-time" show, the one with the biggest audience. My coworker was a real professional, smooth, deep-voiced, and unflappable. In addition, he knew the record business intimately, while I did not. The show was to be called, "Harv Moore and the Redhead." Poor Harv needed me as much as he needed a hole in the head.

My assignment was to make witty, sexy comments after the records ended. Often, I would quickly write little ditties as the record played and then read them afterward. Harv and I were supposed to engage in the utterly moronic "happy talk" format that was sweeping the country. But he and I were on totally different wavelengths and talked at, rather than to, each other.

There were other problems. I simply couldn't function at five in the morning, which was the start of our shift. I'd had enough trouble with those hours in New Bedford. Now I was working late into the night with my free-lance reporting, so I couldn't get to bed at eight p.m., as required for an early morning shift. The biggest obstacle, however, was my utter disdain for rock music, at the time. (I have now mellowed, since I have a son who is a rock musician). I like classical, easy listening, or country music. But the incessant, unrelenting beat of rock drives me up a tree and distorts my senses, making me forget things I really know. Such as the case after we finished playing the new Beatles hit, "Come Together." It had to be one of their most suggestive songs. In their first version, they had a phrase about "Walrus Gonads." Later, they must have re-cut the record, and the phrase was changed to "Walrus Gogules." Now, at the age of 25, I knew what gonads were, though I didn't know what walrus ones were, especially at seven-thirty in the morning. But I made up a poem about them, which I read on the air when the record ended. That morning, there were hundreds of "fender-benders," as commuters listening to me laughed so hard they momentarily forgot they were driving.

That was my swan song on WPGC. I was fired before my shift ended, and my illustrious one-week career as a disk jockey was over. Actually, that was more funny than traumatic for me, because the job was not a serious one, in terms of furthering my ultimate career goals. A similar incident was far more serious for a colleague of mine years ago on WAVA. He'd made his reputation as a very conservative, very proper Southern gentleman. Somehow, the first "take" of one of his news reports made its way to the air during the afternoon rush hour. In it, he had read a few sentences, made a mistake, and said, "Aw, s---!" He kept his job, after a one-week suspension, but his reputation was shattered.

But for me, WPGC was my last fling at a staff job on the Washington market. There continued to be occasional guest appearances on interview shows, and celebrity auctions for the benefit of WTEV public television. It finally began to dawn on me that I could actually make a long-term living as my own boss, and didn't have to be officially employed by anyone. That concept was nearly unheard of in the early 1970s. In fact, there was such a stigma against free-lancers that I had to fight very hard for some of my press credentials.

By that time, I'd had my White House press credentials for several years. Those are the hardest ones to get. You need to prove you spend part of most days at the White House (which I do); get several letters from news directors saying you work for them; and survive a thorough security check by the Secret Service. I also had my credentials for the State Department and for the U.S. Congress. These are the most important news credentials, and I'm very proud of them. I am also very careful not to abuse the privilege of having them by misusing them in any way.

But the free-lance nature of my business caused me problems when I tried to renew my local Washington, D.C. press credential. The "powers" who evaluated my application wrote to me stating that a free-lancer couldn't get one. I wrote back a blistering letter, pointing out that I was a legally incorporated news bureau in the District of Columbia. I added that I had contracts from all my stations around the country and was their correspondent in Washington. Then I told them I needed my credential to cover the news in Washington. I warned that if they didn't give it to me, they were interfering with my right to work, and I threatened to take them to court. I was dead serious about this, as they apparently realized. My local credential (which I'd had for two years, for WAVA and WFAN) was renewed the next week. Ironically, I let it lapse years later, when I stopped doing any local news. The first three were the ones I really used each day as time went on. The experience, however, reminded me that free-lancers were still a new concept and regarded by many as second-class. From then on, I was careful to identify myself as a bureau chief and the Washington correspondent for several stations. Today, however, it pleases me to see colleagues proudly sporting credentials proclaiming "free-lance" dangling from the chains around their necks. And I feel vindicated when I hear CBS announce "So-and-So, a free-lance correspondent on assignment to CBS News." The day of the independent may not have fully arrived, but it's certainly well on its way.

Sex in the Senate (Or, Too Many Hormones on the Hill)

I now settled down comfortably into my routine of covering the U.S. Congress on Capitol Hill, and making daily trips to the White House to attend major events and briefings. In fact, I discovered that the White House was a marvelous place to go in the evenings, rather than wasting time at parties or in bars. (I don't drink anyway, and found smoke filled bars boring and loathsome). Often there was a dinner or state function to cover. Some of the most important quotes can come as the President or a visiting dignitary offers a toast. There was relatively little competition to sell the story, because many of the other reporters were burned out by the day's events and didn't want to cover anything else. But I was pleased to join the ranks of the "old girls." These are some of the formidable female reporters who grow old covering the White House. They live and breathe that beat, and are there from early morning until late at night. Even in my mid-twenties, I thought that was an excellent way to age in a career and be part of history at the same time. I admire the staying power of these legendary women who have grown gray performing the public service of keeping Presidents on their toes. Now, since I have been covering the White House since 1968, I am rapidly becoming part of the legend!

To me, the most memorable of those evening events was the time Israeli dancing was performed in the White House East Room during an Israeli State visit, soon after the Camp David Accords were signed. I was also deeply moved by the Christmas parties to which some reporters are invited. It is remarkable to sit in the splendor of the ornate Red Room, enchanted by the Christmas tree decked with handmade ornaments. We sit on plush red couches near a cheery fireplace, while white-gloved servants ply us with food and drink. We can look at the brightly-lit National Christmas Tree in the park across from the White House. Visitors stream past that tree, often singing Christmas carols as they go.

The Christmas buffet is also sumptuous. You can judge the state of the American economy by calculating the quantity of shrimp and roast beef served at each Christmas dinner. As an added payoff, the invited reporters and guests get a picture of themselves shaking the President's hand in the receiving line. Most of my pictures are just ghastly, and cry out for captions like, "Beast Lady Meets the President." In an early one with President Reagan, the President is holding my hand and appears to be pointing at the veins in my arm. I call that one, "When Did You Stop Mainlining?"

One of my earliest White House dinners took place during Lyndon Johnson's presidency. The dinner was held to honor the American space industry. All the astronauts and the major figures in American aeronautics were invited. The director of the Boston Opera, Sarah Caldwell, was invited to conduct the operetta of Jules Verne's *From the Earth to the Moon*. Later, while socializing, I asked her how she enjoyed performing in the White House. President Johnson hovered near us, apparently anxious to hear her answer. She bellowed to me in her rich voice, "Can you imagine the thrill - performing here in the White House, in front of ... Charles Lindbergh?" Poor Lyndon Johnson was abashed, and slunk away dejected.

While stories abounded about President Johnson (and John Kennedy before him) taking liberties with the female members of the White House press corps, I never witnessed any of these events firsthand. Of course, they did not hold a candle to the disgusting sexual activities of Bill Clinton in the Oval Office. But in the Congress, especially during the 1970s, there were no holds barred.

Now, I'm not particularly pretty or sexy and can't hold a candle to some of the truly glamorous creatures who work on Capitol Hill or in the television industry, but I was unmarried and in my mid-twenties. In addition, many of the lawmakers or staff members on the Hill consider anything in a skirt (or nowadays even in pants) fair game. Some of this still goes on, as witnessed by the scandals involving Congressmen and their teenage pages, and some Governors, and Senators accused of accosting staffers and lobbyists. And little can hold a cigar to Bill Clinton's Monica Lewinsky affair, or "fooling around," as she called it. But it really is much less prevalent than before. Congressman Gary Condit, who reportedly violated other bodies, broke hearts, and was involved with Chandra Levy, is a notable exception. Condit was forced to admit to a relationship, but denies he had anything to do with her murder. The scandal, however, caused his political downfall, much to the relief of many in Washington.

Since then, it is known that former Senator and Presidential hopeful John Edwards fathered a child out of Wedlock, and tried to cover up the affair, while his wife was fighting deadly cancer. And Governor Mark Sanford has an affair with his "soul mate" in Argentina, when he was supposed to be taking a hike on the Appalachian Trail. Governors of New York and New Jersey have had their interesting sexual entanglements, with partners of both sexes. So, in some cases, "the beat goes on." What is it about some public personalities?

Despite this, there is a new breed on the Hill; legislators who are much more serious, intense, harder working, and better educated. They also seem - at least on the surface - to be much more moral. Presidents George W. Bush and Barack Obama appeared to be moral family men. Still, political life is very disruptive to families, causing frequent separations. And, needless to say, no human being is immune to loneliness.

I began to learn that everything concerning the Hill had mildly sexual connotations. To get a parking space, one had to spend some time flirting with the guards, or with the powers in charge of assigning parking. I found these shenanigans increasingly frustrating as time went on. I was becoming busier each day, with more deadlines to meet and less time to flirt, what with rushing to get to a Congressional hearing on time. Even at the hearing itself, it's important to be extra nice to the guards to get in, even if your press credentials are in order. I really like people, and I enjoy smiling and being friendly - even flirting on occasion. And some of the Hill policemen really are my good friends. But sometimes, if one is rushed, civility gives way to preoccupation with the business at hand, and the guards can take this very personally. Before long, you become known as an "old battle-ax," rather than a coquette. I must say, I much prefer the parking system at the White House or at the State Department. There, you might spend long minutes looking for a parking meter and running back to it when your time expires; often your spot is blocks from the destination, which is an irritation when the weather is inclement. But the situation is more straightforward, and you know you will be able to park your vehicle and cover your story. On the Hill, if the guards don't want to help you park or allow you to double-park, you could be prevented from covering a crucial event. (Of course, the situation is much more difficult now – everyplace in Washington, with the security precaution and restrictions in place after the 9/11 terrorist attacks).

I frequently applied for a permit to park in one of the many places allotted to Congress, but was told I would have to wait five years or more for it. Then, a savvy friend suggested I visit Fishbait Miller, the Doorkeeper of the House. He was the short, squat man, who shouted, "Mr. Speaker, the President of the United States," before escorting the President to the podium for the State of the Union address. But the Doorkeeper has many additional duties than the one millions of people watched him perform.

The Doorkeeper has a vast array of little-known powers. He can control entry to major events and can dole out a number of highly paid patronage jobs and important parking spaces. Fishbait also had a reputation as a real "ladies-man", and I had to sidestep his advances more than once. But we struck an interesting arrangement. Once, in his office, I saw a huge jar of Georgia pecans. I mentioned to him that I loved the nuts and made a terrific pecan pie. He grinned and said, "If you'll bake me a pecan pie each year, I'll see that you get one of the best parking spaces on the Hill."

True to his word, Fishbait wrote me a letter, asking the guards to help me with parking whenever they could. Thanks to him, I often got the first spaces on the Plaza, just a few feet from the House chambers. The system worked beautifully for years. Sometimes, however, there were interesting complications. One involved a lawyer who was charged with running a highly successful prostitution ring on Capitol Hill.

Early one morning, I received a phone call from the Federal Bureau of Investigation. The agent on the phone was young and probably more nervous than I. At first, I thought it was one of my friends joking around. After a few minutes, however, I became terrified as I realized it was no joke. I knew I'd done nothing illegal, but J. Edgar Hoover was still running the Bureau in those days, and I knew they kept some devastating files on people. Here's how our conversation went:

ME: "Are you calling me about a story I did?"
AGENT: "What are you talking about?"
ME: "Didn't you know I'm a reporter?"
AGENT: (after a long, pregnant pause):"Er, no, it's something else."
ME "Then are you calling me about my relationship with the Attorney General?" (At that time, I was dating the Attorney General of the United States, who was an excellent news source. I wasn't married; he was, but he started the whole thing.)
AGENT: (after a longer pause, and probably in a state of shock):"Look, I think I'd better come and see you today."
ME: "You can't. This is the day I bake a pecan pie for the Doorkeeper of the House of Representatives."
AGENT: "That's okay. My wife bakes a terrific one. She'll make it."

I reluctantly agreed to receive the agent, fearing he would subpoena me if I refused. At the same time, I also invited two friends to visit my apartment in the exclusive Watergate complex, where I lived in a kind of "commune" with my huge dog and two other roommates. Both my friends were lawyers, and the young FBI agent was very quick to catch on to that fact. He did bring the pie, which I delivered to Fishbait the next day.

It turned out that the agent was investigating the lawyer I'd used to incorporate my news bureau. Phil Bailey was accused of running a thriving prostitute ring in the Congress. My name was in his address book, and the FBI was looking into everyone listed in the book. The agent showed me photos of some voluptuous-looking girls. In some cases, they were shown in compromising positions with other congressional employees. The agent asked if I could identify them. In fact, some of them did look familiar, but I was reluctant to become involved. Besides, the young ladies in question looked like typical sexy Capitol Hill staffers to me. I couldn't believe that I'd managed to choose that particular lawyer to incorporate me. Who would have thought it? Phil Bailey had even once been a seminarian and prominently displayed on his apartment wall was a picture of himself with the Pope. Sadly, he was eventually convicted and jailed, and a promising legal career was ruined.

I had met Phil around the swimming pool at my first apartment complex near Capitol Hill. Most of the residents were connected to the Congress in some way, and led interesting lives, to say the least. One Senator who lived there was mugged in the parking garage. He became one of the few ex-Senators to serve time in jail, on charges of improper financial dealings. His top assistant was actually murdered in front of the apartment by a ten-year-old boy who shot him in the back of his head while the man's poor wife watched helplessly.

The management of the apartment complex had adopted some tactics that would do any sleazy Congressman proud. One of my landlords - a Congressman - would call me up in mid-morning, suggesting that he drop by for a private visit. He implied - not too subtly - that I would not have to pay the rent if I were hospitable to him. I never took the bait; in fact, I allowed very few people into my apartment. Once, things got so bad in my building that several of the neighbors started a rent strike by putting our rent money into an escrow account. But instead of cleaning up their act and trying to make improvements, the owners threatened to take us to court. I was mortified when they attached a legal warning to the door of my apartment. Imagine their surprise when my friend the Attorney General called them and advised them to drop any legal action. (So you see, it really is "who" you know in Washington!) That was about the time I decided I'd had enough. I paid up, moved out, and went to the exclusive Watergate. The owner of that Watergate "commune" worked as an exterminator for Washington's Department of Rodent Control, and assumed many of the characteristics of the creatures he pursued. But the Watergate was still a better choice than my old neighborhood. The view over the Potomac River was spectacular.

Meeting the flirtatious Attorney General provided me a golden opportunity to cultivate my own private "Deep Throat" or well-placed source in the government. In fact, I wouldn't be surprised if he were one of the *real* "Deep Throats" who helped The *Washington Post* expose the Watergate scandal. (I believe they had more than one high-level source). The Attorney General was delighted to give me some private insight into government affairs, or meet me "spontaneously" on the steps of the Justice Department to conduct a television interview. My bosses were impressed by my knack for running into him and surprised (as I was) that he singled me out for so much attention.

Thankfully, it ended one Saturday evening, when he phoned me at my apartment around ten o'clock. At the time, I was rolling around on the floor, watching a horror movie on TV and wrestling with my boyfriend (and future husband), Steve. He caught me off guard by using his first name, and at first I wasn't sure whom I was talking to. When he asked what I was doing, I said, "Playing Dracula with my boyfriend; we're about to suck each other's blood." At that, a shocked and shaken Attorney General hung up the phone, and I never heard from him again. Another entry for Mr. Hoover's FBI files!

But I later learned that my friend the government servant had idiosyncrasies of his own. I was told, by other women who knew him well, that he set his clock radio to wake him at five in the morning, when "The Star Spangled Banner" blasted him awake. He allegedly sprang out of bed, stood at rigid attention, in full erection, and saluted until the music ended!

The Watergate Years

They say that timing is everything, and I had the good fortune of moving into the Watergate apartment complex several months before the notorious break-in at the Democratic National Committee offices, which were across the green common area from my apartment. The Watergate is more than just an office building. It is a large development on the banks of the Potomac River consisting of three apartment complexes, one hotel, two office buildings and several shops, including a fantastic bakery. Next to the Watergate is the Kennedy Center, a large square marble mausoleum that has served for years as the region's major cultural and performing arts center. Some of my neighbors used to joke that the Kennedy Center is the box the Watergate came in.

I enjoyed the luxury of the Watergate, which was built for people for whom time is money. Most of my neighbors were extremely wealthy Republicans, some of whom later were implicated in the cover-up of the break-in, even though many of them at first believed they were doing nothing illegal. But I really moved in because I needed a home for my German shepherd, Tracy. Most high-rise apartment buildings did not allow dogs. I had been living in a townhouse, which had proved attractive to burglars whenever Tracy and I left town. Two of my friends invited me to live with them in the Watergate, and offered me an attractive arrangement: I would pay full rent, and they would take care of my dog during the months I was on the road covering the 1972 Presidential primaries then underway. Best of all, I had the prestige of a Watergate address, which added a degree of class to my new stationery and business cards. Of course, the value of that address multiplied tenfold after the break-in and the worldwide publicity that followed.

I left the Watergate for a month to cover the first primary in New Hampshire. It was a harrowing journey. During a blizzard, my car began to careen down a steep mountain road. I couldn't use the brakes on the sheet ice and, in a panic, wildly turned my steering wheel from one direction to another. If I veered too far to the left, I would crash into the side of the mountain; too much to the right would propel me through a thin wire barrier and over the cliff. My velocity kept building, and by the time I reached a gas station at the bottom of the mountain I was going over a hundred miles an hour. Shaken, I pleaded with the attendant for chains for the car, which he cheerfully produced to the tune of a hundred dollars. They lasted only a few miles, however, snapping on the bare patches of the highway and wrapping around the axle of the car. I gave up at three-thirty in the morning, abandoning the car and trekking through the snow-lit night in below-zero temperatures. Somehow, I managed to limp, half frozen, into the nearest town. After that experience, I traveled more sensibly, riding the press buses as often as I could.

Once again in the company of my fellow reporters, I spent time following President Nixon, George McGovern, and other candidates around New Hampshire. As is usual in the early stages of a campaign, there were a plethora of fringe candidates who set up shop in the main hotels. One was a millionaire from Hawaii who ran on a ticket espousing legally sanctioned wife beating and polygamy. There was also the useful assortment of socialists, libertarians, and other hopefuls sprinkled in. Most of these would not make it past the first or second primary.

I returned to Washington after the New Hampshire primary with the intention of working from the White House for a few months and then going on to the other primaries on the West Coast. But one morning I woke up, looked at *The Washington Post*, and learned about the "third-rate break-in" (as the White House called it) into the Democratic Campaign Headquarters, located a stone's throw from my own apartment. Although there was no mention of any White House involvement during the first report of the incident, I remember my instantaneous reaction: Attorney General John Mitchell, I thought, would stop at nothing to win the election. Mitchell, who was also the chief campaign advisor, was one of my neighbors, but his apartment was in the complex closest to the office building that housed the Democratic Headquarters. Always ecumenical in my thinking, my second reaction was to consider that perhaps the Democrats had done the deed themselves, to cast suspicion on the Republicans.

It took months for the story to completely unravel, thanks to the thorough investigative efforts of *The Washington Post*. Like most other reporters at the time, I tried my best to discover the truth about the break-in and the extent of White House involvement in it and the subsequent cover-up. Living in the Watergate gave me a decided advantage. I could go anywhere I wished in the complex and spend endless hours outside the apartment doors of the men implicated in the affair. Often, I would invite in other reporters, and we would take turns "door-stopping" the men. They hated it, of course, and called the management, demanding that the "damn reporters" be forced from the building. Management responded that their hands were tied. By this time, I'd moved into my own apartment in the Watergate and had a year left on my lease.

I had mixed feelings about hounding my quarry. On one hand, I felt sorry about the mess they'd gotten themselves into. I knew they were suffering, and deserved some privacy to search their own consciences and try to explain the situation to their anguished families. (Martha Mitchell, John's outspoken wife, appeared to be most deeply affected, and once had to be subdued by some strong-armed thugs who injected her with a powerful tranquilizer. In her account of the episode, she wrote that she never knew for sure who had hired the men to subdue her, but she believed it was her husband.) In some cases, I had come to know the wives and children quite well and really sympathized with them. On the other hand, these were public officials and appeared to be abusing the public trust. Rather than acknowledge the truth, they did their best to camouflage it. The Nixon Administration had truly erected a "stone wall" between itself and the public. Most of us - both press and public - were united in our conviction that they should not get away with it.

By this time, we residents had also lost our privacy. I had trouble refusing visits from my friends, who wanted to photograph the crime scene from the balcony of my twelfth-floor residence. By now, the Watergate was attracting more tourists than the White House. It was hard to find parking spaces for our cars, and often difficult to sleep late in the mornings, with the incessant noise from the visitors. At one point, a reporter friend of mine asked me how I liked living in the Watergate during this period. I thought we were talking "on background" (off the record), and said to her, "Now, when my boyfriend and I loll around in my waterbed, I see the tourists on the balcony of the Kennedy Center, peering through the window and taking pictures of us." I never thought she would use that quote in her newspaper, but she did. At that time, I was hoping to marry that boyfriend (who did in fact become my husband a few months later). I'd wanted to impress his parents, who were wonderful folks, proper and refined. Unfortunately, Steve's father read the article. Our names weren't mentioned, but he quickly realized it was referring to us.

The entire Watergate affair dragged on for many years. Most of my European friends - used to a parliamentary system of government - couldn't understand why the Nixon Administration didn't topple earlier, as the criminal charges began to multiply. Every day, it seemed, brought a new revelation to top the previous one. I was able to contribute a small part to the unfolding bits and pieces of the story, thanks to my contacts in the Watergate apartment building and to my personal "Deep Throat" in the Justice Department. Even some of the perpetrators' family members, anxious to put the whole mess behind them, gave me invaluable bits of information.

Covering the Watergate era demanded reporters with mettle, but I was able to report on the major and most dramatic events for my stations. There were the famous Senate hearings with the colorful Chairman Sam Ervin; the House Judiciary sessions chaired by Congressman Peter Rodino; and the two trials of the "plumbers" and the top White House advisors, presided over by Judge John Sirica. In each case, I became very close to the main Senators and Congressmen involved as well as to the fair-minded Judge Sirica, who probably did more to get to the bottom of the scandal than any other public official by imposing long jail sentences to force the participants to tell the truth. I admired the thorough, conscientious job these officials were undertaking. It was no easy task to investigate the top White House advisors and the President of the United States, and it took a great deal of courage to eventually call for the first impeachment or resignation of an American President.

While I hated the cover-up, I could not help but feel sorry for President Nixon and his family. Here was a ruthlessly ambitious man, publicly coming apart at the seams, protesting to his constituency, "I am not a crook." Richard Nixon truly had the potential of becoming a great President, despite his personality flaws. I remember sitting in the White House press room the morning he announced "Project Independence" aimed at freeing America from its reliance on outside sources of oil. Here was the man who had reestablished contact between Mainland China and the United States.

Nevertheless, the fact remained that he was also the President who had ordered the relentless bombing of North Vietnam and Cambodia. It also emerged that he had apparently authorized other espionage operations, similar to the Watergate break-in, when he was a California politician. His chief aides and executioners at that time as well bore familiar names like Bob Haldeman and John Erlichman. They and their fellow senior White House advisors like John Mitchell and Charles Colson appeared for all the world to be men of ice, roundly despised and distrusted by the press and many others. In some cases, even their wives deserted them after suffering through the humiliation and agony of the very public Washington trials and subsequent jail terms. The wives showed up at every session of the trials, well groomed and stylish, only to be spat upon and scorned by the public as if they shared responsibility for the sins of their husbands.

Paradoxically, some of the participants were surprisingly warm and human. Pat Nixon, for one, was an extremely tender person. I doubt that she knew my name, but whenever she saw me at a White House function she came over to embrace me. This was in great contrast to her image as "Plastic Pat," a First Lady deficient in the emotions department. On the other hand, her successor, Betty Ford, was also totally different from her public image. She came across in the media as sincere and gregarious, although in private she was very tight and tense. She slowly measured every word she uttered, struggling to gain control of herself. It was only after she left the White House that we learned she was addicted to drugs and alcohol. There were reasons for her dependency. Mrs. Ford had undergone surgery for breast cancer. In addition, like most political wives, she had faced the task of raising her children practically on her own, while also campaigning and entertaining for her husband. The demands of this arduous and largely unsung job had broken many First Ladies before her. Happily, Mrs. Ford conquered her dependencies, and through the Betty Ford Center she founded, she worked to help others with similar problems and addictions.

The men I grew closest to during the Watergate trials were the Cuban refugees who had actually participated in the break-in. I discovered that they were cultured, educated gentlemen who had acted out of a misguided sense of patriotism for their adopted country. Yes, they knew it was wrong to break into an office building. However, they believed their boss, G. Gordon Liddy, had received instructions and assistance from the CIA, where he'd once worked. The Cubans were so grateful for their new life in America following Castro's ascension to power in Cuba that they were eager in some way to repay their new homeland.

I had numerous conversations with the Cuban defendants over lunch in the basement cafeteria of the District Courthouse. We made an odd assemblage in that depressing, roach-infested eatery: the judges, lawyers, reporters, and defendants, Mitchell, Haldeman, Erlichman, John Dean, Fred LaRue, Charles Colson, and the others. By this time, the White House advisors, bent on self-preservation, were at each other's throats. They usually sat at separate tables, with their individual lawyers. Of course, the only one missing was President Nixon himself. He was largely insulated from the threat of trial because of the power of his office and later through the pardon granted to him by Gerald Ford shortly after he assumed office. That pardon was bitterly received by many Nixon staffers who faced jail time and the ruination of their own careers as lawyers because of their association with him.

The trials progressed, commanding a great deal of my time. One day, I was simply too exhausted to brave the Washington heat and humidity to get to the courthouse. My girlfriend, artist Nancy Wolf, wanted very much to attend the proceedings, but courtroom passes were impossible to come by, truly one of the most difficult commodities to obtain in Washington at the time. I allowed Nancy to use mine, on condition that she would phone in reports to me so I could get updates on stories about the day's proceedings. When I didn't hear from her for several hours, I became furious, for I was missing many crucial deadlines for the Canadian Broadcasting Corporation as well as my other stations. At last she called me, hours beyond deadline time. It seemed that a prisoner had broken out of the basement jail cells adjoining the restaurant. He'd stolen a gun from one of the guards and held several people hostage. Courthouse officials were in a frenzy, and Nancy was trapped with the rest of them. Still, I was angry she didn't call me instantly with an eyewitness account of the hostage taking.

When the long Watergate trials finally ended, the Cubans and John Dean received the longest jail terms, though eventually their sentences were reduced. But the other senior White House advisors came out much better. They were sent to minimum-security prisons (often called "country clubs"), many of them close to their homes and families. Although they endured loneliness and humiliation, their predicament was less bleak than that of the prisoners locked in overcrowded cages of more traditional institutions. After their terms were served, most of these men went on to earn vast sums writing books and doing the lecture circuit. Some, such as the infamous Chuck Colson, even became "born-again Christians." He now heads a very important and worthwhile prison Ministry.

With his aides marching off to prison, it was astonishing that President Nixon was able to hold on to his office as long as he did. But he clearly was not functioning as a President should. It was widely believed that Chief of Staff Alexander Haig was really running the country during the last tortured months before Richard Nixon was forced from office. Finally, with the House Judiciary Committee on the brink of calling for his impeachment, President Nixon became the first American president to tender his resignation. Thus his presidency came to an end in the middle of a steamy week, on August 9, 1974. Many of my colleagues had left Washington for their annual August holidays, only to rush back frantically when the rumors of the impending resignation began to surface. I was too poor, and too ambitious, to leave Washington during that period, as events rushed toward their inevitable dramatic climax. Instead, I spent many nights working in the White House pressroom, waiting for something momentous to happen. One of my most memorable nights there was Nixon's last night in the White House. For about thirty minutes that evening, he locked us in the pressroom so he could walk, undisturbed, across the White House lawn.

He returned from the farewell stroll and delivered his nationally televised resignation speech to the American people and the world. President Nixon was still very much in personal control during that speech, although his features were puffy and distorted. Shortly afterward, the White House photographer caught him in an unguarded moment, embracing his daughter Julie. It was a poignant photo that accurately captured the angst of the Nixon family. It was published in many newspapers, and it touched me deeply, for it evoked memories of the travails my own father had endured in business and politics.

The White House was charged with emotion and none of us knew what would come next. We had no more access to the Nixon family that night, as they retreated to the family quarters for their last night in the great house and office they had struggled so hard to attain. But most reporters were reluctant to leave. I personally feared that the President would be unable to live with his decision, and might commit suicide. Whatever happened, I was determined to be on hand to witness it. So I spent the night in the cramped, paper-strewn White House pressroom, resting my head on one of the small desks. Some of my colleagues sprawled out on one of the worn green leather couches. Others fought for space on the floor, covered with ashes from used cigarette butts and smudged papers of newspapers. Outside the high fences of the White House, often boisterous crowds had gathered all week, chanting for Nixon's resignation. This night, they were uncharacteristically silent, subdued, and somber. They were the ghouls outside, and we were the ghouls inside. But all of us knew we were witnessing history being made.

The following morning, President Nixon delivered his final nationally televised speech from the ornate East Room, where the White House staff and his family were gathered. By this time, there wasn't a dry eye in the house. All of the Nixon family - usually so disciplined and undemonstrative - sobbed with him, as he tried to say his good-byes and thank his staff. Of course, many of his longtime senior advisors were not there; they were already in jail. My fellow reporters were crying, but not because we were sad to lose Nixon. Ours had been a strained relationship from the start. But we were all deeply affected by the family tragedy unfolding before us, the spectacle of a man who had clawed his way up, all his life, to achieve one overarching goal. Then, when he had it, he lost it all. We may never really know for sure whether President Nixon actually authorized the Watergate break-in, or simply created the climate for it to occur. But most legal and political experts believe he played a major role in the cover-up, and was saved from prison only by his successor's pardon, issued shortly after Ford assumed the presidency.

After his farewell speech, President Nixon took his last walk up the red carpet to the helicopter stairs. He then turned and waved farewell for the last time as President. Then, at some point over the skies of mid-America, he ceased being one of the most powerful men in the world, joining the ranks of former Presidents. At that same moment, mild-mannered Gerald Ford, former Minority Leader of the House of Representatives and later Vice President, became the leader of the Free World. It was only by a twist of fate that he was next in the line of succession. President Nixon's first Vice President, Spiro Agnew, had been forced from office following revelations of corrupt practices earlier in his political career. In fact, when Agnew was fighting to save his own political neck, I remember posing the forbidden question during one of his news conferences in the Executive Office Building of the White House. I asked him whether President Nixon and his cronies weren't really trying to publicize and leak stories about his political problems to divert attention from the unfolding Watergate scandal. As expected, Agnew discounted this theory and reaffirmed his loyalty to President Nixon. But to many in the room, his protests fell flat.

Gerald Ford bought himself a period of grace and goodwill in his first public remarks as President when he declared, "Our long national nightmare is over." For a few days, relieved Americans basked, if somewhat uneasily, in an era of harmony, tranquility and goodwill. People the world over could relax, free from any fear that a despondent Chief Executive might push the "destruct" button as his last act in public office. But President Ford shattered the air of normalcy during his first month in office when, by acting during a weekend to minimize the impact and publicity, he granted a pardon to Richard Nixon for any crimes he may have committed during the Watergate break-in and cover-up. He told Americans that the nation had been through too much, and should not have to endure the spectacle of a former President undergoing trial and perhaps being sent to prison. The pardon in itself was so unusual and dramatic that Nixon's acceptance of it was widely viewed as an admission of his own culpability in Watergate.

The morning of the pardon, I received a phone call from an important source at the White House. He told me what was about to happen, and urged me to get there as fast as I could. I leapt from my waterbed, kissed Steve good-bye, and raced off to the Executive Mansion.

The tip from the source presented me with a major professional dilemma, which once again underscored how difficult it is for a reporter who is expected to defer to someone else. Network and newspaper reporters are all too familiar with the problem, but as a free-lancer, I'm usually my own boss, and am free to broadcast what I can get as soon as I get it.

For the past few years, my prime station had been the Canadian Broadcast Corporation, which I considered one of the top companies in the world. I was one of the few free-lancers under contract to CBC, and was quite well known in Canada, since I was doing many stories for them on a daily basis. (Once, when I met a Canadian family on a beach in Florida, they asked me, "Are you really *the* Connie Lawn?" It was a heady experience for me. The problem was, I was also breast feeding a son at the time, so there was an embarrassment factor!) The setback with the CBC was that I was not really my own boss. They maintained their own bureau in Washington, as well as their own correspondent, whom I was supposed to assist. The correspondents rotated every three years. By the time I finally established a smooth working relationship with one, it seemed, he or she was sent away and I had to start all over with someone new. I had a free hand during the Watergate years, because the resident correspondent had drinking problems and thus didn't function as energetically as he otherwise would. Because of this, I could report some of the major stories with little interference from him. When we did work together, he was generous and good-humored about his problems. He remembered being so confused one day that he had even broadcast the name of the American director of the FBI as *Herbert* Hoover (a long-dead American President) when he meant to say *J. Edgar* Hoover.

When Gerald Ford moved into the Oval Office, this correspondent returned to Canada, to be replaced by a man who was ambitious, eager to make his mark, and very turf-conscious. If he hadn't been on the scene, I would have instantly phoned Canada with a story reporting the imminent pardon of Richard Nixon. We could probably have scooped the world with that story, by putting it out to the news agencies after we had broadcast it. If at the time we had said, "The CBC has learned that … " we would have beaten everyone else by a number of hours. But I couldn't do the story, because the new reporter would have been furious, and probably would have tried to get me fired. So I felt compelled to phone him and tell him what I had learned before I left for the White House. I assumed he would put it right on the air, and we would still beat the rest of the world. But unfortunately for both of us, he didn't do it.

Finally, several hours later, he joined me at the White House. By that time, President Ford had made his announcement, which I reported to some of my smaller stations in the United States. I gave the Canadian reporter my tape of the announcement, and he agreed to pay me for it. He then spent a great deal of time editing it before finally sending it to the central newsroom in Toronto. The editors there were angry because it had taken him so long. He told them he'd delayed only because the tape had just been made available to him, which was not at all true. We all have to cover ourselves at times in this as in any other business. But I didn't want to be made a scapegoat for someone else's tardiness, and was furious and frustrated, knowing I would have already had reports on the air for them in the last four newscasts had I been on my own. But I was caught up in the classic trap of having to subordinate my efforts to the whims of someone else. How happy I was when, a few years later, I was able to develop excellent news outlets in New Zealand, Australia, Israel, and other countries. In those situations *I* was the Bureau Chief, and had no superior in Washington to take credit for my efforts.

My heart goes out to my friends in the networks who experience that type of frustration every day. It's true that they make much more money than I do, and are seen as major stars in this country. But too often, several top network reporters will work together on a story, only to see it aired by the anchorman or by another major superstar. They have been "bigfooted." They also experience the frustration of working for days on a story which never sees the light of day. At least I have the satisfaction of seeing ninety-five percent of my efforts get on the air, which is a far higher percentage than my colleagues are able to realize.

The incident at the White House was not the only time I was personally hurt during my ten-year relationship with the CBC. Although they stayed with me in my early days with the news business and paid me quite well (for which I am grateful), they often treated me like a hired hand rather than a colleague. Perhaps this is attributable to sexism, or maybe it was an outgrowth of the rivalry between Canada and the United States. Canadians are often resentful of the influence of their huge neighbor to the south, and this is a pity, because Canadians as a whole are fine people. In fact, I was so pro-Canadian in those days that I often toyed with the idea of emigrating and taking a full-time job with the CBC in Vancouver or Montreal. Toronto was less appealing - too flat and cold. Moreover, I like to maintain a creative as well as a literal distance from my executives, and Toronto was the corporate headquarters.

No matter how well the CBC paid me, they were reluctant to accept me as part of their family. When I was invited to an office party, I was virtually ignored. During the gala dinners held by the Radio-Television Correspondents Association of the U. S. Congress, I was never invited to sit with the other CBC reporters or executives at their table. Once, when I specifically asked to join them, they refused me, even though I was doing nearly all of my work for them at the time.

I stayed with the CBC for several more years, even though the slights continued to hurt my pride and, to my mind, reflected their low regard for my professionalism. Once, at a party, the Bureau Chief grudgingly introduced me to someone by saying, "This is Connie Lawn. She occasionally does some stories for us." (Quite an understatement - I was averaging three stories a day for them at the time.) But he introduced a male reporter, who did stories about once a week, as "one of our top free-lancers in Washington." Another time, during an important function at the Canadian Embassy, a rival free-lancer had several drinks too many. He tore into me, accusing me of making up stories - a charge that so shocked the Canadians that they actually sided with me. In fact, I even considered taking him to court to sue him for defaming my reputation. But my CBC bosses urged me not to, assuring me he would never again work for CBC News after that outburst. I was gratified by their show of support in this instance, and they were as good as their word regarding this free-lancer.

On balance, they were an excellent organization to work for. But as the years wore on I found there were more important aspects to a career than just making money - things like self-respect and personal freedom - and I was having trouble attaining either one as a subordinate to the bureau chief. In addition, as I married and had babies, I could no longer meet the rigorous demands imposed by the CBC. When there was a riot or a plane crash in the middle of the night, they expected me to go to it in person, as I'd done for them for over a decade. But with small children in the house, I couldn't just pick up and go. Breast-feeding was hardly a job for my husband.

It was hard enough working for the CBC when I was pregnant. I was very sick in the early stages of my pregnancies, and could barely wedge my huge belly and my tape recorder into the CBC broadcasting booth on Capitol Hill. The cubicle was located in the basement of one of the Senate Office Buildings, and I had to walk several exhausting blocks to get to it. It was dark and isolated, and I often worried about being mugged by some of the street people who were always in evidence. Making matters worse was the heat, which typically registered a hundred degrees that summer.

The broadcasting booth was not the only hardship I endured for the CBC. Once, the Bureau Chief asked me to stake out and interview the then - Prime Minister of India, Moraji Desai. As he spoke into my microphone, the skinny old man's breath nearly knocked me out. Needless to say, it did little to alleviate my morning sickness. Afterward, as I fed the tape, I mentioned his breath to the editor, who wasn't surprised. It seems the good Prime Minister had once told a national television audience that he drank a cup of his own urine each morning for breakfast. Desai was a vegetarian, and believed he needed the liquid pick-me-up to augment some vitamins and minerals he would not otherwise get from his diet.

****

While the Watergate affair wrecked many political careers, it enhanced those of many reporters, including mine. It is a classic, perverted truth that one person's misfortune is someone else's fortune. My reputation was growing, helped along by some of the scoops I'd gotten, stories which were reprinted by the wire services (AP, UPI, or Reuters). They used my name, and that of my news bureau, when adding the tidbits of information I provided on the Watergate affair. In addition, I was gradually becoming accepted into the "old boy network," a loose, unofficial grouping of free-lance reporters worldwide who report to many of the same stations in Europe, The United Kingdom, the Middle East, Canada, Australia, New Zealand, and Africa. Few women had penetrated this male bastion, with the exception of my good friend Judy Lessing, a New Zealander living in New York. Judy and I became unofficial partners, sharing many of the same outlets.

It was wonderful to be accepted by this distinguished fraternity of international broadcasters. It was also gratifying to have friends and colleagues report that they had heard me on the air in far-flung areas of the globe. One broadcaster said he heard the same group of people wherever he went, and began to think there were no other reporters in the world.

One of my favorite international outlets was, and still is, the British Broadcasting Corporation. The two BBC bureau chiefs under whom I worked in the early days, Angus McDermott and later Clive Small, were classic Englishmen. They often included me in their social events and treated me as a member of their family. This sense of being a part of a team is very important for a free-lancer like me, who often gets tired of working completely on her own.

I've always worried about whether my listeners on the other end would accept and be able to understand my accent. There are always variations in pronunciations, customs, weights, and measurements, and one must be mindful of unique vocabularies in order to make sense. It is also imperative to learn as much as possible about the country one is covering, and project sensitivity to the people and their special customs. For that reason, nothing beats a long trip to the country in question, or even a temporary residence there, if it can be worked out. On the other hand, you have to hope there will be no major crises at home when you are away.

Another difficulty in working with the international stations is the result of the time differences. It can take several weeks to get used to working with stations that can be five, eight, fourteen, or sixteen hours ahead of you. In later years, as the number of my client stations increased, the work came to be nearly nonstop. Even Sunday was not really a day of rest, because that was Monday in two of my countries. Dinnertime coincided with the major noontime shows in Australia and New Zealand. In my case, dinner was frantic enough, what with trying to cook, monitor network newscasters, and cope with two young sons. Adding a deadline pressure to that was a strain on my whole family, but we have adapted, and managed to live with it for a number of years. Our mealtimes, needless to say, are a far cry from the placid, relaxing ones frequently depicted in the fictional media. Many a boss or assignment editor has called me during dinner to talk about next week's assignment.

The hardest aspect of working with a number of different countries can be the accents. For several years, my best editors throughout the world, originally from Edinburgh, Scotland, turned up in Canada, Israel, and New Zealand. I would often get a phone call at three in the morning from someone with a sonorous Scottish brogue, frantically telling me about a plane crash or a war breaking out somewhere. He would demand a story, and then slam down the phone. I hadn't a clue who had just phoned me, so the best remedy was to investigate the story and file reports to all of my people.

One of my favorite editors of all time was Eric Moncour, who really launched my career with the CBC. A hot-tempered Scotsman, he yelled at me often, but it came with the territory and I respected him a lot. Once, on a 1973 business trip to Israel, I overheard two Scotsmen conversing on a beach. I went over to them and said, "I haven't been yelled at by anyone with a Scottish accent for more than two weeks. Will you please yell at me?" They obliged with good humor, and probably added the incident to their repertoire when they talked about batty Americans.

Israel in 1973: War and Marriage

To be sure, 1973 was a landmark year for me, both professionally and personally. It was the year I gained Israeli Radio as a client; this enabled me to focus my efforts on foreign affairs, and begin to develop a special expertise on the Middle East. This was very important, for it would allow me to gradually dispense with the "scatter-shot" approach of covering every breaking story of regional interest for my stations in the United States. I could shift to coverage reflecting my primary interest, international affairs. I would be able slowly to wean myself away from the confused, breakneck pace of Capitol Hill, and concentrate on more in-depth stories on developments emanating from the White House or State Department. Finally, I could abandon my American local stations and focus on the international ones.

I have nothing against local radio, and am proud of the special ski stories I now broadcast occasionally on WTOP All-News Radio, in Washington. And, it is great to work for IRN/USA Radio. Their reach is national and, in some cases, international.

This new strategy, I reasoned, would enable me to better utilize my time. Moreover, for some reason, I have generally preferred working with people from other countries, often finding them more interesting and better educated. From my perspective as a reporter and broadcaster, they have proven, generally speaking, to be far more honest with me and more appreciative of my work than have the Americans.

IRN/USA Radio News, Radio America, and the Voice of America, are fine, honest organizations. But, I have learned the hard way to be especially wary of the New York stations, which have been disappointing to work with. One network still owes me over $16,000 for reports I provided from the State Department as their diplomatic correspondent. I accepted at face value their verbal promise to pay me $25 per story, but without a written agreement I would have little chance to make a successful claim in a court of law. Sad to say, some of the smaller stations in London followed the New York example, and tended to short change payments to free-lancers. (I hope this has now changed). But, this is not true of the BBC, for whom I am proud to provide occasional talk-backs and commentaries. They are among the best!

Again, it is difficult to prove one's case, but unethical behavior has come back to haunt those who have a reputation for cheating free-lancers. Our only hope in a situation like this is to get the word out to our colleagues, so that experienced, reliable reporters will keep their distance.

Another reason 1973 was an important milestone in my year is that I would finally abandon the overrated "glamour" of the "Washington merry-go-round" and wed Steve Rappaport, the charming, handsome, accountant I had met during a Christmas ski trip to Vermont.

Steve and I shared a ski cabin there with a number of friends. I had been dating a neurosurgeon who lived in the Watergate at the time, but he was playing the field with a couple of other women. When he sent us all pink poinsettias for Christmas, accompanied by the same messages, it was too much for me. I left in a righteous huff and signed up for the ski trip. But I also invited a date, so I wouldn't be alone over the holidays. I phoned Howard, a friend from New York who had his own twin-engine private airplane. He has often invited me on cross-country trips, and was used to flying to Vermont for getaway weekends. He was happy to be asked, and promised to fly up a few days after Christmas.

Meanwhile, I drove up to Vermont with two dogs in my car - my faithful shepherd, Tracy, and a roommate's cocker spaniel. Steve arrived at the cabin in the middle of the night, and was greeted by my canine companions before he met me. By the time Howard arrived five days later, I'd fallen in love with Steve. It was a delicate situation; I tried my best to discourage Howard from coming, but dreaded telling him the truth. I phoned him to say the snow was no good, and complained that the cabin was filled with dogs (Howard hated dogs, as Steve does now). But Howard flew up anyway, and I handled the situation terribly. In the end, I couldn't bear to be separated from Steve, and poor Howard had to sleep with the dogs.

A few months after I met Steve, I was invited to go to Israel for a journalists' seminar. I jumped at the chance to visit Jerusalem, the city that was to me one of the most special and sacred in the world. At the same time, I was filled with the pangs that accompany the unique, painful early stages of love, and it hurt in a nearly physical way to leave Steve. I left tears halfway across the Atlantic. This was a hard-boiled reporter? But flying on El Al, the national airline of Israel, provided enough distractions to bring me out of myself. I began to feel the stirrings that heralded the personality changes I always undergo when I travel.

Airport security was extremely tight, for El Al flights are always an attractive potential target of terrorists. All the passengers were escorted to tiny rooms and body-searched by stewards or stewardesses, since electronic screening devices had yet to be installed in most airports. By the time I actually boarded the plane, I felt as if I had been recruited into the Israeli Army. Such thorough searches, regarded as nuisances by some, nevertheless afforded peace of mind to the passengers who could travel in confidence that there were no bombs aboard.

Security precautions notwithstanding, I found the male stewards charming and helpful, and everything about the service was excellent. It was moving to witness the Orthodox Jewish men put on their prayer shawls and pray at sunset, while they were several thousand feet over the ocean. Somehow, that also made me feel safer. When the plane swooped into Israeli skies, hundreds of excited passengers began to sing songs of welcome, and some even performed Israeli dances in the aisles. It added a festive note to the last stages of our journey.

The one drawback, from my own perspective, was my seatmate, one of my WNBC editors I had informed when I was originally invited to the seminar. Not to put too fine a point on it, she was a stereotypical neurotic, pushy New Yorker. The woman - whom I will call Esther - asked if I could also wrangle an invitation for her, and I was able to oblige. Unfortunately for me, it turned out that she was a real white-knuckle flyer. She screamed and clutched my hand in terror during most of the eight-hour flight. Even after we landed in Israel, she proved to be insecure about being in a strange land, an inexperienced babe in the woods … and frankly, not terribly bright.

When the journalists in our group were touring the old city of Jerusalem, Esther managed to pick up an Arab merchant who had a false ear. He'd lost it in a fight, he said, and replaced it with a plastic one. However, the prosthesis was three shades lighter than his skin, and it gave him a grotesque look. Like most Arabs, however, Abdul was very smart, and he certainly knew a sucker ripe for plucking when he saw one.

Abdul told Esther and some of the other news hens on the trip that he sold jewels, and they stupidly informed him they had a lot of American dollars to spend on gold. He promised to bring some fine samples of gold rings and chains to their hotel tomorrow, if they would be so kind as to tell him where they were staying. Since I was Esther's roommate, I didn't like the sound of this arrangement at all.

This was a few months before the traumatic 1973 Yom Kippur War, and Israel was in a very tense period. We'd all been warned to report anyone who acted in a suspicious manner, or who offered to provide us with packages or gifts. The Israeli authorities knew such offerings could contain bombs or, at the very least, drugs - a surefire ticket to jail for the long term. I told some of the Israeli security guards about the situation, and they advised the women in our party to tell Abdul he couldn't come to the hotel after all. Undeterred, he suggested instead that we meet him elsewhere, so he could give us the jewels and some other items.

I had no intention of accompanying them to their rendezvous with Abdul. The situation seemed dangerous to me; second, I preferred to attend the seminars and go sightseeing, instead of buying trinkets. By now the security people were quite alarmed. They asked Esther and me if we would actually meet Abdul and accept the package from him; they also proposed that we lure him to the coffee lounge of the King David Hotel, which they said had hidden cameras concealed in the ceiling. It was no small trick to persuade Abdul to meet us there, but when he did arrive he showed up with his brother ... and no package.

I had prearranged with the guards to signal them when we got the package. I would do this by taking off my eyeglasses and laying them down on the table. Then the guards would emerge from their hiding places in the corners of the lounge and examine the package. If there was nothing unacceptable in it, there would be no further questions.

Unfortunately, I was inexperienced in such cloak-and-dagger routines, and to make matters worse, I had a nervous habit of unconsciously removing my glasses and putting them down. This gave the guards a start, and they began to rush toward us. I tried - none too subtly - to motion them away. After I'd taken the glasses on and off a dozen times, one of the exasperated guards motioned me to join him. I excused myself and met him on the way to the ladies' room. I informed him that there was no package, but reported that we'd been invited to go to their home to pick it up. He sternly warned me not to do so, and I assured him I had no intention of going.

I returned to the table, and told Esther and the two Arabs we could not come to their home and had to leave immediately. As we were leaving, Abdul did take out a small gold puzzle ring from his pocket, which Esther bought at a greatly inflated price. She was very proud of her purchase, until it turned green on her finger three days later.

We saw no more of poor Abdul after that, and never did learn what he actually wanted to sell us. But the security men were by no means finished with us. By now, they thought we were either conspirators or too naive to be left alone in Israel. For the next few days, they followed us everywhere. If we got on buses, they followed. We felt like something in a James Bond movie - running on and off buses, and into side streets, trying to elude them. One night, when Esther and I returned separately from late evening events, the security men confronted us. They took us to individual rooms and grilled us for hours about our contacts with any Arabs in Jerusalem. Ironically, Esther had just returned from having dinner with a very important Israeli legal official, but that didn't save her from the third-degree treatment.

The following day, our group took the long bus ride south to the stone fortress of Massada in the desert. There, we were both enthralled and awed by the dramatic, history-laden structure which jutted upward into the clear blue sky. Beneath us lay the rugged desert and the Dead Sea; from our vantage point above the desert, we could see Jordan across the water. As we watched new Israeli soldiers take their oath of office on the same spot where, centuries ago, nine hundred Jewish zealots had committed suicide rather than face Roman enslavement, we noted that some of the soldiers looked familiar. Our inquisitors, presumably determined to protect us from ourselves had followed us to Massada. In retrospect, I respect their dogged thoroughness. And, since this took place only two months before the 1973 war - which was to be a great tragedy for Israel and for the oil-consuming world - I now sometimes wish they had been even more vigilant. At the time, however, their machinations scared the hell out of us. Since we were doing nothing wrong, we didn't like being followed and hounded like common criminals. I felt like a character ripped from the pages of a Kafka novel.

Still, we didn't allow our bloodhounds to ruin our visit to Massada. Our journalists' group spent hours exploring the baths, cisterns, and caves where the religious faithful had lived, flourished, and eventually died hours before the Roman soldiers scaled their walls to capture the fortress. It was a marvel of architecture and engineering, built centuries before by King Herod and his slave laborers.

At one point, we descended a steep side of the cliff on a wobbly rope bridge. As we were inching our way down, the guide described how King Herod kept some of his concubines hidden in the caves dug into the sides of the steep mountain. But he was so fat that the only way he could visit them was to be lowered down to their quarters by ropes. At that point, one member of our group froze. He was a very prominent

Washington attorney, whose wife held down a top job in the White House. But all the high-flown connections in the world were of little use up there. He was heard to mutter, in Hebrew, "Oh, my God - ropes!" He blanched, turned white, and was unable to move, either up or down. His terror spread. There we were - ten reporters and a handful of lawyers - stranded in the blazing sun, caught between the Dead Sea and the desert and an electric blue sky. Our rope bridge swayed precariously from our combined trembling, and we were paralyzed with fear. It took a full forty minutes to coax the lawyer down to King Herod's playroom. But to this day, when I see a rope, I think of the incident at Massada.

While I was in Israel, I made it a point to visit the English division of Israeli Radio, to ask if I could free-lance for them from Washington. They had an excellent correspondent at the time, but his forte was magazines and newspapers, rather than radio. When they agreed to give me a try, I felt pangs of guilt. After all, I've never been the type of reporter to crawl over anyone else's body to get a job, and I'd been known to fight like a vixen when anyone tried to "steal" a client from me. There is a strict unwritten code of ethics among independent reporters, and one of the first commandments is: "Thou shalt not steal thy colleague's bread and butter."

Thus when I returned to Washington, I contacted the correspondent, Charles Fenyvesi, to let him know that the Jerusalem news director had asked me to assist in coverage, with the understanding that Charles was their main correspondent. To my surprise, he was wonderful about it. Rather than try to block me, he was gracious, and helped me a great deal. We tried to coordinate stories without duplicating our contribution. The English Division was already getting some news from the Hebrew-language correspondent and from the Voice of America, so it was a four-way split in any case. But it was an arduous assignment, and the most difficult I ever had.

In the first place, the Middle East is a dynamic, confusing, and complex region. There is always a crisis somewhere in the area, and news emanating from Washington is always of crucial interest to the region. Often the very survival of Israel depends upon what the policy makers are thinking in Washington. It is the region that is truly the oil barrel - and the powder keg - of the world. To make coverage even more difficult, the phone system in the Middle East was still rather primitive, compared with that of Australia, New Zealand, Canada, or South Africa, any of which can be accessed in seconds. When you called the Mideast, it was often hard to get a circuit, and you have to fight through endless recordings informing you that "all circuits are busy." I often imagine that phone calls must be routed by camel over the desert, rather than via phone cables or satellites. When only moments to go before a major deadline, the last thing a reporter wants to hear is excuses. Finally, when you do get through, the line often sounds as though Hannibal and his legions were stampeding over it. Another complication: I had to learn to shout out the extension numbers I wanted in Hebrew. Over the years, I acquired a working vocabulary of curses in Hebrew and Arabic as well as in English.

I signed on with Israeli Radio at a time of intense crisis. This allowed me no time to make a systematic round of the policy makers who dealt with the region. I also had no official entree to the American Jewish leaders and their organizations, or to the key personnel in the Israeli Embassy. I would have to hit the ground running, and build momentum from there.

Why the rush? A number of successive crises befell Israel. As soon as I returned to Washington, one of Israel's top diplomats was assassinated outside his home in suburban Washington - a killing that to this day has never been solved. I began to cover the story immediately, following up with law enforcement agencies and the Federal Bureau of Investigation. Then, as I was finally getting into the rhythm of my job, the Egyptians invaded Israel in the surprise attack of October 6, 1973. The Yom Kippur War was underway.

The invasion meant the very existence of Israel was at stake. It was essential for Israel to know whether it would get American support and receive it in time to make a difference. As reporters, we had to try to answer that crucial question as soon as we could. Our reports were vital, because they gave hope to the Israelis listening to us. But we had to be accurate; any misstatements could conceivably cost lives. In addition, the English Division had a wide audience in the Arab world. There, the listeners could pick up hints on the future direction of the war. English-speaking diplomats, reporters, and residents in those countries, as well as in Israel, often got the first news of what was happening (or could happen) from us.

The correspondents for the Israeli and Arab media representatives in Washington worked frantically, broadcasting and writing stories almost continuously. In the ensuing days, it became even more essential for the Washington-based reporters to produce material to fill up the broadcasts and newspapers. Back in Israel, most of the editors and reporters had been called into the Army. The women too were doing their share to support the war effort. The Israelis could not spare the personnel to do the reporting, so it was up to us, in the United States, to fill up the fifteen- to thirty-minute broadcasts.

All of this came at an especially hectic time for me. Steve and I had decided to get married on November 11, 1973. I was so frenzied, overworked, and exhausted that I offered to postpone the wedding to a quieter time. But my new editors told me it was bad luck to take such a step, so I compromised by changing the location. Instead of planning for a wedding in Washington, the city I called home, I asked my parents to make arrangements for it to be held in New York. It was quite a sacrifice, because in Washington we may have been able to use Congressional connections to allow us to be married in the chapel of the U.S. Capitol. Instead of going there to cover a story, I could have gone in that day to cover my own marriage!

The ceremony eventually took place in the ornate Plaza Hotel, off New York's Central Park. It was a beautiful event in a magnificent setting. But I was still required to do some broadcasts a few hours before and after the ceremony. I even took my tape recorder to the wedding, where it was set up on the virginal white bridal table to record the sounds. The straight steel microphone looked positively phallic, jutting sharply from its nest in the white bouquet atop the satin Bible. The first sounds the microphone picked up, as the strains of the Wedding March died down, were me asking Steve, "What am I doing here?" His answer: "Damned if I know!"

We managed to squeeze in a short honeymoon in the bridal suite of a nearby hotel overlooking the resplendent fall foliage of the park. It was the Essex Hotel. Ironically, the letters, e and s lost their electricity, so that night it proclaimed itself the SEX Hotel! The next morning, we hired a horse and carriage and took a stately drive through Central Park to my parents' Fifth Avenue apartment. I felt like a movie actress, riding in an open carriage, clutching my wedding gown. It was an enchanted feeling, as we were driven up the circular driveway in front of the apartment. It was also incongruous with the long line of girls waiting to have an abortion at the clinic that was housed off the lobby of the building.

We returned to Washington later that day, as the full reality of the tragic war was beginning to set in. Both sides were suffering severe losses; in Israel, they were especially traumatic. Every family had either suffered its own loss or counted a friend or relative among the dead or injured. It was only years later that the devastation of the 1973 war made any sense at all, because it enabled President Sadat of Egypt to claim a victory, and then take the magnanimous step of going to Jerusalem to propose a peace.

Washington in the Seventies

The years between those peace negotiations and the climax of the Camp David Accords continued to be difficult ones for me, but they were also filled with joy and satisfaction. By now, I was frantically dividing my time between the Capitol, White House, and State Department. To my surprise, some of the more lascivious legislators seemed to find me irresistible now that I was married. One, a very prominent Southern Senator, was also the chairman of one of the most powerful committees on Capitol Hill, the Senate Foreign Relations Committee. He was one of three very influential politicians who were always asking me to dinner, or inviting me to meet them in their private underground offices in the Capitol Building - invitations I always managed to sidestep. This particular Senator was more than just a lecher; he was also widely thought to be approaching senility. In press conferences, even with all the television cameras rolling, he managed to position himself close to me. He then lifted his arm and rubbed it across my breast. Trapped in a tight pack of reporters, I managed to duck away with difficulty. In the process, I often interfered with the cameramen's shots, which understandably was a source of irritation to them.

The septuagenarian Senator was such an incorrigible ladies' man that he went after anyone in skirts who crossed his path. Once I introduced a lovely, sophisticated BBC correspondent to him. Carol was thin and petite, and no match for the tall, gangling legislator. After I introduced them, he extended his hand, as if to shake hers. Instead, he quickly lowered it, dipping it into her waistband and fondling her bare butt. She screamed loudly, "Senator, what are you doing?" All of the Senator's ninety-nine colleagues on the floor heard her, and were momentarily diverted from their monotonous debate to see what they were missing.

On another occasion, I waited for several hours to interview Senator Hubert Humphrey on a very important piece of legislation. Humphrey, who had always been a perfect gentleman, finally arrived, and we began the interview. A few moments later, my lecherous Senator arrived and interrupted us. Humphrey, ever the gentleman, said, "I will leave you with the Chairman." I responded firmly, "Oh, no, you won't!"

Abashed, the Chairman slunk away. An astonished Humphrey asked what that was all about. I explained the situation to him, adding that his virile 74-year-old colleague carried a newspaper with him less for edification than to place over his lap should the women reporters arouse him. The paper had a tendency to rise to attention as he became excited.

The idea of my having any sort of intimate relationship with this Senator was unthinkable, but he somehow fantasized it was so. Thus, the day came when he was shocked when I walked into a committee hearing he was chairing. He noted my belly, now swollen with the child I was carrying. He stopped the hearing, came over to me and said, "My God, you're pregnant. I didn't know you were pregnant." Clearly he believed he was responsible, and I tried to reassure him that he had nothing to worry about from me. When I later told my husband, he joked that perhaps we should nurture the Senator's delusion after all, and sue for child support.

Another politician who made rather mild overtures to me was Wilbur Mills, the once powerful Chairman of the House Ways and Means Committee, which introduces all the nation's tax legislation and plays a large role in controlling the country's finances. Mills was an austere man who positively reveled in the intricacies of the monetary system. He was said to read the income tax laws in bed each night, and eat bankers for breakfast. Mills was really quite subtle and gentlemanly in his approaches to me, and largely confined his advances to giving me exclusive interviews, which he denied the other reporters. Indeed, he was so subtle that I was honestly oblivious to his signals. But Congressional staff members who knew him insisted he was sweet on me, in his courtly Southern way.

How shocked we all were when the Washington, D.C. police arrested Mills one night. In that notorious episode, he was driving home with Washington stripper Fanny Fox, who fled from his car and leaped into the Tidal Basin, a scenic spot which is bordered by the Jefferson Monument and the Japanese Cherry trees. Neither Mills nor his erstwhile paramour took notice of their shimmering beauty on that cold winter night, and the police did their best to shelter the couple and keep them hidden from reporters. But this was Washington, and keeping things quiet proved impossible. Soon the country learned that poor Wilbur Mills was not only an alcoholic, but that he had a taste for the strip joints along the District's notorious 14th Street, which he frequented, spending lavish sums of money. So the nation learned that its resident tax expert apparently found the seedy nightspots a tad more stimulating than the dry pages of tax bills that kept him company by day. The Congressman was like Ashenbach in Thomas Mann's *Death in Venice*, the super-disciplined professor who lived his life like a clenched fist. It eventually burst open, unleashing a tide of perversion and passion. The Chairman was eventually stripped of his power and authority, and the Tidal Basin became known in Washington as "The Old Mills Stream."

Sometimes, Congressmen and Senators become close to reporters to fulfill human needs not necessarily related to sex. I established a special rapport with former Vice President Hubert Humphrey toward the end of his life, as he was suffering from bladder cancer. Humphrey had resumed his life as Senator, having lost his race for the Presidency. To visit the men's room off the Senate floor, the Senators had to cross the area where the press waited to interview them. Poor Humphrey was in considerable pain by this time, and had to cross that area every five minutes. Finally, I confided in him that I too had a long history of bladder problems from childhood (aggravated by my run-in with the Chicago cop - ironically, the night Humphrey won the Democratic Presidential nomination).

Humphrey opened up to me, and we spent some time on several occasions commiserating with each other on the agonies we endured because of our condition. I told him that after twenty years of searching, I'd finally found a doctor who operated on me and cured the painful condition. But Senator Humphrey was an intensely loyal man, and never one to change staffs or doctors. He remained with his original physician and postponed surgery until his cancer had advanced to a deadly stage. I often think that if he had sought the advice of another doctor and had the surgery earlier, he may have survived. But Humphrey was a brave man, and his courage in the final months of his life was an inspiration to the many who admired him. He walked the halls of his hospital - ever the master politician - trying to cheer his fellow patients.

With everyone aware of his impending death, the nation was able to honor him at countless memorial dinners and other events. He and his wife even realized one dream of spending a weekend at the Presidential retreat at Camp David with President Jimmy Carter. Senator Humphrey joked that after all the tributes heaped upon him, there would be nothing left to say at his funeral. But when that sad day arrived, the funeral became an occasion for nationwide mourning. Those who had scorned him for his support of American involvement in Vietnam, others who had derided him for his nonstop, if eloquent, chatter - all were united in tribute for a great man who died before he should have.

Of the many who honored him shortly before his death, Israeli Prime Minister Golda Meir probably paid the greatest price. She paid him a farewell call on a cold, wet winter morning. The visit had special significance for me, for ironically it took place in the lobby of the apartment building where Senator Humphrey and I both lived, Harbor Square in Southwest Washington. It was hard to control my emotions as I watched while the two old warriors, who had lived life with such intensity, bade each other farewell. But only Golda Meir knew she would soon follow Humphrey to the grave. She, too, was in the last stages of terminal cancer. But unlike the more public Humphrey, hers was a private battle with the disease. Thus, her own tributes would not come until after her apparently unexpected death.

The Camp David Talks

There were so many stories to cover in the late seventies and eighties that reporting became a question of very relentless, grinding hard work. Most of the events lacked the excitement and glamour that made digging for stories exciting. This is not to say that I didn't remain a dedicated and hardworking reporter; but in journalism, like marriage, it is hard to sustain the romance and fever pitch of the first few years. Nevertheless, to me, reporting is the best game in town, and I knew I wouldn't give up my career for anything. I've been extremely fortunate, for I've been able to combine my reporting career with marriage and child rearing, although all three have suffered on occasion by the compromises.

Steve and I started our family after four years of marriage. As noted earlier, my severe morning sickness made things difficult; there also were logistical problems, such as when my ballooning body found the Canadian Broadcasting booth a tight squeeze. Once, my mother warned me that I might have to stop working after the baby was born. I shot back, "I'd rather die first." In fact I did work, right up until the last minute, and even filed a report on the Sunday interview shows for Israeli Radio moments before my labor began. We rushed to the hospital, seven miles away, and made it a scant two hours before my son David was born. He was pronounced healthy and normal, and I thought he was the most beautiful child I'd ever seen. A few hours later, I watched the evening newscasts, and took notes about a major train crash and chemical explosion in Texas. I phoned my newly acquired stations in New Zealand and Australia, Radio New Zealand and the 2SM chain, and did the broadcast. Only months later did I tell them I had a baby; I'd worked for years to get New Zealand as a client, and had just landed the Australian station, and was afraid both would fire me if they learned they had to share my time with a brand-new infant.

When I got home the next day, I realized I would have to change my pattern of working. I could no longer run around to cover every story; I'd have to depend more on the telephone and radio, less on my own two legs. Within a few weeks, I managed to get to the White House, State Department and Capitol Hill each day. But I had to work with greater efficiency, so that I could make my rounds and be back home with David within five hours. I wished I could take him to work with me on a regular basis. Now, of course, childcare facilities are incorporated into a number of office and government buildings, but such amenities were unheard of in 1977. In addition, they pose a danger. Many innocent infants perished in the cruel bombing of the Oklahoma City Government Building.

Despite dangers, sometimes I did take my children with me to work. One day, having been assigned to cover a news conference at the Department of Transportation, I experienced the universal nightmare of every working mother: the sitter didn't show up. So I loaded ten-day-old David into his little plastic bed and set off on my rounds. Even then, he was a quiet, serious child, and I was able to place him on the table right in front of the Secretary of Transportation. He (David, not the Secretary) was so distracted by the new sights and sounds that he didn't even gurgle during the news conference. Truly a media professional - even at ten days old!

I soon learned that I could exist on only four hours of sleep a night and established a new routine. After awakening for the four a.m. feeding, I turned to the phone and did some more broadcasts. My editors wondered what I was doing working at that hour, but I found this arrangement financially lucrative. An added bonus was that stories written at that ungodly hour also tended to be more reflective and analytical than those written during a daytime deadline frenzy.

The children made many contributions to our married life, for they've brought to Steve and me new dimensions of love and understanding.

But even before his birth, little David probably played some role in enhancing my own brief political career. Since I was still very active in covering Capitol Hill developments, I wanted to participate in formulating the rules and customs governing the Congressional correspondents. After all, the people in the Congress had really done a lot for me over the years and I thought it was time to give back some of my time to them. I ran for an executive position in the Congressional Radio-Television Correspondents Association. To be eligible, I had to gather on a petition a number of names of people willing to back my candidacy. Of course, there was a lot of behind-the-scenes politics, as there is in any election. The candidates from the biggest news organizations typically had the largest body of voters from their own networks. There was usually a spot left open for the independent reporters, but if you represented a one-person bureau, even a total of a hundred percent support didn't get you very far. I rallied most of my support among the other international correspondents, convincing them they needed representation on Capitol Hill, even if they didn't actually cover the Congress every day.

When Election Day arrived, I got the same number of votes as a rival woman reporter on the Hill. She and I were hardly the best of friends. She had a large body of listeners on a U.S. FM radio network, and a rich organization to back her up. She eventually went on to win the election in later years, but that year I managed to edge her out with a three-vote margin in a special runoff election. As some of my friends told me later, they wouldn't dream of voting against an eight-month-pregnant woman - it would be like casting a ballot against Motherhood, Apple Pie, and the American Way.

My year on the governing board was an immensely satisfying experience. Some of my initiatives - such as special phones in the Senate for radio reporters to use in broadcasting - are still in effect today. We also curtailed the amount of smoking in some of the press areas, so we wouldn't all be subjected to the proverbial smoke-filled rooms. This was never instituted as a law, at that time. But over the years, legal and social pressure began to create a separation between smokers and nonsmokers. Years later an Israeli cartoonist, observing the new American penchant for running and health care, said, “They’re all crazy in America. No one is smoking, and everyone runs around in their underwear!”

One of the nicest benefits to serving on the Radio-TV Board is the opportunity to sit at the head table during the annual Correspondents’ Dinner. This is one of several gala events held in Washington each year. It also includes a glittering array of guests such as the President or Vice President, most of the Cabinet, the Congress, and as many thousands of reporters, lobbyists, and assorted hangers-on as can squeeze into the ballroom of the elegant Washington Hilton Hotel. After the former dinner, the “tuxed-and-gowned” hordes storm into the network hospitality suites, where they continue to drink, eat, politic, and socialize until the early hours of the morning. It is a great chance to see your favorite network anchorman in his cups.

I must say, it was a heady experience, sitting at the main table with Jimmy Carter and some of his top Cabinet members. The table was raised on a podium looking down at the hundreds of tables below. It was an ego trip to peer down at thousands of friends who, like me, had scrambled to positions of success (or at least survival) in the Washington jungle. It was also nice to watch the few who would have preferred to have my back turned, offering a tempting target for their daggers.

The only problem I had that evening centered about my anatomy. I’d delivered David only five days before, and was breast-feeding him. Within two hours into the dinner, my breasts - no doubt mindful of the time - swelled to the bursting point. After three hours of endless speeches and a great deal of laughter, the laws of physics prevailed. Milk began to squirt into my red low-cut gown. I’m not sure whether President Carter noticed, or whether the down-home country boy would have lusted in his heart if he had. The good news is that at least my contact lenses didn’t pop into my soup.

The opportunity to sit at the head table solved a painful problem I always faced at these dinners. As an independent reporter, I belonged to no one, so I was never invited to sit at anyone’s table. The networks and the major American radio chains reserved large blocks of tables for themselves. Most of my stations were either too far away or too poor to send a delegation to Washington and then shell out $60 for each dinner ticket. (Incidentally, the price has gone up: it's now over $200.) So in past years, if I paid for a seat, I was assigned a table in Outer Mongolia with the other independents. For our money we got to see the waiters and security agents come and go between the tables, bathroom, and kitchen. Although I enjoy working on my own, I also miss the sense of being part of a team – a void that I feel much more on occasions such as these gala press functions. (Later, at the White House dinners, I organized my own table of prominent people from around the world; it is a huge event each year, and associates came from New Zealand, Australia and California to join me.)

Needing to belong is one reason it's so very important for me to visit my far-away stations. This enables me to meet the other members of the team, as well as gain a better understanding of the product we are putting out together. I've sometimes spent more hours on the phone with these editors than with my own family. Over the years, we've shared our personal as well as business problems. Often I find myself intensely frustrated because I can't scramble through the phone lines to be with them personally. When I am able to arrange my overseas trips, I look forward to productive mutual exchanges that draw us together, both professionally and in friendship.

The following year, I also sat at the head table - with the same politicians and my fellow Executive Board members. This time, instead of having just given birth, I was pregnant with my second child. Of course, I endured the usual old jokes: "Surely you must know by now what causes this," and so on. Even my parents warned me that I couldn't keep doing this each year. In time I decided to give up on Capitol Hill politics, and stop having babies. Somehow the two seemed to go hand in hand.

My children are a continuous source of joy and, beyond everything else, the greatest pleasure in my life despite the complications created by commingling career and motherhood. When David was a few months old, the Camp David peace talks began in earnest. In fact, during a crucial White House visit by Israeli Prime Minister Begin shortly before the Accords were signed, I brought little David to the White House. There I covered the Carter-Begin meeting. He fell asleep on the couch in the press room, among the tape recorders and used rolls of film. An alert photographer took a shot of him, diapers showing and belly exposed. It appeared on the front pages of many regional newspapers with the caption: "King David, asleep at the White House."

While David, by virtue of being my first baby, became quite well traveled during his infancy, his brother Daniel witnessed far more exciting events while he was still in my belly. He actually went with me to Camp David each day as the talks progressed. But getting there was half the battle. Most of my friends were reluctant to make the two-hour drive with me, especially as my pregnancy neared the end. They knew we had to travel through an hour-long stretch of rather desolate farmland and woods. If the baby came then, they feared they might have to serve as midwife. The rest of my friends were even nervous about my running around the White House in my condition, for fear that I would go into labor there. Actually, I think it would have been nice to deliver the baby in the White House or at Camp David, but my sense of history was thwarted in the end, when I barely made it to the George Washington Hospital, a few blocks from the White House.

The only reporter who was brave enough to accompany me when I drove to Camp David was Clive Small, my friend from the BBC. Such daring shows the true mettle of the British. Once we arrived at the presidential retreat, working conditions were far from ideal. The press briefing room was absolutely jammed with reporters from around the world. The room was actually a large meeting chamber in the American Legion Hall in the town of Thurmont, Maryland, about a ten-minute drive down the mountain from Camp David. Each day at high noon, White House Press Secretary Jody Powell descended from the mountain camp to brief us on the progress of the talks. Thank goodness he was prompt; my deadline for the main evening newscast in Israel was one p.m. Washington time, or eight p.m. Israeli time. As soon as the briefing ended, I would scramble for an unreserved phone at the end of the stairs. There, I competed with other reporters for the right to get a circuit for an international call before launching into my usual shouting and cursing at operators in my peculiar polyglot English, Hebrew, and Arabic. Somehow we managed to get through with about two minutes to spare. I would scream out my story, trying to block out the noise behind me. At the other end, in Jerusalem, my editors taped it. Then they would run down the steps of their centuries-old stone building to the studio two floors below. Somehow, we got our stories on the air a full hour before anyone else in the Middle East, and often before anyone in Europe or the United States.

The tension of these harrowing shenanigans sent us reporters to unwind with drinks, lunch, a few more hours of briefings, background interviews, and finally the long drive back to Washington. Often we had to be creative to fill up the voracious maw of radio. Since we were not privy to what was actually going on, we had to analyze, hypothesize, or spend endless minutes rhapsodizing over the fall foliage of the region. At such times we sometimes resort to interviewing each other on the air, in hopes of rounding out the program and convincing the audience we know more than we actually do.

Occasionally, it wasn't necessary to drive to Camp David, since the State Department or the United States Information Service provided a bus for reporters to cover special events. I took it one day because we were invited to visit the inner sanctum of Camp David that night. The military honor guard was putting on a review for Presidents Carter and Sadat and Prime Minister Begin. This, as well as a later visit to the Gettysburg Cemetery at the end of the week, provided some of the few opportunities for the television types to get good pictures of the Camp David participants. The rest of the time they had to content themselves with footage of the boyish Jody Powell, or the still shots of the Heads of State provided by the White House. But now that we actually had the chance to get into Camp David itself, most of us jumped at the opportunity to go.

My husband drove me into Washington early in the morning so we could make the bus. En route, a traffic policeman who wanted to ticket us for speeding stopped us. I pretended to be in intense labor, thrashing and groaning in agony. Instead of giving us a ticket, the policeman insisted on escorting us to the hospital. There we had to wait until he left, so we could detour back to the State Department. I barely caught the bus in time.

The conveyance to Camp David was reminiscent of the hundreds of buses I'd ridden during campaign trips. The reporters told the same dirty jokes and sang the usual ribald songs. This time, however, there was a difference, since our fellow passengers were correspondents from many countries. It was amusing to hear them gamely trying to sing American football cheers in Japanese and Afrikaans.

The bus driver was a lovely, warmhearted, protective black man from Washington. He stayed with us all day and late into the night, while we were paraded around through the woods and secluded cabins of the very private Presidential retreat. We got close enough to the three leaders to shout questions at them, but the answers were conveniently drowned out by the blare of military music, as a full honors ceremony was performed for the world leaders. It was hard to tell whether they enjoyed it, but Carter, Sadat and Begin stood ramrod straight throughout the performance. The cameramen had a field night, and scored some excellent footage of the men framed by their three flags and silhouetted by the full moon and the forest. After the ceremony, we stumbled down the narrow dirt road in the dark and poured ourselves into the bus, exhausted.

Three hours later, the buss arrived on schedule at the darkened and deserted State Department. There we were disgorged and expected to find taxis to take us home. None of us had left cars, since it was impossible to find legal parking spaces in that area for an entire day. Most of the male reporters banded together and headed for the Watergate Hotel fifteen blocks away, hoping they would find taxis there and not get mugged on the deserted Washington streets.

It is at times like these that being pregnant has distinct advantages. Our wonderful bus driver was afraid to leave me alone in my condition, and insisted on driving me to my home, seven miles away in Virginia. The poor man didn't know what awaited him - nor did the three Japanese reporters who were quietly sleeping in the back.

We crossed the bridges and drove down the highways to the residential sections of Virginia. Eventually the houses gave way to woods, and the cement roads became dirt trails. As we crept through the woods to my hideaway home, the bus driver's eyes began to widen with fear. He'd heard terrible stories about lurking Ku Klux Klansmen lying in wait in the Virginia forests. His panic grew when the three Japanese journalists woke up, looked around them, and began to scream, afraid they'd been kidnapped. Finally, the twenty-ton bus made it to the circular driveway in front of our home. But recent heavy rains had turned the driveway into mush, and the bus bogged down in mud up to its axle. The hapless driver got out and tried to figure out how he could dig his bus from the mire.

At that moment, my husband woke up and was startled to see a huge bus outside his bedroom window. Since we were in a rural area with little traffic, it came as a double surprise to him. Steve stumbled out of the house wearing his baggy underwear and carrying an evil-looking shotgun. He never thought to ask whether I was all right; instead, he yelled at the poor driver for ruining his driveway and getting deep tire tracks in the grass. The driver - whose black face had paled with fright - quickly found the strength to dig the bus out, rev the motor, and leave. He refused to accept any payment for his kindness and trouble.

There was one other occasion during the meetings for us to see the participants at reasonably close range. On a Saturday, Jimmy Carter "liberated" the men from their Camp David fortress and took them down the mountain to a nearby graveyard. They toured the Gettysburg Battlefield, the scene of some of the bloodiest action of the American Civil War. Dutifully, the men traipsed up and down the hills, examining vantage points and rusted old cannons. The message could not have been more explicit: President Sadat and Prime Minister Begin must have been reminded of the many similar battles fought on the sands of the Sinai between their countries. They thought of their many relatives, friends, and countrymen who had died, only to have the scenes of their final struggles obscured by the timeless, unforgiving desert. President Carter appeared to be telling them: "This will happen again to you, if you don't reach a peace agreement."

On a more personal level, the day became a pleasant family outing for my family and me. Since it was a weekend, Steve was there to drive our nineteen-month-old son and me to Maryland. David delighted the officials and other reporters by climbing on the cannons in front of the press hall. Steve even took him downstairs to the bar, which was crammed with the folksy townspeople and other reporters trying to recover from the cold of the wind-swept hills of Gettysburg. Young David, fascinated by the sight of a bartender wearing a big white apron, chastised the barkeep, calling him a "big baby" for wearing a diaper all over his body. The embarrassed - and very macho - bartender took the scolding well, and refilled our son's milk bottle.

Nowadays, fewer reporters would have the firsthand experience of covering a "photo opportunity" a hundred miles away from their own base of operations. With the advent of cable, all-news television, such events are broadcast live. And you can get a lot closer to the characters on a television screen than you can from the exclusive vantage points of the press locations. In the end, nothing can beat the intimacy of the camera, although you do miss the full flavor of the event and the companionship of your colleagues if you aren't there in person.

I see the proliferation of all-news radio and television formats, and the internet, forever changing the nature of the news profession. I fully approve of them; they bring more news and information to the public, and provide more employment for journalists in some cases. On the other hand, however, fewer employers in small organizations will spend the money to cover events in person. They know the public will see or hear the same event as it happens. Young reporters now find the system much more passive. They do not have to struggle to find phones or parking spaces, and they don't have to endure exposure to wind, cold, heat, or rain. The practice of "borrowing" from the all-news outfits may not be quite legal, but it's now done with increasing frequency.

The Camp David talks dragged on for several weeks, past the deadline Jimmy Carter had set. Finally, under pressure to conclude them, heads were "banged together" and the parties made significant compromises. President Sadat would recognize Israel, establish full diplomatic relations between the countries, and encourage trade and tourism. For its part, Israel would do the same, as well as return the Sinai desert it had captured from Egypt. In doing so, it would give Egypt the expensive oil fields Israel had located and developed. This concession was extremely difficult for Israel, because it had grown dependent on the oil from the region and the extra security provided by the Sinai and the major new airfields it had constructed there. Thus far no oil reserves have been discovered in Israel. As former Prime Minister Golda Meir was fond of saying, "Moses led the Jewish people in the desert for forty years, and then settled in the one area in the Mideast which had no oil." The Camp David Accords also included an Israeli promise to destroy the modern settlement of Yamit, which had been developed at great expense and sacrifice in the desert. With Jewish soldiers forced to destroy a town developed and inhabited by their own countrymen, this provision caused a serious rift in Israeli society.

Unfortunately, the promises of Camp David have not been fully kept. The Accords may have contributed to the assassination of President Sadat. And so far, the truce between Israel and Egypt has led to a "cold peace," with a return of anti-Israeli or anti-Egypt cartoons and editorials in the antagonists' newspapers. But the night the talks ended was an occasion of nearly universal jubilation among the press corps assembled there.

Early that day, most of my colleagues had dutifully trekked up to Thurmont, Maryland, expecting the end of the meetings to be announced from there. But my instincts told me President Carter and his men wouldn't make such a momentous announcement in the bare surroundings of the American Legion Hall, when they could instead use the grandeur of the White House as a backdrop. Staging, I felt, would be an important aspect in planning the occasion. So I stayed close to the phones and the briefing rooms in the State Department and White House. Finally, we got the word that the talks had ended and that a major announcement would be forthcoming later that night at the White House.

Frantically my colleagues rushed home at breakneck speeds from Camp David. They had to contend with a driving rainstorm and always-impossible rush-hour traffic. Some of them never did make it back to the capital in time to cover the big story. For their part, the participants had no trouble; they flew back on the wings of government helicopters.

Once back at the White House, we received a long, detailed and technical background briefing from the National Security Advisor, Zbigniew Brzezinski. Then we rushed to the East Room for formal statements from the three leaders. Somehow, we radio reporters were expected to assimilate this highly sophisticated material and digest it into stories lasting from thirty seconds to three minutes in length. It can be terribly frustrating in such instances to have to weed out most of the details one has struggled so hard to amass. No wonder many reporters take the easy way out, and rewrite the stories they hear coming over the air from other newscasts. The problem is that those stories do not always place emphasis on aspects important to your outlets. Moreover, if the person you copy from is wrong, you too have made a serious error to be witnessed by your audience of millions.

After broadcasting volumes of short stores and some longer analysis pieces, I staggered out of the White House press room at about three o'clock in the morning. With me were some of my colleagues from Israel and Egypt. Suddenly, the enemies of thousands of years had become friends and allies. Most were jubilant over the promise of the accords, and euphoria enveloped them. We literally danced our way down the middle of Pennsylvania Avenue, mixing Arab with Israeli dancing as a full moon shone above the White House behind us. I had great trepidation about the pact, even as I celebrated with the others, but it was a moment to rejoice and we did. What a sight I was, very pregnant, tape recorder dangling from my shoulder, leading an Israeli circle dance in front of the President's mansion!

Regrettably, the announcement did not signal the end of the negotiations. For months, teams of Israelis, Egyptians and Americans continued to wrangle over details, language, and compromises. President Carter even had to make a final trip to the Middle East before the parties agreed to return to the White House in March 1979 to sign the Accords.

Meanwhile, we reporters were subjected to a daily round of briefings. This is where our own internal politics came into play. Most of the briefings were "on the record," and therefore open to everyone. But several were closed. Sometimes, the State Department official who controlled such things would invite the Israeli press and not the Egyptian reporters, or vice versa, to briefings that were crucial to all of us. At other times he would leak vital bits of information to a favored reporter. In some briefings, reporters who needed particular information were excluded for no apparent reason, other than the official's own petty likes and dislikes. Indeed, there are always times when more powerful reporters are given "leaks" which others are not privy to; this is an occupational perk - or hazard, depending on your point of view - and always has been. Usually, leaks are strategically placed as a means of floating a trial balloon, or to get across one point of view. Because it is easy to get burned by reporting leaks, the reporter is wise to double- and triple-check whenever possible, before airing the story.

In this case, the pattern of leaks was consistent. When I felt I had been excluded from crucial briefings once too often, I made the matter public. During the regular State Department briefing, I complained about the official. I accused him of running the State Department like an exclusive club, and insisted that he had no right to do so with an office funded by our - the taxpayers' - money. My voice trembled as I led the protest, and my whole body was shaking. Such behavior did not constitute accepted protocol in these conservative, striped-pants surroundings. But thankfully, some of the senior reporters came to my aid, and supported my accusations. One of them, Bernard Kalb, had long served as diplomatic correspondent for CBS and later NBC News. He eventually went on to become the Department's spokesman under Secretary of State George Shultz. He quit on a matter of principle, a few weeks before the Iran-Contra scandal broke out. Bernie and his brother,

Marvin, represent the best in thorough, seasoned diplomatic reporting. When he stood up and accused the man of "mishandling the Mideast Division" from the beginning, it added great weight to my protest. Since the State Department briefings are broadcast to every U.S. Government building in the nation and transcribed afterward, the beleaguered man got a lot of publicity. For months thereafter officials across the country offered me their congratulations on the protest I'd led.

I was treated somewhat better after that, by everyone except the man in question. Later, one respected columnist wrote that the diplomat would be "lucky to get a dry posting" in his next assignment. Sure enough, he was sent to a country where the weather averages a hundred degrees each day, and monsoons alternate with dusty, uncomfortable dry seasons.

Another problem with some of the striped-pants set is a bit more delicate. Many, many of my friends are homosexuals, and I am sympathetic to their situation. Often, I argue passionately for their civil rights. But every once in a while, I encounter a gay man who is a flagrant misogynist, and find myself on discrimination's receiving end. Often, the pressure is worse than any casting couch. During the Camp David talks, I encountered such discrimination with one such official. He clearly favored the male reporters over the female, even though some of the top Mideast reporters were women. The more handsome the man, the better his access to good stories. Often, a good-looking man got gifts he hadn't sought. One day, a particularly dashing Arab correspondent was late in joining our regular group of Israeli and Arab reporters for lunch. He arrived carrying a big, fancy fruitcake - a gift from his admirer. The reporter did not understand the symbolism, and was surprised we hadn't all been given the treats. With great glee, we dissected and consumed his special, hard-earned Mideast fruitcake!

Another Son and New Work Methods

A funny thing happened as I was about to leave for one of the Mideast briefings. I experienced sudden, and quite violent, labor pains and decided I'd best detour to the hospital, rather than to the State Department. My second son, Daniel, had clearly decided to put in an appearance … three weeks earlier than expected. Fortunately, a live-in nanny from England had arrived a few weeks before, so my twenty-month-old son, David, was being attended to at home. Steve had gone to work, and I knew there was no time to phone a taxi. An ambulance would have taken me to the nearest suburban hospital, but I wanted to go where my doctors were, and where my tests had been taken and my medical history known.

So I stowed away my tape recorder, picked up my suitcase, and waddled off to the car. Just as I got in, another sharp pain hit. David and my dog, Tracy, were quite concerned when they saw me kneel down in the driveway, doubled over in pain. When the contraction passed, I calculated that twenty minutes had elapsed between the two major spasms. If I was lucky, I reasoned, I could just make it into Washington, seven miles away, before another one hit. If the pain struck while I was driving down the highway, I hoped I'd be able to pull over to the side of the road until it ran its course. I also counted on meeting a policeman, who could drive me into the city at high speed.

As the saying goes, you can never find a cop when you need one. I did my best to be stopped, by driving thirty miles an hour over the speed limit and traveling in an express lane, reserved for four-passenger cars.

But no policeman was lurking in the shadows to catch me, and I listened for the sirens in vain.

Miraculously, I arrived at the George Washington University Hospital just as another contraction hit. I had to get out of the car so that I could double over to relieve the pressure. Passersby-by stared, aware that I was in trouble, but no one stopped to help. When I could stand again I parked the car in a space reserved for the handicapped. I wrote a note explaining that I had gone into the hospital and would try to move the car once the baby arrived. I put my missive on the windshield.

At least I'd made it to the hospital in time. Daniel was positioned incorrectly, and his birth was very difficult. If there hadn't been a doctor present to perform an episiotomy, the poor child might have been brain-damaged, trying to force his way into the world. So, I later reflected, it was a good thing I hadn't had the baby at Camp David or the White House after all. As it was, Daniel and I survived the trauma, but I'm not sure some of the young doctors in the delivery room did.

Since George Washington is a teaching hospital, there are always student doctors present during a procedure. One of them had never witnessed a delivery before, so he was keen to interview me, much as I interview a politician at work. At first I was cool and dispassionate, and tried helpfully to answer his questions. I tried to describe the pain in the third person and remain aloof from the whole business. But as the pain of the contractions intensified, I fell to pieces. I began to scream and curse at everyone around me, including my husband, who had been called at work and who barely made it to the hospital in time.

I became even more frenzied when I learned that it was impossible to get any painkilling medications because everything was happening too fast. Steve and I had attended natural childbirth classes, but were among the worst students there. Somehow, the breathing exercises never did much for me. And as Steve often said, he would have preferred to sit the whole thing out in a bar. As Daniel was finally born, I screamed so loud they could almost hear me at the White House, a few blocks away. Even in the midst of my agony, I actually began to laugh when

I heard my doctor - Allen Weingold, the Chief of Gynecology at GW Hospital - say, "This natural childbirth is for the birds!" Bless him; he never lost his sense of humor, despite his reputation and expertise.

An hour later, I rejoiced in having been blessed with another healthy, normal son. Two hours later, determined to maintain my record, I phoned in a story on the Mideast negotiations. It was especially difficult getting an outside line from the recovery room, but in no time I was yelling at the poor international operators. Things were back to normal.

With two young sons at home, and a longer recovery period to look forward to, I once again found that I would have to work at home. I'll always be grateful to my friends at one network who had a direct line to the State Department briefings. They let me phone them each day, and gave me a "feed" while the briefing was in progress. This way, I didn't get too far behind on the flow of news. At the same time, I discovered that working from home had its advantages, a lesson that had been driven home to me soon after David, my first son, was born.

In March 1977, the Hanafi Moslems, a small and fanatical black group, shot their way into three Washington buildings. They occupied the ornate Mosque, which served the mainstream Moslem community; the District Building, which housed the offices of the Mayor and the City Council; and the B'nai B'rith Building, where the largest number of hostages were taken. For most of those hostages, the experience was especially traumatic. Many of the employees in the Jewish Service Agency were survivors of the Nazi concentration camps in Europe. Others had fled Europe, a few hours ahead of invading Russian or German troops.

When the Hanafis burst into the buildings, they shot their way from floor to floor. Some of the employees tried to barricade the doors and hide behind desks. But the terrorists burst in, and systematically rounded up each group, imprisoning them on the highest floors. Some of the people were shot, and carry physical - as well as psychological - scars to this day. One black radio reporter was shot to death in the District Building.

The hostages were held for thirty-nine hours, until the Hanafis agreed to free them after official and ecumenical groups from Washington spent many painful and harrowing hours convincing them to do so. When the hostages were finally released, church bells from every part of the city rang out together, to celebrate their liberation. I was almost overcome by the emotion of seeing the city I loved so much united in a sense of triumph and jubilation. The feeling of joy that united the city that day is usually reserved for only one other occasion: when the Washington Redskins football team wins a major victory.

The Hanafi siege represented a painful period for me on a personal level. Not only was I worried about my friends imprisoned in the District and B'nai B'rith buildings, but I was frustrated by my inability to cover the event firsthand. I was still weak and bleeding from David's birth and couldn't walk the long blocks necessary and then stand around in the cold for several hours awaiting developments. So I had to do the job by staying home and monitoring the news bulletins as they came in. Occasionally I was able to get a phone call into one of the B'nai B'rith offices and interview one of the hostages or a Hanafi guard. Thus, I added to the total coverage provided of the event.

In many ways, I served my stations better by staying at home. I could phone in several reports each hour, whereas ironically, if I had been standing on the street, staring at the building, I would not have been able to report. There are never enough phone booths around, and those available are sealed at the mouthpiece. You can't unscrew it, so you can't send tape reports through the phone. The best you can do is shout through your story, which is never as good.

Gone are the days of the steel hats, antennas, and fifty-pound mobile units of 1968. To broadcast, you do best with an expensive van, to provide live coverage to your television or radio station. With the advent of cable television and satellites, those reports are broadcast instantly to stations around the country and around the world, provided they can afford to pay for the satellite time. That can run several thousand dollars for a three-minute transmission. But if you work on your own, with a limited budget, you can't give the same instantaneous coverage from a location without the equipment or, at the very least, a telephone. Now, you can also use a cell phone and internet. But, again, those technologies did not exist for us in the 1970's and 80's. So you were reduced to monitoring the other newscasts, if you could not be on the spot. It isn't very satisfying, but it's the way thousands of other reporters throughout the nation are also forced to work. At least you are always at the other end of the phone when your station needs you for a broadcast. You are not standing on a windswept street corner, out of reach. And, in my case, I was home to breast-feed a baby when he needed it, even if I was holding a microphone in the other hand at the same time.

The Air Florida Crash

While I now do ninety percent of my reporting "on the scene," I had to use this at-home method during one other crucial incident, the January 13, 1982, crash of the Air Florida jet into Washington's Potomac River. It took place in the midst of a furious Washington snowstorm, when visibility was nearly zero. The snow and ice built up so fast on the windows and wings of the plane that it was nearly impossible to keep them clear. Families of some of the 78 victims later testified that their relatives were afraid to fly that day but board the plane because they had schedules to meet, or were concerned about losing the money they'd paid for the ticket if they canceled.

Sadly, the pilot did take off, lost altitude, crashed through part of the 14th Street Bridge, and plummeted into the ice-filled Potomac River. Most of the passengers died instantly, as did five people driving their cars across the bridge who were also crushed or swept into the river by the plane. One victim in a car was decapitated, as the plane sliced off the top half of his vehicle. Another man died soon afterward in the freezing water as rescuers tried in vain to reach him. He sacrificed his own life by grabbing the rescue ring from the helicopter and passing it to fellow survivors in the river. Two courageous passersby also won the admiration of the world by jumping into the river to assist the professionals in their rescue attempts.

As if the plane crash and ensuing traffic jam weren't bad enough, the Washington Metro also suffered a disaster – a tragic crash underground. Three people were crushed to death as the train slammed into a cement wall. Both stories were gruesome, but they were big news that had to be covered. The subway crash became more or less a sidebar to the more dramatic horrors unfolding in the Potomac River. And both stories became even bigger because they occurred in Washington, where thousands of reporters could cover them. A plane crash in remote, snow-covered mountains would not get the same on-site coverage, with the world watching transfixed as survivors and victims were pulled from the wreckage. In the same way, hostage taking in Lebanon is not as dramatic as the same type of incidents in Washington, because unfortunately, it has become mundane in that violence-prone area of the world.

Fortunately from a professional point of view, I was able to cover the crash story for my clients, but only because I had made the decision to stay home and be a good mother. My children are my prime responsibility. If I were not there to pick them up from school, they would be stranded. My husband may be able to get them at six o'clock, but by that time they would be frustrated and scared. And, on a night like this, they would have had to remain at school until nearly ten p.m., or later, when the traffic from Washington to Virginia finally began to flow again. I could not let that happen.

After several years of living in the Washington area, I knew the city descends into chaos at the first sign of snow. There are several reasons for this. First, Washington is not really accustomed to large snowfalls, and the city doesn't have as much equipment to handle it as, say, Boston or Minneapolis. Second, Washington is a melting pot if ever there was one, with area residents hailing from all corners of the world, from Texas to Ethiopia to India to Argentina. Many are ill equipped to drive in the snow because they are unused to it. Such drivers are timid and unskilled at responding to skids, ice formations and adverse road conditions. Traffic backs up until a "gridlock" is formed; one street is blocked by the cars stalled on the street ahead. Literally, nothing moves for hours, except the horns and fists of frustrated motorists. Often, commuters sit in their cars all night, unable to get home while the snow and frigid wind swirl around them.

As a mother, I vowed never to drive to Washington when it snowed, or threatened to snow. I could not afford to leave my children in school, or with a baby-sitter, with no one to pick them up at closing time. So on the day of the fateful crash, I'd stayed home with my two young sons. I wrote stories for several hours on political topics and on the worsening weather situation. Then David, Daniel and I went sleigh riding for two hours. We came home frozen, exhausted, and the two boys went right to sleep.

Suddenly, radio and television were filled with bulletins about the Air Florida crash. I jumped to the phone and broadcast without a break for the next five hours. It is a morbid way to make a living, on the tragedies of others. My stomach churned as I considered the victims, especially the young mother who survived, while her husband and infant son died in the crash. On a personal level, I was also worried about my husband Steve, who was someplace in the bowels of Washington, in the subway system, during the crash. It was more than five hours before he could get out and make his way home, by walking part of the way in the blizzard and hitchhiking the rest. I knew there had been some deaths in the subway crash, but no names had been released at that stage. Others around me waited tensely as well, wondering like me if their husbands or wives had been swept off the 14th Street bridge by the plane. Friends from New Zealand, Australia, and Israel who had relatives in the area whom they could not reach pleaded with me to try to find out if their loved ones were still alive.

Somehow, in the midst of this horrifying limbo of waiting and not knowing, I did my job as a reporter, and kept my listeners around the world updated on the unfolding tragedy in Washington. Some of my frustrated colleagues, caught in the traffic jam, couldn't get out and send reports until several hours later. The next day, as the traffic and storm abated, I was able to go to the bridge myself and watch for a few hours as the derricks pulled parts of the fuselage from the river. It took days for frogmen to locate and recover all of the bodies. Sometimes, as parts of the plane were lifted up to the bridge, bodies of the crash victims fell from the seats and tumbled back into the river. It was a gruesome, blood-curdling business, and a terrible ordeal for the rescuers and the reporters who had to endure hours and days of bitter cold on the wind-swept bridge. The only relief was offered by a small Salvation Army truck, which provided a warm shelter and hot coffee to the personnel working at the site. I captured with my tape recorder several descriptive pieces from the bridge, but had no means of broadcasting from there. Thus I was still required to return home to transmit the story; but in this case, because the immediate emergency had passed, the delay was acceptable. In fact, it gave me more time to do colorful, descriptive stories with the sounds of wind, rescue equipment, and other planes in the background. While the rescue operation was progressing, planes departing from and landing at National Airport passed over the bridge every three minutes. I thought that few passengers could fail to notice the grisly scene beneath them.

Working onsite at the bridge made it necessary to combine my personal and professional roles in a way not everyone would approve of. At the time, I had nowhere to leave my children, since baby-sitters would not come to work that day. Now that the highways were relatively clear, my husband had returned to his business in Washington, so I had no choice but to take the boys with me.

First, to amuse and exhaust them, I took them sleigh riding for an hour. Then we headed to a motel where the Federal Aviation Administration conducted a briefing. They had established an emergency press room near the crash site. Afterward, the three of us - along with an Australian reporter whom we had initiated into the joys of sleigh riding - headed for the bridge. I didn't tell the boys what was actually going on, of course, and left them in the warm back seat of the car while I went out to observe the scene and record the stories. As much as I wanted my sons to know as much about the news business as possible, I knew this was not the time or the place for children of two and four years of age. Thankfully, they have never had to experience such a tragedy firsthand, and I pray they never will.

The Ethics of Leaks

The Washington routine continued for many years, with occasional dramatic events to punctuate the pattern of methodically grinding out stories each day. This stage was much more professionally satisfying - and financially rewarding - than were the years I spent bumming around the nation and the world. But, the excitement levels certainly were not as high! During Jimmy Carter's presidency, I continued to divide my energies between the White House and the State Department. Most of the foreign affairs stories came out of State. But sometimes, when they emanated from the White House, the officials there proved to be extremely thin-skinned and - in my view, at least - unprofessional.

This opinion is illustrated by a situation in 1978, when the Carter Administration waged a bitter uphill fight to get Congressional approval to sell sophisticated F-15 warplanes to Saudi Arabia. Carter prevailed, despite vigorous efforts by Israel and its friends in the U.S. Congress to defeat the move. Critics of the plan argued that the planes and missiles could be turned against Israel, a country threatened by war with Saudi Arabia. When the final debate was underway, I spent an entire day in the Senate, providing nonstop coverage. That night, the vote was finally taken, and I wrote a four-minute wrap-up piece, in which I noted that White House Press Secretary Jody Powell and advisor Hamilton Jordan had "gloated about breaking the back of the powerful Israeli lobby." I really considered it almost a "throw-away" line, and used it to add color to the piece. I had two excellent sources, who had sworn to me that they'd heard the statements made during a Washington cocktail party the night before. It may be that my sources were lying, but it is standard procedure to go ahead with a piece if there are two independent sources to verify it. Sometimes, however, even that precaution is inadequate, especially if the sources in question have an ax to grind and are working together to air a story for their own purposes.

The Carter White House was enraged when they heard the broadcast. My report was heard overseas, while National Public Radio broadcast a similar report in this country. Powell and National Security Advisor Zbigniew Brzezinski did their best to get to our sources. They summoned the NPR reporter and her boss to the White House, where they were read the riot act. Jody Powell saw me daily there, and for the next two weeks he tried to get me to reveal my sources. When that failed, he harangued me with phone calls late into the night.

One day, I finally agreed to see if my sources would come forward and speak to him. He offered to let me use his White House phone to call them, but even I was not naive enough to fall for that. When I did consult the sources later, I was disappointed; they refused to talk to him, and I began to wonder whether their story was true after all. In any case, my one-liner would have died a quiet death if the White House had not chosen to blow it up out of all proportion. I felt they acted very unprofessionally by behaving like a dog with a bone over what was essentially a trivial incident. It was akin to President Carter's oft-noted obsession with detail, which extended even to his personal supervision of the schedules for the White House tennis courts. On the other hand, the incident definitely taught me to be a lot more careful about leaks. People who leak stories to you always do it for a reason, and I have now learned to think four times before airing their point of view.

Sometimes, the game of leaks can be particularly brutal. Witness the time I became an unwitting player during the brief tenure of Richard Allen as President Reagan's National Security Advisor, the first of many who would hold that position. I believed I had established a rapport with him during the official transition period between presidential administrations, and covered him during several news conferences. I requested a personal interview with him, but was put off. Then, to my surprise, one day into the new administration, his secretary phoned to tell me I could come in. Flattered, I jumped at the chance and accepted immediately. I thought the interview would be "on the record," since she never said to me it would be "on background," or not for attribution.

The next day I came in, but was forced to cool my heels for several hours in the waiting room next to the top-secret National Security Council headquarters. That office lies on a basement floor of the White House, and it really looks no different from any other set of offices anywhere else in the world. Only the pictures of political leaders on the walls and the style of the flags in the corner give any impression of the special nature of the place. I was annoyed by the long wait, but as we were all to discover many months later, Richard Allen was unusually busy at the time. This was the same day he had arranged an interview with Mrs. Reagan for some Japanese reporters, who expressed their gratitude by giving him a very expensive wristwatch and some money for his help. He was supposed to report the gifts but later claimed he was so busy he put the items in his safe and forgot about them. The fact of the gifts was eventually made public, and created a minor scandal. This incident, as well as internal feuding among White House staff, led to his forced resignation from his powerful post. Perhaps my presence for the one-on-one interview created one more distraction for him and contributed to his failure to report the presents. Personally, I doubt it, although Allen certainly conveniently forgot some things about our interview and the conversation that preceded it.

When I was finally ushered into his office - heavily decorated with all the trappings of a super-patriot - I got out my tape recorder and began the interview. Allen jumped on me, insisting our meeting was "on background," and that no tapes would be allowed. I argued that I needed to at least tape for note purposes, to better ensure accuracy. He remained adamant, although most officials do not object to taping if it is done openly.

Thus we conducted the interview, focusing mainly on the Middle East. It soon became clear to me that Allen was trying to send a message to Israel: that the Reagan Administration would not abandon that country even though it might announce some very unpopular positions in the upcoming weeks of the new administration. I took notes as best

I could, while his secretary made her own record of the conversation in shorthand. At the end of the interview, I asked Allen how he could be identified in my broadcast. He instructed me to say, "White House sources." This was a clear indication that he understood that I would do a broadcast on the basis of the interview. Again, this is standard White House procedure.

The next day, I did something journalists are not supposed to do. I called his secretary and read my story to her, as a means of crosschecking my own notes as well as showing them every courtesy. She agreed that my notes were correct, and I informed her that my story would be broadcast in two days. The secretary made no effort to dissuade me and certainly had adequate time to inform her boss if she wanted to.

Two days later I aired my report, which reached my audiences throughout the Mideast. I also sold it to radio stations in America. That Monday, Richard Allen called me and gave me hell. He fumed that I was never meant to do a story on the basis of the interview, and I reminded him that he'd never stipulated this, and had even said I could refer to him as "White House sources."

In any case, each of us suspected the other of lying. Despite the fact that by that time I'd been reporting for fourteen years, I was shocked by the incident. But I became somewhat more sanguine about it when a very distinguished newspaper colleague of mine told me he'd had a similar experience. He had conducted a "background" interview with then-Secretary of State Alexander Haig (who, incidentally, also was forced to resign twenty months later). Everyone was aware of the interview, since it was published and displayed in the daily State Department schedule. The next day, my colleague published his story - attributed to "sources" - on the front page of his newspaper, which is one of the most respected journals in the United States. At the regular White House and State Department briefings, the press spokesmen spent nearly twenty minutes each, denouncing the story and its veracity, suggesting that the reporter had been "misinformed" and had spoken to some "bad sources." The reporter in question, who was much tougher and more self-assured than I, just sat there during the briefings, with a big smile on his face. He knew he was being used as a pawn in the old Washington game in which officials want to get across a point of view but then don't want to take responsibility for it. It's a vicious practice, at least from a reporter's perspective, but it goes on every day in the Nation's Capital. Perhaps, though, the appointees who endure in office are those who are the most straightforward in their dealings with their fellow officials and with the media.

President Reagan appeared to display the twin ideals of openness and honesty, until his Administration was torpedoed by the Iran-Contra arms scandal that was uncovered in 1986. Dubbed by Congresswoman Pat Schroeder as the "Teflon President," he seemed to lead a charmed existence with the public and the media until the secret arms sale to Iran was uncovered. The Administration had concocted the scheme to gain the release of the American hostages from Iranian-controlled factions in Lebanon. Prior to that scandal, none of Reagan's other foreign policy debacles seemed to stick. He'd survived the bombing of the U.S. Marine barracks and the American Embassy in Beirut, which claimed over 250 lives. The public was not outraged when he authorized the bombing of Libya, and was complacent about the invasion of Grenada, even about the channeling of public and private funds and arms to the Contras in Nicaragua. Everyday Americans did not seem to mind that he frequently rambled and missed the point, and sometimes even rewrote history, during his public news conferences. After all, the indulgent rationale went, here was a 76-year-old man who had survived a serious shooting and major cancer surgery. We did not know, at the time, that Reagan probably suffered from the early stages of Alzheimer's disease. He was warm, open, friendly, folksy, and devoted to his wife, Nancy. He was everybody's favorite uncle. He didn't sleep around, or insult women, as had several of his predecessors, and successors, in the White House. President Reagan was indeed the Teflon President, to whom no adversities stuck ... until the "Irangate" affair. Now, there were charges that he may have presided over the most duplicitous administration in modern American history; at least on the part of some staff members. With virtually all of his staffers contradicting each other, it was impossible to tell whether the lies were emanating from the White House, the National Security Council, the

CIA, the State Department, or the Pentagon. The scandal also opened up a very serious debate: Why do lawmakers often consider themselves above the very laws they are sworn to protect and uphold?

The lies and cover-ups also underscored the Machiavellian nature of politics that has been evident for centuries in every country around the globe. Consider, too, the eerie case of the former Director of the Central Intelligence Agency, William Casey, who had major brain surgery following weeks of testimony before the Senate committees investigating the scandal. Legislators contended that Casey's testimony was incomplete and misleading. But before Casey could be recalled, his cancerous brain tumor was discovered and surgery performed. That surgery severely impaired his ability to think, speak, and move. Doctors insisted that the timing of his operation was purely coincidental. But to some observers, that medical coincidence ranks on the same level with the efforts to silence Attorney General John Mitchell's wife, Martha, during the Watergate scandal, or with the fact that President John Kennedy was assassinated in Lyndon Johnson's home state of Texas.

Regardless of how one feels about the revelations of the hearings, it is indisputable that the Iran-Contra scandal was a personal tragedy for Ronald Reagan, precisely because he was perceived by his constituents to be such a decent guy. As many commentators noted, President Carter had to try hard to like people, while Reagan had to try hard not to like them. Ronald Reagan's natural warmth was always in evidence, even in the midst of formal news conferences that were viewed by as many as 60 million people at a time. Even during the mad scrambles to ask questions of him, Reagan managed to make each reporter feel he had established eye contact with the President.

When Reagan did recognize me for a question - a supreme honor during these well-publicized events - I felt as though he and I were alone in a room together, having an intimate chat. In similar situations with past presidents, my whole body would shake when I asked a question, and I feared my voice would give way and my knees would buckle. Perhaps I was just more experienced by the time I attended those Reagan press conferences, but to me Reagan seemed adept at generating a sense of relaxation. Contrary to the "Great Communicator" moniker promoted by his aides, he could deliver long and rambling discourses in answering questions, and he certainly made many mistakes. He tended to trail off in mid-sentence. This once caused me to interrupt him for a "follow-up" question in the midst of his response, because I couldn't tell whether he was about to go on or stop. If I hadn't jumped in with a follow-up, I would have gotten no news out of his answer, and another reporter would have rushed in to ask a question on an entirely different topic.

On the whole, President Reagan did get along quite well with the news media, at least before the scandal broke. It's a pity so many of his appearances were stage-managed. In the beginning, he called on whomever he chose; then he began to arrive at his news conferences equipped with a list. Those he expected to call on were supposed to be in pre-assigned seats. It didn't always work that way, because reporters sometimes left their seats to get closer to him. On occasion, he might call on one of the sixty or so reporters present, only to get someone else sitting in the wrong chair. Once, he called on a male reporter, who happened to be home that night, watching the event on prime-time television. The reporter later said he stood up automatically in his own living room, and then burst out laughing. Meanwhile, a woman reporter stood up to be recognized, even though President Reagan had clearly called out a man's name.

During earlier administrations, the biggest reporters, or the ones with the loudest voices, had the advantage. But the Reagan presidency sought to maintain proper decorum. For that reason, reporters could no longer jump up and shout; they had to raise their hands and cross their fingers. One news director friend of mine, an executive at a major network, once suggested I would have better luck if I dramatically changed my approach. He sent me an oil painting, clearly depicting former President Nixon and most of my professional colleagues, who were shown shouting to get the President's attention. In the painting, I could be seen standing, a buxom redhead, stark naked, raising my hand for attention. It never happened in real life, but I was often reminded of that painting when I failed to be recognized for questions.

Actually, most reporters are rather tame and respectful during news conferences. For many years, we never went through any particular security checks and were just ushered through, provided we had proper credentials. Fortunately, however, we now go through metal detectors so that no one can smuggle in any dangerous object. There are always reporters from fringe groups around, and there's always the danger that some nut wearing a press pass will try to shoot the nation's Chief Executive. Ultimately, our access to President Reagan was sharply curtailed because one reporter accosted him, grabbing his arm as he was leaving a news conference. Traditionally, we had an opportunity to talk with him informally as he was leaving the room, but after that incident, which scared the hell out of the Secret Service, the President changed the entire seating order in the East Room. He used to stand in the back, and then wind his way out through all of us. But the seating was rearranged, and his podium backed out into the red-carpeted hallway. After the conference, the President had only to turn his back and walk quickly away. The first time the new arrangement was tried, he stumbled, nearly falling flat on his face. But he soon got the hang of things.

The incident with the journalist who overstepped her bounds presented a real dilemma for us. Often, reporters will use a news conference to harangue an official and bring national attention to their cause. These advocates have press credentials because their organization may sponsor a newsletter, even if it is a tiny one. In some cases, however, the newsletter is distributed to thousands of cult followers across the country. Some of us have supported the curtailment of press credentials among those who use them simply to promote a cause. But the flip side of that argument is that by limiting even those fringe elements, freedom of the press is compromised. Everyone has enemies, and everyone could be hurt by stricter controls of news credentials. I reminded the officials of the Supreme Court Justice's phrase that "A man does not have the right to shout 'fire' in a crowded theater." We all recognize when reporters are clearly misusing their privileges, so it us up to us all to police them, criticize them, and prevent them from abusing those privileges. Sometimes, that takes guts and nerve. Some of the fringe movements can be quite vicious, and have tried to harm the families and even the pets of other reporters who have criticized them. One organization stole the stationery of an investigative reporter, and then wrote an extortion letter on it. That reporter was about to go to jail, after enduring years of trial and trauma, before she was found innocent. We must all take a stand against these abuses, which further erode the reputation of a profession that is easily tarnished.

While the press conferences are regulated, "stakeouts" or "photo opportunities" are not. On those occasions, while the press is ushered in to watch the President conferring with a distinguished visitor, the reporters with the booming voices try to shout out questions on any topic of the day. Usually the staff will cut off the President midway through his response. Or, if he is leaving for Camp David or some other destination, the engines of the helicopter conveniently rev up, drowning out his answer during a crucial response, or an embarrassing question. Sometimes, the questions can be most irreverent. The unofficial leader of the press corps was Sam Donaldson of ABC television. Sam possesses an overpowering voice, and nothing intimidates him. Shortly before Christmas one year, allegations emerged that a close friend and unofficial advisor of the Reagans', the late millionaire Alfred Bloomingdale, was a sex pervert. None of these charges were ever proven, but, in newspaper reports, he was accused by a former mistress of stripping girls bare and riding on their backs, drooling all the while. When that bored him, Bloomingdale allegedly bound their hands with his expensive ties. The former mistress who spread these stories was later beaten to death. After one formal news conference, as President Reagan was leaving the room, Sam shouted to him, "That's a nice tie, Mr. President. Did it come from your friend, the late Alfred Bloomingdale?" The President rushed from the room; he may not have heard the question, but some of his aides certainly did.

Sam also had a running feud with some of the older female reporters who have covered the White House for nearly half a century. One day, a diminutive white-haired woman reporter was hit by a bus, and spent several days in the hospital. When she returned to the White House, Sam bellowed out, "Welcome back! Was the bus hurt?"

Some of these wisecracks paled in comparison to the comments made when President Reagan's rectal surgery was announced. At first, simple surgery was scheduled to remove a small polyp. Then it became major cancer surgery, with a good deal of his intestine removed. White House news secretary Larry Speakes tried his best to be serious and professional, but he was met by a barrage of gross questions such as, "What are the doctors gonna use, Larry - a Roto-Rooter?" Actually, few of the reporters could have survived the surgery with the strength and courage displayed by President Reagan.

While most of us consider such jokes in good fun, they often reflect an underlying frustration with the way the news is managed and spoon-fed during every administration. All too often, the White House can become a very passive beat. That's why White House reporters can burn out quickly, even though they get more air and print time than their colleagues assigned to other beats. But there is little opportunity for investigative, in-depth reporting in the White House. During the Watergate years, it was the reporters outside the comfortable confines of the White House who managed to dig for and unravel the truths that lay underneath the cover-up. The White House reporters can be extremely aggressive and intelligent, but they're often hampered by their position. They know that if they step on too many toes, they might lose their sources inside the hallowed halls. Even worse, they may lose their priceless White House press credentials, the most coveted commodity among the Washington media.

Covering the Reagan White House became a matter of routine: attending briefings, photo opportunities, and endless stakeouts in the cold, snow, heat, or rain; and waiting to interview people who had met with the President. The Reagan White House was a bit livelier than other administrations, because Larry Speakes had a rapier wit, and enjoyed parrying with the press, even if the arguments are serious ones. His successor, Marlin Fitzwater, employed the same light touch with the press. Sometimes, these "newsmeisters" rewarded us by bringing in a top sports or show business figure to conduct the briefing. Once, Speakes brought in Mel Blanc, the longtime voice of Bugs Bunny and other cartoon characters. He was introduced as "Professor Lapin," and conducted a highly technical briefing with a thick French accent. For several minutes, we struggled frantically to take notes, until he lapsed into his "Bugs" accent, and we realized that our collective legs had been pulled.

The Reagan Presidency: An Assassin Strikes

The Reagan White House experienced a dramatic break in routine that had occurred only on a handful of occasions, following the tragic shootings of Abraham Lincoln, James Garfield, and John Kennedy, all sitting Presidents. On March 30, 1981, Reagan and three other men were shot and seriously wounded, less than three months into his presidency. Fortunately, all the victims survived, thanks largely to modern technology and an efficient Secret Service.

The shooting took place just as President Reagan was exiting from the Washington Hilton Hotel after delivering a speech there. Ironically, the would-be assassin, John Hinckley, Jr., was the son of a wealthy businessman who had been a generous backer of the Republican Party. Young Hinckley clearly was mentally disturbed, for by killing the President he hoped to gain recognition and earn the admiration of film actress Jodie Foster, with whom he was obsessed.

Hinckley failed to kill anyone, but he seriously wounded press secretary James Brady, who was struck in the head. The image of Brady's large, inert form, lying bleeding on the sidewalk, was soon flashed over nationwide television. Two other men, a Secret Service agent and a policeman, were also hit by flying bullets. A horrified nation later saw clips of one of them convulsing in a fetal position and moaning in agony. All recovered in a few months except for Jim Brady, who underwent numerous major operations and spent every day in painful therapy at the hospital where doctors had struggled feverishly to save his life.

Brady was partially crippled, and his speech has been affected. But he still manages to attend the most important Washington social functions, where he is escorted in a wheelchair. In later years, an important piece of gun control legislation was named after him, and President Clinton named the White House press room, the "James Brady" room.

Indentations from the bullet scar Brady's forehead. But "the Bear," as he is affectionately known, has not lost his warmth or sense of humor. He jokes that Hinckley was such a lousy shot he couldn't hit the broad side of a barn. But he did hit Brady, who was in the wrong place at the wrong time, as was his primary target, the President of the United States.

As for Ronald Reagan, he didn't even realize he'd been hit until he was back in the limousine, speeding toward the White House. He thought the Secret Service agent who pushed him into the car had injured him in the ribs. But when the President developed intense chest pain, began to panic and experienced difficulty breathing, he was rushed to George Washington University Hospital, where he and his friend Brady underwent emergency surgery. Miraculously, the excellent medical teams at the hospital were able to save both men.

From our perspective as reporters, covering the story proved to be a matter of catching up and trying to sort out conflicting accounts. We rushed from the hotel, where we tried to interview witnesses. Then we fought our way through the traffic to the White House, or to the hospital, where press officials gave briefings to reporters who gathered outside in the torrential rain. It was there we learned officially that President Reagan had been wounded, and was undergoing surgery. Back at the White House, amid the confusion, Secretary of State Alexander Haig ascended the press podium to announce he was in charge, until Vice President Bush could return to Washington. In the ensuing flap, Haig explained he'd done so to calm the nation, and to assure the world that someone with more authority than White House staff members was running the show.

Meanwhile, the Defense Secretary put American troops on alert, in case the shooting turned out to be part of a wider conspiracy, or in the event the Soviets tried to take advantage of the perceived chaos and lack of leadership. Most diplomatic reporters thought Haig had acted reasonably; but the White House staff was infuriated. Many of them thought they were in charge, and the line of succession would not go immediately to the Secretary of State in any case. It would go first to the Vice President, even though he was in an airplane en route to Washington.

Many of the staff members communicated their anger to the regular White House reporters, who spent months afterward trying to make mincemeat of Alexander Haig. He was never able to overcome his image on national television that day, trembling and perspiring, as he announced, "*I am in charge.*" What may have been a perfectly necessary and logical action on his part was to become one more nail in his coffin, forcing his resignation several months later.

My stations naturally were scrambling for up-to-date accounts of the shooting and its aftermath. I tried to phone in reports whenever I could, but it was a haphazard enterprise at first. In a major story like this, my practice was to call in a bulletin number and ask to be put on the air live and immediately. I didn't bother to write a script, but just asked the anchorman to fire questions at me. This is invaluable, because it guides the flow of my description. Often, the anchorman can slow me down, if I am losing the listeners or not giving enough details. In addition, he or she may have access to bulletins from other reporters or from the wire services, and can fill me in on details I may have missed. There is nothing to match such teamwork, especially in the midst of a breaking story. When a major crisis is unfolding, I am also relieved of the necessity of finding a phone I can unscrew to attach my alligator clips. I just rush to a pay phone (which is sealed and cannot be dismembered) and shout my story into the receiver. The quality isn't nearly as good, but it adds authenticity, and the listeners understand everything cannot be broadcast in the controlled atmosphere of a studio or recording cubicle.

Despite the excellent teamwork I enjoyed with my stations in New Zealand, Australia and Israel, Canada wanted me to be several places at once. If I was at the hospital, they wanted me at the White House. When I was at the White House, they wanted me in their studio. I was really reluctant to change locations, because it meant I was out of contact with my clients while en route from one location to another.

Finally, after a two-hour vigil at the hospital following the shooting, I decided to head for the White House. It seemed a better base from which to work. In addition, I was chilled and miserable, drenched to the skin by the constant rain. Fortunately, I chose to drive to the White House just as the networks flashed the erroneous bulletins that James Brady had died.

Had I been near a phone, I probably would have reported it without checking any further, assuming that with so many people on the job the American networks would be certain of the facts before putting the story on the air. But caught up as I was in the unyielding Washington traffic, I couldn't do an update. By the time I found a parking space and slogged about five blocks to the White House, the networks had returned to the air, saying they had made a grievous mistake. They apologized to Brady's family for reporting he had died when he was, in fact, still clinging to life on the operating table, undergoing delicate and complex brain surgery. One superb newscaster - ABC's Frank Reynolds (who has since died of cancer) was so furious he slammed his fist down in front of millions of television viewers, glared at his staff, and said in tense, clipped tones, "Let's get this thing *nailed down*!"

Fortunately, I was saved from perpetuating the rumor that poor Jim Brady had died, but I did have to explain the inaccurate report to my editors. Then, firmly ensconced in the White House for a long vigil, I had to turn to my friends for help. They came through splendidly, once again underscoring the importance of keeping friends in this business. Three of my stations wanted me to give live updates at the top of the hour. I often had nothing new to say, but had to come up with some exciting new angles to keep the listeners' interest. At a few moments before the hour, I borrowed phones from three of my friends so I could call my stations in Canada, New Zealand, and Australia. Then, on the hour, I talked as fast as I could to each one. As soon as I finished an update to one station, I hung up the phone and repeated the process for the next one. Fortunately, the anchormen on the other end were true professionals, and helped to keep the conversation going. I'm not sure which countries I talked to, in which order, but they all had British accents.

At the end of five hours, I had to do a long wrap for Israel. I covered it as an ongoing story, since I had already done several newscasts for them on earlier bulletins. The editor on duty, however, wanted me to write it as a breaking story, starting from the beginning and detailing everything that had happened. By that time, I was exhausted, and verging on pneumonia thanks to my wet clothes and exposure to air conditioning. We argued frantically (a not uncommon occurrence with some of my hotheaded editors). Finally, he killed my story and wrote his own. I was furious when I later heard about it, but it's one more frustration that goes with the territory. Reporters cannot always have their own way, and the editor on duty has the final say. In addition, a human being can stretch only so far. By midnight, I was exhausted, and could barely drive the seven miles to my home, much less write another long story.

My colleagues also experienced similar frustrations as they covered the aftermath of the shootings. We ran around like fish in a feeding frenzy, trying to learn the truth. We bumped into each other at the White House, walked in front of each other's cameras, and got tangled in each other's cables. The smoke was thick from the reporters who still relied on cigarettes, causing irritation among the growing legions of militant nonsmokers. Food was brought into the White House, which was soon strewn with trash and leftover Chinese food, tossed around by several hundred reporters. There is little glamour to the job at times like this.

The White House press room is in a basement area, which had once been an indoor swimming pool until it was covered over and made into expanded press facilities. However, because of the location, the press room had a problem with rats and mice. Even so, the rats are not as large as are the ones in the State Department, which was built in a swamp known as Foggy Bottom. There are rats (and I mean the four-legged variety) as large as small dogs. They can be seen scampering in the cafeteria, or as far up as the top officials' offices on the sixth and seventh floors.

In the White House that night, I managed to hold most of the mice and rats at bay. But I was very nervous when I retreated to the small broom closet to find some quiet in which to record a long story. That closet was permeated with the ripe smell from the men's room across the way, and several times during the course of the story, I screamed as a cricket or cockroach scampered across my lap.

The tragic assassination attempt on President Reagan helped afford a friend of mine from New Zealand a unique personal view of Washington events. Don McKinnon (later Foreign Minister and Deputy Prime Minister), who was then the Junior Government Whip, was in Washington on an American Government fellowship. It is my usual practice to invite any visiting officials or friends and their spouses to accompany me on my rounds or social functions. The evening after the shooting, I was invited to a party in honor of the incoming State Department news spokesman. I phoned Don at his hotel and invited him to join me. He answered the phone in a weak voice, saying he was sick and dizzy. Alarmed, I decided I'd better help him, and spent the next half-hour phoning doctors, including my family physician. Back home in Virginia, I recruited my husband to make calls as well. But we found no one willing to make an emergency hotel call. An ambulance seemed a bit premature, so I decided it best to take him to the hospital emergency room. Fortunately, when I got to the hotel he was able to walk. I'm used to carrying around several pounds of radio gear, and could pick up my forty-pound children, but I can't carry a 200-pound, six-foot-four-inch man, even in an emergency.

We drove to the George Washington University Hospital, which was the closest and most familiar to me. But I had momentarily forgotten the President was there, until I saw about three hundred of my colleagues, with numerous television cameras, standing in the grass of Washington Circle across from the hospital. They were on a round-the-clock vigil, hoping to pick up any scrap of information they could about the President or Jim Brady.

Of course, some of the entrances to the hospital were blocked, so I had to run barricades to get to the emergency room doors. By this time, Don was white as a sheet, and becoming sicker by the minutes. I helped him out of the car, and tried to support him as we walked toward the hospital. About fifty policemen besieged us, demanding to know what we were doing. I explained I had a very sick foreign dignitary on my hands, and wanted to leave him off so he could get emergency care. Several of the police tried to wave me off and send us to another hospital, about a half-hour drive away. I was concerned Don might become even worse, so I tried to barnstorm my way in by displaying my White House pass. This further enraged the cops, who accused me of trying to pull an end run around them in order to get close to the President. By this time, Don really looked sick and nearly passed out. I was able to identify him, because we'd had the foresight to bring his passport, which indicated his official status. The police finally took pity on him and allowed him to be admitted, but I was unceremoniously shown the door. If they treated us this way, I wondered what they did to women in labor, or victims of serious accidents, who also had to use the emergency facilities.

In any case, the doctors ushered Don into the examining room. He had been there only a short while when he heard a commotion in the halls. Mrs. Reagan and a phalanx of Secret Service agents came flying down the hallway, en route to the President in the intensive care unit. Don said to himself, "My God, man, you're a Member of New Zealand Parliament - you can at least stand up and greet the First Lady of the United States." He struggled to his feet, and nearly vomited all over the President's elegant wife.

By the next day, Don had completely recovered from his exhaustion and dizziness, and continued his frantic round of appointments with American officials. His scary medical condition turned out to be nothing more than a classic case of Foggy Bottom flu. President Reagan also recovered eventually, and left the hospital after a few weeks to return to an emotional welcoming ceremony on the White House lawn. His recovery was remarkable for a man of seventy, and he continued to improve, becoming stronger and healthier than ever. He later even survived major cancer surgery in robust health. He attributed his resilience to diet and an exercise regime, which included cutting firewood, riding horses, and "pumping iron." How tragic that in the last years of his life, Reagan's often absent-minded behavior turned into full – blown Alzheimer's disease, and he was kept from public view as he continued to deteriorate.

The other two wounded men eventually returned to work, and James Brady divided his time between his painful physical therapy and a few hours of work each week at the White House. There, he tended to correspondence and continued to offer the President the benefit of his own political experience and insights, which were not dulled by the serious brain injury inflicted by the near-lethal shot. Brady was still listed as press secretary, and a stuffed teddy bear - his trademark - sat on the fireplace in his office. But others handled the functions of the news spokesman on a day-to-day basis.

The attempted assassin, John Hinckley, Jr., is now a very expensive guest of the U.S. taxpayer, in residence at St. Elizabeth's, a Washington mental hospital. His parents, showing their great strength of character, are now devoted their lives and fortune to the study of mental illness. They travel the country, giving lectures and trying to alert other parents to the signs of mental disease, so that they will not suffer similar tragedies.

As President Reagan recovered, he seemed to enjoy a golden Presidency, despite some problems with personnel and foreign policy. Many were appalled by some of his policy decisions, especially the invasion of Grenada, the stepped-up U.S. involvement in Central America and, most disastrous of all, the dispatch of the Marines to Lebanon. Although nearly three hundred were killed before the Marines were finally taken out of their vulnerable position in the Beirut airport, the American public generally forgot those incidents. But to the parents, wives, and children of the dead Marines and sailors, the loss can never be recovered by a policy reversal. They can never forget that their loved ones died as they slept in a barracks destroyed by a suicide bomber; were shot like sitting ducks in their position at the Lebanese airport, or killed trying to guard the American Embassy, which was also destroyed by a suicide terrorist attack. These policies were only a prelude to the major failure, which nearly brought down the Reagan Administration in its last two years - the sale of weapons to Iran and the diversion of some of the funds to the Contras, who were fighting to overthrow the government of Nicaragua. But those events came later.

We reporters were continually pessimistic about Lebanon, and thought the United States should not become involved. I was perhaps the most vocal in my criticism. Many were the days I walked into the State Department, with tears streaming down my face, cursing the presence of the Marines in Lebanon, because I thought it was a tragic waste of American manhood. Surprisingly, Secretary of State George Shultz even allowed me to interview him on this topic and other flash points, despite my oft-expressed criticism. I guess that says something positive about the stature of the man. As a former Marine, he must have been agonized by the situation in Lebanon.

An exclusive interview with the official in charge of foreign policy is considered a major coup. It is unlike the situation in Congress, where one can nearly always get a Senator or Congressman to talk, simply by sticking a microphone under his nose.

Some politicians also disagreed with Administration, but buckled under White House pressure for several months and didn't fight as strongly as necessary to get the Marines out. Only Senator John Glenn showed a significant amount of backbone early on. During one Senate hearing, he predicted that the Marines would be brought out in body bags, if sent to Lebanon under those conditions. But the Administration persisted in its macho "can do" attitude, and stayed the course for several months before shifting policy.

Despite the foreign policies, and cutbacks in social programs that caused massive unemployment and homelessness until the economy eventually turned around, the President remained personally popular. Some of the more tragic stories were often supplanted by the antics of his advisors. After Richard Allen was forced out as National Security Advisor, Judge Bill Clark was named to that extremely sensitive post. He was brought to Washington from California, where he had seemed proud of his lack of knowledge about foreign policy. He was at first named to the number two position at the State Department, some say to serve as a White House spy on Secretary of State Haig's camp. But during his confirmation hearings for the position, Judge Clark shocked the Senators by confessing he did not know the name of the Prime Minister of South Africa, the head of Zimbabwe, or the philosophy of the British labor unions. On the latter question, he didn't even attempt a guess. The State Department officials who had prepared detailed briefing books for Clark, a former member of the California Supreme Court, cringed when he failed to answer the questions. The skeptical Senators said that President Reagan could make his own appointments, but they did not really think the man was fit for the position. (State Department positions needed Senate confirmation; members of the White House executive staff did not, although there remains pressure to change that tradition).

Bill Clark's qualifications were somewhat equivalent to those of Interior Secretary James Watt. He called Indian reservations "drug-infested examples of the failures of socialism." Watt also caused a stir by refusing to allow the Beachboys rock group to perform during the huge annual Independence Day concert at the Washington Monument, professing his belief that the rather moderate group was "immoral." President Reagan, his wife, and Vice President Bush all came to the singers' defense, and the President gave Watt a bronzed statue of a foot with a hole in it. It was the "Shoot Yourself In The Foot" award, but it didn't prevent Watt from putting his other foot squarely into his mouth.

Watt's downfall came when he described the representatives of his coal advisory panel as consisting of "a woman, a black, two Jews, and a cripple." After that outrageous statement - which drew the ire of advocates of the handicapped - public pressure mounted, and he was fired despite strong backing of his Conservative supporters. James Watt announced his resignation as he and his wife sat on horses in a cow pasture out West. Shortly afterward, Bill Clark left his National Security post (which he was awarded after mastering the State Department in a few short months, having been declared a "quick study"). Now Clark, an instant expert in foreign affairs, was shifted to an area he knew better, the great outdoors. He became Secretary of the Interior when Watt faded from the Washington scene.

This game of musical chairs may have been rather benign, except for the loss of life suffered in Lebanon. But numerous other Administration appointees also quit, were investigated, or faced allegations of financial irregularities or abuse of the public trust. These included the former head of NASA and the number two man in the Department of Defense, among others. Toward the end, there was mismanagement and betrayal in the White House and the National Security Council, under Donald Regan, John Poindexter, and Oliver North, who were implicated in the notorious Iran-Contra affair.

President Reagan managed to stay above the fracas, until he was hit with the Irangate scandal. He remained as handsome as the movie idol he once was, vigorous and youthful, even in his mid-seventies. Most of the country - including reporters - continued to like and respect him. Overall, Reagan got a free ride from the press during his tenure. At the most, we suggested that although he might be too old or senile for the job, his wife Nancy could probably do a better job running the country anyway! Jimmy Carter correctly observed that some presidents are cursed with a bad press, while others seem to spend their terms on a pedestal. We did criticize President Reagan, but our chastisements were characteristically mild, and largely ignored by the public. He did create a rather noisy flap when his aides scheduled a trip for him to the Bitburg Cemetery in West Germany, where some Nazi SS soldiers were buried along with hundreds of other Germans. The trip deeply offended many Jewish Holocaust survivors, as well as thousands of American veterans who had fought the Nazis. But President Reagan did not want to lose the support of the West Germany leadership, so the trip went ahead as planned. Within a few months it was forgotten, as President Reagan underwent cancer surgery and other news events intervened, such as the hijacking of a TWA plane in Greece. Most of the Americans on board that plane were eventually released, although one Navy frogman was brutally beaten, tortured, and murdered. But by the time the standoff ended, the terrorists had gained massive amounts of worldwide notoriety. In a sense, we journalists were all held hostage by the Amal terrorists, by feeding their insatiable demands for publicity. We responded, because we had vast amounts of airtime to fill up. It is a bad system, but I see no early end to it.

Despite the problems and crises, there was an easygoing rapport among the reporters and Administration press staff prior to the Irangate affair. The White House press staff gave us plenty of access, paper, and information, making our job almost too easy. Generally, there was mutual respect between us. Of course, there was the time when President Reagan muttered a reference to the press as "those sons of bitches." But even that was turned around when Larry Speakes insisted he'd really meant to say, "It's sunny, and you're rich." Soon the reporters had printed up huge shirts that read, "SOB." Underneath, in smaller letters, was the caption "Sons of Basement," meaning the basement area of the press room. The President took it in good humor. This sort of rank talk and leg pulling might have gone on in the John Kennedy era, but would have been difficult under Nixon and Carter.

New Zealand and Australia: Alpine Golf, Anyone?

Some months after President Reagan was shot, our family suffered a terrible personal crisis. My beautiful, artistic sister, Margo, died after a heroic two-year battle with cancer. She left behind her husband, Ken, her three children, my parents, my brother, Richard, and me. All who knew her were broken-hearted. To this day, we never really got over the heart break. It intensified, as her magnificent children grew into wonderful adults, with successful careers and families. How cruel for Margo to have missed these milestones. It puts into perspective the tragedy of others who have lost close loved-ones; sometimes the pain can never really heal, and the death cannot be put out of ones' mind or heart.

Throughout her illness, despite the pain, fear, and degrading medical treatments she suffered, Margo had managed to keep alive her extraordinary sense of humor as she fought to extend her precious time on earth. Even with Death waiting silently nearby, we shared some good laughs. We recalled, for example, the time Margo attended the funeral of an Uncle who had once been a professional arsonist. As the casket was opened, and solemn prayers were being intoned, Margo opened a book of matches. Slowly, she began to throw them, one by one, into the casket. It was impossible to maintain a sense of respectful decorum after that.

Another time, as I was holding down my first "glamorous" job in New York Governor Nelson Rockefeller's reelection campaign, Margo came to visit me at the headquarters in the New York Hilton. She sat down at a front desk, pretending to be an official. At one point, some politicians came in asking to see the financial men involved in the Republican Rockefeller campaign. Margo calmly directed them across the street, to the offices of a rival Democratic candidate. These warm memories of Margo, her extraordinary family, and her beautiful works of art will endure, keeping her alive forever in our hearts and minds.

Some will think me quite callous, but as poor Margo lay near death in a coma in her final hours of life I found myself using the telephone of a patient next door, to broadcast to Israel a story about an interview given by the Prime Minister. I was not really as hard as I may have seemed at the time. Everyone, it is said, must deal with tragedy and crisis in his own way, and broadcasting the radio report was the only way I knew to maintain my sense of sanity. My work had been an anchor in my life for over thirteen years by that time, and I now turned to it for stability. In the neighboring patient's room, where I used the phone, I learned from her some heart-wrenching details about the last hours of my sister's life, before she went into coma. I shall carry the horror of those memories with me always.

As Margo lay dying, I rushed to catch a plane to Washington, so we could round up the family and return to New Jersey. As luck would have it, the car I was in broke down on the highway on the way to Newark Airport. Desperately I resorted to hitchhiking - a dangerous venture anywhere, but even more so in that crime-ridden state. A longhaired hippie type picked me up in his convertible. I must have looked like a kindred spirit, since in addition to my suitcase I was carrying a large drum. The drum had been languishing for years in our New Jersey house, and I'd hastily grabbed it as a present for my sons (a gift, I might add, which they never used). I pleaded with my driver to get me to the airport safely, and explained the circumstances to him. Fortunately, despite his spaced-out looks, I had nothing to fear from my rescuer, and I made my flight without incident.

Margo's death plunged me into despair, and may have prompted me to do things I would not have considered had I been in a better frame of mind. While I was accustomed to traveling - in fact thrived on it - I had not taken any major trips since my first child was born five years earlier. But the death of a close friend or relative always makes me acutely aware of my own mortality. There were some things I intended to do before I died, and one of them was to take a trip to New Zealand and Australia.

It was a big decision for me to leave my children for that long, because I tend to be an overprotective mother. So I arranged for an excellent live-in nanny to substitute for me for a month. Having her and my husband to look after things ensured that the house would run smoothly, and I would be phoning them nearly every day I was gone.

I felt foolish making such a big deal of the trip. My girlfriends, who are network correspondents covering the White House, leave their children most of the year. Some of them annually spend only a few weekends at home; this is especially true in an election year. They stay with their children - in spirit anyway - through the photos they always carry. Having already done a lot of my traveling, I now was committed to spending as much time as possible with my kids before they grew up and went off on their own.

I'd planned to sponsor the trip myself, but to my surprise, when I told my radio bosses I would be coming down, Radio New Zealand volunteered to sponsor the trip if I would agree to deliver a series of speeches, interviews, and seminars. Astonished by their generosity, I was only too happy to accept. I had long felt that my association with Radio New Zealand was the best thing that ever happened to me professionally, and this confirmed it. This arrangement, on the other hand, also increased the pressure on me. I knew I couldn't cancel, even if a war broke out. Fortunately, the nanny showed up as scheduled, the world scene remained relatively stable during my absence, and none of my children got sick.

As I prepared to leave Washington, I learned that New Zealand's Ambassador to the United States, Frank Gill, was waging his own war with cancer. Gill had been treated for the disease before coming to Washington, and had undergone extensive surgery. Then, apparently in remission, he seemed to enjoy robust health for the next two years. He engaged in spirited battles with American politicians over dairy, lamb, and beef quotas and tariffs. Despite the intense pressures on him, he had many occasions to display his ribald, lusty sense of humor. Sometimes this got him into hot water, and onlookers who could not see the steel beneath that facade considered him a buffoon.

In late 1981, Ambassador Gill returned home to New Zealand over the Christmas holidays, and then made the long flight back to Washington, arriving to a very harsh winter. He must have known this was his last trip back, and struggled until the end to push aside his health problems. But when I saw him soon after his return, I sensed with despair that the cancer would soon overcome him. He had the sallow complexion and gaunt look I had seen in Margo and others whose bodies are ravaged by the disease. Little was said at the time, but Gill missed a series of important events at the Embassy and the State Department, as well as a White House dinner for Ambassadors. His fine wife, Barbara, believed he was suffering from a nasty case of flu, or from the fatigue of the long trip back. At one diplomatic function at the New Zealand Embassy, I asked her about his health in general. She told me he had received a clean bill of health during a recent physical. In fact, she said, he had recovered so well that he might go and lecture to other victims of bladder cancer, to give them hope.

It was clear to me that Mrs. Gill was in no way trying to cover up the situation that was unfolding. I believe her husband knew he was dying, but concealed it from everyone to spare his family unnecessary suffering and grief.

Professionally, I found myself torn. On one hand, I had a tremendous desire to respect the privacy of Ambassador Gill and his family, and not add to the tragic developments. Yet, he was a public figure, and the truth had to be told at some point. Finally, about two weeks before I was to leave for New Zealand, I returned to the Embassy for a personal interview with him. Although he assured me that his health was improving, it was evident from the weak sound of his voice on my tape that he was a very sick man. I ran the interview without comment, leaving it to the most sensitive listeners to distill the truth for themselves.

Of course, I didn't intend to hurt him in the interview, but I'm afraid that's what happened. At one point I asked him whether, since he was recovering so well, he had considered his wife's suggestion. "What was that?" he asked.

"To lecture to other cancer victims," I replied, "and inspire them."

A long silence ensued, and the interview drew to a close. A few moments later I saw him downstairs, at the front door of the Embassy. He was standing in the bitter cold and snow, waiting for his car to take him to the Pentagon. He looked thin and ashen, stooped as if laden with a terrible burden.

A few days afterward, Ambassador Gill again was forced to stop working. I phoned the Embassy daily to find out what was happening. Finally, I received a tip from an Embassy official, who told me he was in the hospital for tests. I spoke with the hospital, with other Embassy staff, and with Barbara Gill. I knew I had to do a story, but first I wanted to talk with her to ensure that her family in New Zealand knew it was coming. The Embassy also needed time to formally notify the Prime Minister, although he probably knew what was happening - and may have been aware of Frank Gill's condition for a very long time. Contrary to popular notions, then-Prime Minister Muldoon may have appointed Gill to the post in part as an act of loyalty and kindness.

Late that night, I was preparing to file a detailed story on the nature and extent of his cancer. I'd been told he would make his final trip home to New Zealand as soon as he was strong enough to make the plane trip. To my surprise, I received a phone call from Gill himself. In a weak voice, the Ambassador thanked me for everything, and predicted he would soon be fine. He promised me that we'd visit the bars of Washington together once he recovered. That occasion, in February of 1992, was the last time I spoke with him.

The next morning, I kissed my boys farewell, and Steve drove me to the airport, where tears flowed freely all around. My mother was particularly upset to see her only remaining daughter venture off to a destination halfway around the world. She also was angry with me for filing the story about the Ambassador's cancer. Sometimes, reporting entails an undeniable cruelty that is hard to stomach, even for the reporter herself.

My American Airlines flight to Los Angeles was crowded and unpleasant. Once in California, I excitedly made my way to the Air New Zealand First Class lounge. It was decorated with Maori good-luck symbols, and resplendent with sheepskin rugs and large photos of the magnificent country I was about to visit. In the lounge was an assortment of travelers from around the globe. One confused elderly man, en route to New Caledonia, was bundled up in at least three layers of heavy clothes, despite the warm Los Angeles temperature. He spoke no English, and I tried my best to help him out in my American-accented French. Eventually the Air New Zealand hostesses and I steered him to the right plane, but he adamantly refused to take off any of his coats. The last time I saw him, he was muttering blissfully about how peaceful and idyllic the French-controlled island of New Caledonia was.

On my own flight were a lot of New Zealanders from all walks of life. They are usually referred to as "Kiwis," named after the flightless bird and the fuzzy green fruit. The Kiwis included a handful of New Zealand runners, traveling from one world competition to another; and scores of other Americans, as excited as I was to be heading for New Zealand for the first time.

My time aloft on the luxurious Air New Zealand plane was a dream, and the crew was charming and solicitous. This was in sharp contrast to many American airlines, which often have all the ambiance of a cattle car. The eight-hour leg of the journey to Hawaii passed quickly, and there was even room to stretch out and sleep between meals and movies.

I enjoyed myself so much, I was almost sorry I'd arranged to spend the next twenty-four hours in Hawaii. But earlier, the thought of a twenty-hour flight from Washington to New Zealand had seemed more than my body could bear. Landing in Hawaii at dawn, and then carrying my heavy luggage through the endless airport corridors, proved far more exhausting than the flight itself. At that ungodly hour of the morning, there were no porters around to help with the luggage. I was laden with fifty pounds of books and gifts for my New Zealand friends, but with every step I took, it felt more like a ton.

I made my way to a cheap hotel near Waikiki Beach. It was a pleasure to bake in the hot Hawaiian sun. I even plunked down $5 for an exciting outrigger canoe ride, so I could experience the thrill of being swept along by the immense waves without going through the months of training typically endured by serious surfers. I was fascinated by the diversities in the Hawaiian cultures, and often had to remind myself that I was still in America, and not in a foreign country. Waikiki Beach itself was both beautiful and depressing. Every few feet, runaways of both sexes, some as young as ten, solicited tourists for sex, money, and drugs. Watching those kids, I could almost see myself at that age - chafing at the bit to leave home.

All things considered, Hawaii was more spectacular than I had ever imagined. I could see why New Zealand, Australia, and the South Pacific Islands wage an uphill fight to attract U.S. tourists. Many Americans could go as far as Hawaii and say, with justification, "This is paradise - why go any further?"

But New Zealand and Australia are incredibly beautiful in their own right, and their citizens are so friendly and open you find yourself smiling most of the time. In those countries, I sensed an equanimity and serenity of spirit among many of the people that were less evident during my two-day stop in Hawaii. But, you still had many people in New Zealand who suffered from poorly paying jobs, discrimination, alcohol, and drugs – as you have in any society.

I left Hawaii the next morning at sunrise, ready for my eight-hour flight to New Zealand. By this time, however, I was becoming quite exhausted, and was uptight after a restless plane ride. I wasn't sure what awaited me in New Zealand, but I was keenly aware that I would be responsible for press conferences and interviews from the first hours of my arrival. I complained so much about the noise keeping me awake that the crew cajoled me into accepting some strong drinks. Finally, something worked, and I slept fitfully, curled up on the seat with a Kiwi track star until the beautiful green mountains and the long white clouds of New Zealand were visible below.

My sense of excitement reasserted itself when I finally landed and made my way through the long customs lines. Why, I kept asking myself irritably, must I endure all this at dawn? Air travel has a way of creating a surreal effect, and I was suddenly nervous about being charged a monstrous duty for the gifts I was bringing in, especially for a bulky, ten-pound Morantz cassette machine I was smuggling in for a good friend. I'd lugged that damn machine all the way from Washington, carrying it with me out of fear that it would break in the suitcase. I was afraid it would be conspicuous, and I would be levied a small fortune in duties to bring it in. But ironically, a group of rock singers who had boarded the plane with me in Hawaii all carried the same Morantz stereos on their shoulders. Even though theoretically we could have sold them for a profit in New Zealand, we all got through customs without paying a cent.

At the end of the line, I was delighted to see my boss, the exuberant Buzz Harte, standing at the fence to greet me. Buzz, who reminds me of an impish leprechaun, had once visited me in Washington and undergone the baptism of fire of staying in a household with my screaming, mischievous infants and my animals. Buzz also had in tow another executive from Auckland station 1ZB, Rod Melville. It was a wonderful welcome to a magnificent country. The two men whisked me off to the Vacation Motel, where I spent a few precious hours trying to rest and prepare myself for my forthcoming debut as a "public person."

In the early afternoon, I was driven to the 1ZB studios, where I met the other reporters and news directors. Next, I was to give my first news conference. Of course, I'd covered news conferences for fifteen years, but I now discovered that actually giving one was a very different matter. Occasionally, other American reporters had interviewed me for their own radio or television features on the unique type of news bureau I had established. It was easier for me to "sell myself" to strangers than to my colleagues in New Zealand, with whom I had established a special and personal relationship in recent years. I sat there in the bare room of the radio station, looked at the television camera and tape recorders across me, and drew a blank - I didn't have the first clue what to say! I thought, "What can these people possibly learn from me? I should be asking *them* questions!"

Suddenly, it occurred to me that the room looked like the one from which, back in 1969, I had phoned news directors to tell them about the naked black man on top of our television transmitter. I asked my colleagues to turn off their recording equipment, and I told them the story, on an off-the-record basis. This broke the ice, and things became much easier after that. I may have made a fool of myself, but my fellow reporters protected me, and wrote complimentary articles. My hair and dress looked disheveled on television later that night, but then I often don't really project well on the tube. There's a real art to putting across a slicked-down, controlled appearance, and I've always found it difficult to achieve that. It's one of the many reasons I prefer radio to television.

That was just the first of many news conferences and speeches, and I gradually became somewhat more polished. I hadn't thought about that transmitter incident for at least a decade, and had also forgotten many other stories and anecdotes which suddenly came pouring from me. Soon, I realized people were genuinely interested in and entertained by them.

The New Zealand visit was invaluable. It gave me a chance to put my life in perspective. For the first time, I began to think there might be something to be said for committing my experiences to paper, as a guide for aspiring journalists or others who might profit from the lessons I'd learned.

My stay in that magical country brought me another valuable dividend: renewal. In Washington, my spirit had been drained, although I didn't realize it at the time. People work very hard in the Nation's Capital; it's common for many - from professionals to typists – to arrive in their offices at five o'clock in the morning, and leave late at night. D.C.'s worker bees take themselves, and their endless paper shuffling, so seriously they often don't take time to enjoy themselves. My New Zealand friends were open, natural, and possessed a unique and marvelous ability to look at the light side of things. I found myself laughing with them, and relaxing as I hadn't in years.

Toward the end of that first day, one of the Radio New Zealand reporters in Auckland cornered me for a private interview which was to run the next day on "Morning Report," an important show with the largest radio audience in New Zealand. I don't think he was intentionally trying to put me down, but he had only recently come over from Australia, which may account for what happened next.

Although I'd been in the country less than a day, he naturally assumed I was an expert in everything. He asked me how New Zealand should promote its tourism industry, and I babbled something about publicizing the country's unique sporting opportunities, such as Alpine Golf.

Alpine Golf consists of hitting a golf ball from one spectacular New Zealand mountaintop to another. To retrieve the ball, the golfer must descend the mountain, sometimes swim across a fjord, scale another peak, and try to establish whether the ball made it onto the green or lay nestled in a snowy crevice. You see, I knew all about Alpine Golf, because I'd seen it depicted on a dramatic New Zealand calendar. There they were, those incredible greens atop those spectacular mountains. The calendar in question had been hanging on a wall in the office of Wayne Scanlon at the New Zealand Embassy, when I'd visited several weeks earlier. Suppressing a smile, he'd let me glance at the picture for a few seconds, and then, with deadpan expression, explained the procedure to me. The Embassy press attache earnestly backed up Scanlon's explanation of this demanding and little-known sport. I kept exclaiming, "That's incredible!"

But they went on to say that the sport was a combination of mountaineering and golf, and solemnly swore that Alpine Golf would soon be a thriving pastime in their native country. Since Americans know that Kiwis are some of the world's best athletes, I fell for it, hook, line and sinker. With my trip coming up soon, I half expected to meet a race of supermen. Come to think of it, I also seem to recall that Wayne had a bag of white powder stashed in the corner of his office. He told me it was the important New Zealand dairy export, "casein." Now, I'm beginning to wonder about that, too.

The next morning, the interview - Alpine Golf and all - was run on "Morning Report," falling on the ears of several million people. Some of my editors on the show, tricksters that they were, knew I'd been suckered. But they enjoyed a hearty laugh at my expense. Buzz Harte, however, was less pleased. He said he'd heard the tape while still half-asleep in his motel room, and was so startled he nearly fell out of bed. He resisted an impulse to send me packing on the next plane, gently pointing out instead that I was a damn fool. No one in her right mind, he said, could possibly believe in Alpine Golf.

The promotion tour continued, despite the gaffe. Later that day, during a break in the frenetic round of interviews and meetings, I sat on the steps of the 1ZB studio and wrote a poem. Reporter Peter Kingston, as amused as the editors by the incident, helped me embellish it. The poem began:

"You must think I'm quite a doff
About the complex subject of Alpine Golf.
Yesterday I told the Nation
About a figment of someone's imagination.
It was a myth, painted on a calendar vivid,
And when I learned the joke, I was at first quite livid."

After several more stanzas, the poem concluded:

"It could have been worse, I now conclude
If I'd seen calendars of Kiwis walking around nude.
I might have come here naked,
And that would have been very lewd."

My editors, bless 'em, ran the doggerel, and gave me a chance to redeem myself. Since then, I've become an honorary member of several Alpine Golf clubs. I now have my very own calendar, which hangs like a shrine over my bed. I haven't even changed the page. It will stay forever on February and March 1982, commemorating some of the best weeks of my life. A postscript to the episode: Since the interview, several New Zealanders - even one prominent Cabinet member - confided to me that they, too, had at first been taken in by the calendars. The Minister said his first reaction was: "Where are those golf courses? I've never seen them before!"

The New Zealand trip proceeded south from Auckland to Wellington. Many of the stops in between had to be canceled, because I became much busier than expected. Most days began at six a.m., with a breakfast meeting or phone calls. Then I listened to, or visited, the studios of Radio New Zealand to watch as the early morning bulletins or Morning Report went to air. Sometimes my editors put me on live. (Occasionally, I even knew what I was talking about).

My first weekend in the Wellington area included a glamorous dinner with the Radio New Zealand executives in The Windows, a restaurant overlooking the city. Then we drove to the exquisite farm country of the Wairarapa. My figure began to suffer. I was attending at least five formal teas a day, and I was powerless to refuse the delicious pastry and rich dairy products that were offered.

In the Wairarapa, I had some fun playing with their fine farm animals, and took advantage of an opportunity to ride some splendid horses. On a tour of one stud farm, I nearly managed to get trampled by three thoroughbred stallions and their entourage of mares and foals. I observed how skillfully the owner's son handled the steeds, walking fearlessly among their hooves in feet scarcely protected by thin leather sandals.

Later that weekend, I had a near brush with disaster. One of the stops listed on my schedule was at a freezing works. I was unaware that the term is a euphemism for a slaughterhouse. Had I known, I would have declined the honor. Fortunately a strike had idled the plant temporarily, and I was spared the necessity of witnessing the commerce of death. I was impressed with the sterility and efficiency of the facility. I laughed when one of the managers told me how they had bested the representatives of Iran's Ayatollah Khomeini, when they inspected the plant to ensure that the sheep were being slaughtered in the direction of Mecca. On occasion, the devious plant officials would engineer their compasses to point inaccurately in the direction of the Holy City. Now, as New Zealand's trade with Iran and Iraq has become more important, the ploy won't work. The Mullahs stay on duty at the plant, overseeing the ritual slaughter.

My trip to the freezing works left me with other startling images. There were railroad tracks leading up to the plant, and beautiful, manicured flowerbeds in front. For some reason, the sanitized, peaceful facade reminded me of the concentration camp sites I'd once visited in Europe. Nevertheless, hypocrite that I am, I brushed aside all negative images and went off with my hosts to enjoy a delicious New Zealand lamb lunch.

After the Wairarapa, I returned to Wellington for anther dizzying swirl of meetings and interviews. It was quite a novelty to be treated as a celebrity, a heady experience indeed, and I knew it would be hard to get back to earth in Washington, where I was just another working slob. But the interest in me was supplanted a few days later by the sad news of Ambassador Gill's death.

Mrs. Gill had managed to get her ailing husband back to New Zealand the day after I arrived. It was a heart wrenching flight for them, and she later told me she nearly lost him a few times during the long transit. In the end, she was able to get him home to say farewell to his family, and finally to die in the country he loved so much.

I went to the hospital in Auckland as soon as he arrived, and had an emotional meeting with his family, although the Ambassador was too sick to see me. Over the weekend, reports were broadcast on the radio that he was not considered terminal and might yet pull through. I learned from his family, however, that the reports were misleading. But the ever-sensitive Buzz Harte urged me to let them pass, so the man could die in peace.

Word of Frank Gill's death came while we were in the midst of a business meeting in the Radio New Zealand executive offices overlooking panoramic Wellington Harbor. When the news was announced over the radio, I was unable to remain impassive. I had a brief cry, right in front of my bosses. It was the same thing that had happened when Bobby Kennedy died; sometimes it takes hearing the news over the electronic media to give validity to a story, even one we all know is coming.

Radio New Zealand had already assembled an impressive schedule of publicity appearances for me that day, but suddenly the number doubled. Interviewers wanted to ask me questions about the Ambassador's last months, and about the way Ambassador Gill had functioned in Washington. I replied straightforwardly, leaving out some cocktail party stories and off-the-record conversations, in which we reporters had exchanged sometimes tasteless remarks with the Ambassador.

In being candid, I bore strong witness to the Ambassador's work in the States, and his vigorous - sometimes heated - exchanges with U.S. Congressmen and diplomats. He had frequently come out on top, and often overcame their reservations regarding New Zealand imports. I remarked on this, once again providing fodder for the endless debate on whether politicians or Foreign Service professionals make the best Ambassador material. In this case, I suggested, politicians were the best representatives for their times. It is a case by case basis. But I hastened to add that the bureaucratic professionals who had preceded them, representing New Zealand in America, had also proved highly effective.

America, too, is of two minds over the issue of political loyalists versus Foreign Service experts. Often, New Zealand and Australia are considered plum assignments that go to extremely wealthy or influential backers of the President. Such Ambassadors have not always worked out as well as they should. In some cases, I've run afoul of them, but I must have been doing something right. One was decidedly cool to me, suspicious that I was anti-Jimmy Carter. Another accused me of being anti-Reagan. The reality is that my function is to deliver the news, and not be a partisan of anyone, from any country. Thus a bit of criticism from a politician helps keep one honest, although it does infuriate me at the time.

When I learned of Ambassador Gill's death, I resolved to try to attend his funeral, even though it meant canceling a visit to the scenic Lake Taupo region. I didn't say anything to the Gill family, but made plans on my own to take part in the memorial service. A few days later, following a visit with Prime Minister Muldoon in his office, his secretary called me aside. She told me that Mrs. Gill had graciously invited me to the service in Auckland, and asked that I be allowed to travel on the Royal New Zealand Air Force plane carrying the top members of the Government. I was both touched by Mrs. Gill's thoughtfulness, and flattered to be in the presence of such powerful company.

Although the occasion was a somber one, it was also a splendid opportunity to see all the members of the Cabinet together in one place. I was able to say hello to some people who had been left out of my schedule. In mid-flight, I stopped to give my regards to America's Ambassador to New Zealand, H. Monroe Brown, who was seated behind the Prime Minister. Despite the fact that I'd been in the country for over a week, had received a great deal of publicity and had even spoken to a group at the American Embassy, he'd been unaware of my presence. His face paled noticeably when I approached him and he exclaimed, "My God, what are *you* doing *here*?" Actually, he appeared startled whenever he saw me, and was prone to run the other direction when we crossed paths, whether in Wellington or in Washington. The memorial service for Ambassador Gill was impressive and crowded, and was held in Auckland's majestic Catholic Cathedral. Exhausted, I'd hoped to sneak quietly into a back pew, but I was ushered instead to one of the front rows. Soon, the heat and tranquility of the music combined to lull me into a gentle sleep. Midway through the service, somewhere through my stupor, I heard the officiating Archbishop intone that he had not known Ambassador Gill personally, but formulated many of his opinions from the reports he heard about him by the Washington correspondent. I jumped straight up in my seat, even as I wanted to crawl under it at the same time.

After the service, the Gill family again honored me by inviting me to their home for a private gathering. Regretfully, I explained that I would very much have liked to accompany them but I'd promised to return to Wellington by ten o'clock that night for a party and a live radio interview.

The party was lovely but, as usual, I was exhausted. It seemed that wherever I went in New Zealand, I first asked the host for permission to use his bed - for a quick nap. I catnapped my way all over New Zealand, which led to many humorous accounts of my "sleeping around" all over the pacific paradise. If I did, I was certainly too tired to enjoy it. The fatigue wasn't just the result of the intense schedule that in many ways was not quite as difficult as a typical eighteen-hour work-and-family cycle in Washington. The problem was my body clock, which was royally messed up. No matter how tired I was when I poured myself into bed after midnight, I woke up with a start at four a.m. Once I awakened, nothing could get me back to sleep. Poor Buzz even gave me sleeping pills to try, but they only revved me up more. Then, though I'm normally a night owl who usually begins to perk up in the evenings, I'd find myself losing steam at uncharacteristically early hours. In any case, I never was successful at resetting my internal clock.

Another highlight of the New Zealand trip was the chance to meet with the Lawns of New Zealand. I don't really know if we're related, but I like to think we are. Lawn is a very unusual name, and there are only a handful of Lawn families in America. But there are several in New Zealand and Australia, and I was delighted when they wrote to claim me as their own. Various Lawns, along with their spouses and offspring, generously offered to fly to the Christchurch airport from several cities in New Zealand. Our meeting was all too short, for we had only a rushed twenty-minute "reunion," when we exchanged greetings, hugs, and gifts they had brought me for my two boys. Despite the hectic nature of the affair, it was easy to believe they really were relatives. Some of them even looked like members of my family in Europe, England,

and the United States. This kind of experience underscores how close we all are, and how interrelated the world community truly is.

I wasn't able to explore as much of New Zealand as I would have liked, and decided I would need several long return trips to really savor the exquisite beauty of the land. My editors did fly me south to Queenstown, where I spent a memorable weekend along Lake Wakatipu that included a magnificent four-hour horseback ride in the Cascade Mountains. At one point, when an angry bull chased us as we attempted a shortcut through his pasture, I was definitely glad to be on the only thoroughbred in the group. We outraced the others, jumping barriers and dodging sheep and cattle. I felt like a New Zealand cowgirl on a roundup.

Despite the excitement, my weekend in Queenstown was the only time I was depressed during the trip. It's one of the most beautiful areas on earth, and cries out to be shared with someone you love. For the first time, I felt keenly the distance between my family and me. Fortunately, then-Foreign Minister Warren Cooper, who arranged for good friends to fetch me, salvaged the weekend.

John and Trish Davis and their family live in an exquisite home along the deep lake surrounded by the Remarkables Mountains. From their kitchen windows, they can view the morning moon as it descends the sheer cliffs. At the same time, across their house, from the living room they can watch the sun climb the other face of the mountain. At night, relaxing in their outdoor Jacuzzi, the Davises can sit, watch the sun drop, and view the sparkling clear stars of the Southern Hemisphere. Sometimes they can see lights of satellites blinking across the unobstructed skies. Visiting the Davises gave me a greater appreciation of the many satellite stories I cover - stories which otherwise can be quite mundane and technical. Above all, it was the warmth and hospitality of the Davis family that turned the visit into one of the highlights of the trip.

After Queenstown, I staggered onto yet another flight to witness the thundering beauty of Mt. Cook, the highest peak in New Zealand. I am not a particularly brave flier, and was reluctant to board the twin-engine plane that held about twenty passengers. But the pilots of the Mt. Cook Line tried to make me feel better by inviting me into the cockpit. From that vantage point, the panorama was truly spectacular, and the pilots' professionalism and self-assurance alleviated my anxieties. But the hapless passengers in the back were a bit shaken by the rough flight over the rugged, desolate terrain. When I emerged from the cockpit, the faces of the passengers ranged from sickly green to chalk white. A couple of the more fretful Americans asked me in astonishment, "Were *you* piloting the plane?" When I assured them that I had indeed, some groped around comically, as if looking for a parachute.

That flight was nothing compared to what awaited me. Once our aircraft landed safely on the small airstrip nestled among the towering mountains, I checked at the airport about a flight up the mountains. None had been arranged for me, but the airline staff was happy to offer me a free ride. In retrospect, I think *they* should have paid *me* to venture in the small, single-engine plane up the side of the mountain. Some of my colleagues told me *they* certainly wouldn't do it, unless the plane had at least two engines. They were talking to one who is afraid to take even a roller coaster ride! But my bearded pilot, Bruce Campbell, tried to soothe me as we climbed over the jagged Franz Josef Glacier, Mt. Cook, Mt. Tasman, and so many other peaks, glaciers, and steep valleys that I lost count. Time and again, the Cessna headed straight into the mountain, only to swoop up at the last minute. I spent many moments praying that a sudden downdraft or wind shear wouldn't force the plane back into the rocks and snow. Most of the time I was so terrified I clutched like a vise onto Bruce's arm, which didn't do much to improve his flying ability. Eventually, however, I found it impossible to sustain the terror as the breathtaking spectacle of nature unraveled before me, as if on a huge screen.

When Bruce suggested we land the ski plane on the glacier, I protested. "No way!" I exclaimed. But Bruce persuaded me that it would be a chance to compose myself, and actually, I was pleased to feel the solid ice and snow at my feet when we finally landed. Photos we took later revealed we were in the midst of clouds, giving us the ethereal appearance of ghosts emerging from the snow and haze.

For some reason, the return trip was less terrifying, although we were trying to outfly a storm that was closing in behind us - a system that entirely obscured the mountains for the next few days. When we arrived again at the Mt. Cook Airport, Bruce gave me an elaborately executed certificate proclaiming me "an exalted Member of the Unique Order of Ski-Daddlers," entitling me to "boast of the most exhilarating and exciting ski plane landings on one of the Giant Glacier Snowfields of New Zealand's Southern Alps."

It was an experience I'll never forget, and the certificate became one of my treasured mementos from the trip. I felt I'd come closer to heaven than ever before.

From that point on, the trip became more routine in terms of excitement and stimulation. There as more work, more speeches, and a three-day trip to Australia. There I was also wined and dined by my editors at station 2SM - for "Two Santa Maria" - hard-rock station. My news editor took time from his frenetic schedule to drive me from Sydney to Canberra so I could view the lush, rolling Australian countryside. The excursion was worthwhile, but alas, much too brief to do justice to that grand country.

It also did little to further my professional goals. For several years, I'd considered leaving my Australian string of stations - which had a hard rock, sex-and-scandal format - and defect to a more serious news station. I'd hooked up with the 2SM group several years before, when it boasted one of the strongest news departments of any of the commercial Australian stations. I phoned them one day from the White House with a story about Australia. A British reporter was reporting to them at the time, but he suggested that I take over when he returned to England (another example of the importance of friendships and cooperation in this business).

Thus I became their Washington stringer. Unfortunately, despite the other prominent newsmen on their staff in Australia, they wanted sensational stories from me, preferring them to serious items if they had the choice. A classical example of a 2SM story was "Amy's Killer Nanny

Speaks." That was taken from the headline of the *National Inquirer* tabloid, which had interviewed the baby-sitter of Amy Carter, who was then in residence at the White House. Before moving to the Executive Mansion, the nanny was reported to have done time in prison for killing her husband. But President Carter and his family nonetheless thought her qualified for a White House job. After all, some of the President's own cousins had seen the inside of a jail, and the Carters were very forgiving people - sometimes.

I had worked with 2SM for about two years before learning they were the flagship radio chain of the Catholic Church in Australia. I'd just tried to feed a story to them, but was told I couldn't that day because, it being Good Friday, they were broadcasting only sacred music. I was flabbergasted. Actually, I have a great love and respect for the Church, as both as spiritual and a business institution. In fact, my father had once served as a lawyer for a Church diocese. This afforded me an opportunity to associate with many fine priests and bishops when I was a university student. All the same, I would never have believed that 2SM, with its format, belonged to the Church. Considering the irreverent and flippant editors there, I was also taken aback when they phoned me at about four o'clock one morning, Washington time, to ask me to get a reaction to the dead Pope.

I replied, "I know this is typical of your weird sense of humor, but I don't appreciate it at this time of the night." Little did I know that Pope John Paul the First indeed had just died, after one short month in office. For once, my editors did not appreciate the irony of the situation either. They'd just spent thousands of dollars to send a reporter to Rome, to cover the election and coronation of the new Pope. The reporter had just staggered back and barely recovered from jet lag when they had to pack him off to the Holy City again, to repeat the process. Perhaps in fatigue and frustration, he committed a major gaffe in reporting that a Cardinal from Poland had been named the new Pope. He broadcast all over Australia: "For the first time, a non-Catholic has been named Pope!" I suppose it's easy enough to get "Catholic" and "Italian" confused, especially when one is suffering from the terminal exhaustion that is all too familiar to most journalists.

I spent many enjoyable years reporting unusual stories for 2SM and its sister stations in the major Australian cities, but the chain was sinking badly in the ratings. It had been number one when I came on board, and retained those ratings for years afterward. But now, rising competition and changing public attitudes brought its ratings crashing down. It scrambled frantically to vary its formats and, toward the end, I was doing a five minute wrap-up of American news for them each day. It came at a very difficult time here - five p.m. Washington time, which was seven o'clock in the morning in Australia. I had to fight the rush-hour traffic and surmount other obstacles to do the broadcast when they wanted it. Several times, I barely made it from Washington to my sons' nursery school, where I asked to use the phone to call in my broadcast. The phone was shaped like an erect Mickey Mouse, and I had to unscrew its little paw to get my clips in. Against an audible background of fifty screaming children, at least we got the newscast on the air live.

At other times, I had to rush home from a nearby beach, where I'd been entertaining guests for the day. Once those guests included Ambassador Gill and his wife. It might be Sunday afternoon here - supposedly my day of rest - but it was Monday morning in Australia, and the show must go on, even thought I was sitting at my desk in a wet, sandy bikini.

On another occasion, I'd gone for a sail, and flagged down a friend's houseboat. The broadcast was done from the boat's phone, as the owner's cat purred loudly and rubbed against my leg.

Despite our best efforts, the 2SM ratings continued to sink, and I realized I would soon be forced to find other stations, as had my more prominent colleagues. Once I made the decision to do so, I spent a sleepless night out of a misplaced sense of loyalty. Where is ruthlessness when you really need it?

I didn't approach the other stations by phone, and couldn't make myself do so during my stay in Australia because the 2SM managers were so nice to me. They lodged me in a luxury hotel right next to 2UE, one of the stations I wanted to work for. I felt guilty for costing them so much money, and tried to keep my hotel and restaurant expenses down. But my boss had said to spend as much as I wanted, and told me to make as many international phone calls as necessary.

Soon I understood why. Two weeks after I returned to Washington, the news staff was gutted. All but three of us were fired. They kept me on for another week, but soon I had to go too. 2SM would revert to a "rip and read" format; that is, they would take most of their news from the wire services. They would also try to get as many free stories as they could from abroad, by calling towns where a tragedy occurred and doing telephone interviews. But that approach costs nearly as much as hiring your own reporter, so I'm not certain how long this practice lasted. In any event, I had to close the door on my seven years of hard work for 2SM.

Oblivious to the undercurrents of change at 2SM, however, I was able to enjoy the rest of my time in Australia. On my last morning there, I jogged in a beautiful park overlooking Sydney Harbor. The air was so fresh, the grass so green, and the water so sparkling and clear, I felt as though I could run forever. I relished the freedom of being able to run in my bare feet, as I'd frequently done in New Zealand. I'm not a jogger, and seem to have no stamina at all in the Northern Hemisphere. But being there transformed me, and I felt invigorated by the clean atmosphere. It was a near spiritual experience to run and feel part of nature. At one point, a stray dog picked me up and trotted along beside me.

I returned to New Zealand for another round of visits with political and media friends. I spent some time at the farm of friends in Albany, on the North Island, where I discovered that our listeners took their radios into the fields, to hear Radio New Zealand's "Morning Report" as they were tending to the farm animals. I'd always thought our audience were those in bed, in the bathtub, or at the breakfast table - further proof that nothing can replace radio for its universality and flexibility. Television is fine, if you want to be chained to one spot. But for people on the go, radio is the medium of choice.

So people were listening to us while the cows were being milked, or the sheep fed - and this knowledge added to my repertoire of morning radio lore. I relished the stories of numerous politicians and diplomats who told of having cut themselves shaving at a breaking news story I was reporting over the air. In the very early days of my career, Americans were still unaccustomed to hearing women deliver a hard news story. Early one morning, I got a call from a listener who confided he got an erection when listening to my voice. I asked him if that was the origin of the term "hard news." Laughing, I quickly hung up the phone.

Now, after a month in New Zealand and a brief spin to Australia, it was time to tear myself away. Earl Rowell, the manager of 1ZB, saw me off at the Auckland airport. He and his wife had graciously welcomed me as a guest in their home over the last two days. After buying out the souvenir shop, I sadly lugged my self aboard the plane, sheepskin and kangaroo skin rugs dangling from my bulging suitcases.

The long trip home, including daylong layovers in Hawaii and Los Angeles, ended with a redeye overnight flight to Dulles Airport in the Virginia suburbs near Washington. Not wanting to wake my husband up at six in the morning, I was searching for a taxi when I spotted a neighbor retrieving his own luggage. He was Lynn Nofziger, perhaps President Reagan's most influential advisor. Despite the rarefied White House circles in which he traveled, he was still my neighbor, and I was not shy about asking him for a ride home. He was gracious about it, and we spent a pleasant half-hour chatting about political strategy as the sun came up over the Washington suburbs.

We arrived at my front door just as the trash trucks were arriving to pick up the garbage. Some triumphal return! Any neighbors awake at that hour must have wondered what Lynn Nofziger was doing, helping a woman unload suitcases from his car, at that hour of the morning.

***

I had a wonderful reunion with my husband and family, who were happy to have me home again. Later that day, I attempted to do my first story in a month. It took me over five "takes" to give a coherent report to New Zealand. My editor on the other end, my friend Mike Lee, teased me. "A wee bit rusty, are we?" he asked. I also attempted to do stories for my other stations, so they wouldn't forget who I was.

One reason I rushed home was to cover the visit to Washington of then New Zealand Foreign Minister Cooper, who had arrived one day after me. Despite his busy schedule, he, his wife, and his private secretary, Robert Hyde-Smith, dropped by to visit us in our home. Cooper jogged around our seven-mile lake, while his wife, Lorraine, and I attempted to keep up with him. We gave up after a few blocks, but he managed to wind his way along the shore past the dam and the highway, and find his way back to our house. He might have been in a lot of trouble if he'd got lost, and tried to convince the cops he was the Foreign Minister of New Zealand. There's just something about being clad in jogging shorts that strains one's credibility, especially if he's claiming to be a high government official.

In fact, had Warren become lost, it wouldn't have been the first time he had to explain himself out of a tight situation. Sometimes his problems were created not by diplomats, but cooked up by his beautiful, witty, and mischievous wife. Lorraine probably worried about her husband, who often stepped from a plane in a strange city, after an overnight flight, and promptly began to run. Frequently, the physical strain on his body was great, but he would never admit it. He would arrive from a winter climate in the Southern Hemisphere, for example, and plunge right into a long run in the sweltering, humid, hundred-degree weather of a Washington August.

Perhaps as a way of hiding her anxiety, Lorraine would resort to tricks when he finally trudged back, often under escort. In one airport, he was picked up by police for jogging in an unauthorized area half-naked,. Cooper persuaded the cops to bring him back to the Air New Zealand First Class waiting lounge. He led them up to Lorraine, and the police told her, "This man says he's your husband, claims he's the Foreign Minister of New Zealand." She looked at him with eyebrows raised, cocked her head impishly to one side, and cooed, "Oh, is he telling that story again?"

Another time, Cooper was picked up by cops and taken to his hotel room in the middle of the night. It was amazing that he was able to get them to do that; many others have found themselves in a jail cell instead. He led the officials to his hotel door, where they knocked loudly. Lorraine opened the door, and they went through the same introductions. She looked at the tattered group coldly, announced, "I've never seen that man before in my life," and slammed the door in their faces. Poor Warren Cooper could have found himself in quite an embarrassing diplomatic situation, had his wife and private secretary not relented and come to his rescue. Needless to say, the confused cops seldom appreciated the humor of the situation.

The day Warren Cooper visited our home, we invited a neighbor over. Former Congressman Bob Duncan is one of the funniest men I've ever known, and the Coopers enjoyed him immensely. At one point, however, Bob did something that was completely natural to him: he casually pulled out his can of chewing tobacco and put some between his teeth. This is a fairly common practice among many in the halls of the U.S. Congress, where highly polished brass spittoons can be found nestled in cozy corners.

Cooper asked, "Well, now, what's that?" and offered to try some. With the words, "I'm doing this for my country," he stuck a large wad in his mouth. Then, too polite to spit it out, he swallowed it. When last seen, Poor Warren was a mild shade of green when he boarded the gleaming Embassy limousine.

Foreign Minister Cooper became one of several New Zealand and Australian guests to visit our home. They included several Ministers, Ambassadors, and one man who went on to become Prime Minister, David Lange. We had an especially gratifying day "en famille" with Lange, who was our guest shortly before he became Opposition Leader. A few months before visiting America, he'd undergone painful stomach surgery in order to lose weight, but he was still quite large. He kept tilting back on our $200 dinner chair, which was not designed to sustain precarious positions. We rushed to inspect the chair after he left, but he hadn't even cracked it. To this day, however, it is known as the "David Lange Memorial Chair." It nicely complements the bullet hole in our living room window, which had been made by a neighbor fed up with the spotlights the former owner kept on constantly. We kept the window the way we found it, as a fond remembrance of our close ties to the Old West here in Virginia.

Other New Zealand guests included Mike Moore, who went onto become Prime Minister, and then head the controversial World Trade Organization. Then there was my friend Don McKinnon. After serving the longest period of time as New Zealand's Foreign Minister, he moved onto the important and demanding job as Commonwealth Secretary-General, living in an ornate Palace in London, close to the Queen and the Royal Family. Two small-town men who made it big on the World Stage! I invite these guests to our home not as fodder for name-dropping, but because it means a great deal to me to see people in a natural, relaxed context. And I think they enjoy the break from sterile government buildings and pompous official residences. For the same reason, I am pleased when business associates invite me into their homes, whether here or abroad.

Not only officials, but "ordinary tourists" too are invited to come over. Sometimes they pop by unannounced for a swim or dinner. Usually, however, their time is limited, and we arrange to meet at the State Department or the U.S. Congress. When I can, I take them into a briefing or Congressional hearing. Most events are mundane and the exasperated travelers, their eyes glazed over with boredom, ask me, "My God, how can you stand that B.S.?"

But every once in a while we put on a good show. Once, a lovely couple from a small New Zealand town met me at the State Department at just the right time. Outside, several hundred Moslem fundamentalists were demonstrating, in support of the Ayatollah Khomeini. From the sidewalks of the State Department, about a hundred enraged diplomats were cursing and screaming at them. Sporadic fistfights broke out. The usually mild-mannered diplomats were frustrated and furious, because Iranian fundamentalists had been holding nearly seventy of their colleagues hostage in the American Embassy in Teheran. Finally, my guests got past the opposing crowds and entered the State Department lobby. There, a bevy of policemen were guarding the monarch of Jordan, the diminutive King Hussein, who was on hand for an official visit. I managed to score a quick interview with him, but did so while resting on my knees, so I wouldn't interfere with the camera crews. I was quite a sight, talking into his navel. It looked positively obscene!

No sooner had the King left than an Australian Minister arrived. I also cornered him for a hasty interview, before rushing to my booth upstairs to try to make some sense of these stories. By the time I filed them, the situation outside had become violent, as the police tried to prevent serious harm to any of the demonstrators. The interviews and protests provided the ingredients for a very exciting, if atypical day. I hadn't had so much fun since Jimmy Carter's day, when he and the Shah of Iran, not to mention us reporters, were tear-gassed at the White House, where fierce riots erupted because of the Shah's visit. On that day, the riots may have been outside the White House fence, but tear gas didn't respect the high, iron barriers. As President Carter and the Shah attempted to deliver their speeches, tears streamed down their cheeks, and they choked on the tear gas.

In retrospect, I'm astonished that more officials and ordinary citizens aren't killed in the sometimes-tense confrontations that crop up in Washington. Now, security is much tighter, especially in light of the terrorist movements being spawned around the world. But sometimes the security procedures have loopholes the size of Montana. A common practice in the State Department is to seal off or "freeze" the lobby several moments before a foreign dignitary is about to enter. This means people on the outside cannot use the main entrance. Instead, a large crowd builds up outside the red ropes. (It was from just such a crowd of bystanders that President Reagan was shot outside a Washington hotel.) In the meantime, the people already in the State Department building cannot get out via the main entrance. The other doors are quite some distance away, and are useless to someone rushing to meet a deadline.

One afternoon, former Presidents Ford and Carter were leaving the building after meeting with Secretary Shultz. I wasn't very interested in interviewing them, but I was desperately trying to get outside to the sidewalk, where Ray Lilley, one of my top New Zealand editors, was waiting for me. I tried to exit using various elevators, and circulated through four different hallways, hoping to find another escape. But everything was blocked. Finally, I went down to the basement garage. There, State Department Counselor Ed Derwinski and I found ourselves trapped. Just then, we saw a man dressed in a jogging suit run out the garage exit with no problem, even though he passed very close to the lobby entrance. I protested to the heavyset guard, pointing out that the runner could easily have had a plastique bomb concealed on him. Besides, he had no identification, while the diplomat and I clearly displayed all our State Department and White House cards. The guard spat out, "The Secretary says anybody in a jogging suit can go out, and you ain't got no jogging suit on."

Totally frustrated, I took the elevator back to the lobby, where, thanks to the State Department press staff, I was allowed to get into the news "stakeout" area. There, I asked the ex-Presidents a couple of questions, but the answers weren't particularly newsworthy. As the ex-Chief Executives then left the State Department, they waited virtually unprotected, past the crowd of strangers on the sidewalk. One was my editor, who was close enough to touch them or do anything else he may have liked. True, there were no gunmen in the crowd, but there easily could have been.

That wasn't the only time this type of security system backfired. Once, the State Department lobby was frozen off in anticipation of a visit by former French President Giscard d'Estaing. No one was allowed in the building, including a distinguished, well-tailored man who had walked up to the front entrance. He tried desperately to convince the guards he was the former French President, and would now be late for his lunch with the busy Secretary of State because of them.

"Sorry, buddy," they snapped, "we didn't see any limousine." Finally, someone from the Secretary's office came down, searching for Monsieur le Président. He identified his guest and escorted the furious Frenchman upstairs.

Ironically, my unfortunate companion on the elevator had his own tragic brush with State Department security. As I noted, Counselor Derwinski and I had both protested the obvious lapses, but the bureaucracy did nothing about them. Years afterward, a teenage boy walked into Derwinski's office suite with a loaded rifle. He murdered his mother, who worked there as a secretary, and then turned the gun on himself. The killings took place just down the hall from the executive offices. There was little to prevent the boy from killing Secretary Shultz or anyone else, had he wanted to. The mother had repeatedly pleaded with State Department authorities to protect her, and begged them to revoke the boy's family entrance pass. He had beaten her several times, and she was then living in a shelter for battered women to escape him. Still, he managed to enter the State Department garage on a bike. He assembled his machine gun in the garage, took it up to the top floor of the State Department, and committed the murder. It was only after that tragedy did the officials open their eyes and tighten security for members of an employee's family. Today everyone goes through the same kind of metal detectors that have been used for years on Capitol Hill.

Diplomatic security again became an issue later, during the Clinton and subsequent administrations. Overseas, it was truly tragic, as two US embassies in Africa were blown up, with a large loss of innocent life. Back at the State Department, a diplomat was arrested, and accused of spying for the Russians, even though the Cold War was officially over. A bug was actually discovered, hidden in the wall of a State Department conference room! Then, a valuable laptop computer was missing. It was said to contain some of the most highly classified diplomatic secrets. There are likely to be more security lapses, not yet identified.

The point is that security measures should be applied consistently, even if they become more rigorous. At the White House, all visitors now pass through a metal detector, and our equipment and pocketbooks are searched. I think this is a reasonable precaution, and wish it had been instituted years earlier. I must admit, however, that I have been embarrassed on occasion when the guards dismantled some feminine items in my purse. I blush when this happens, but the security procedure takes only a few seconds. And, once inside the White House, we have unrestricted access within the areas assigned to the press. This gives us close proximity to the President and visiting dignitaries when we are covering a ceremony in the East Room, the Oval Office, or on one of the White House lawns. That's why, with some of the loose nuts running around the city, it's probably a good thing we are checked out carefully.

We cannot wander the halls of the White House without an escort, but we are still free to try to reach anyone we can get to by telephone. In fact, that's often a better way to get to a "source" for a story; many will not talk on background when others on the staff can see a reporter in his or her office. On the other hand, there are plenty of White House officials who hang around the press area, and are quite willing to speak with reporters on a non-attribution basis. Often they have their own agenda, a point of view to communicate, but it's then up to the journalists to decide whether the story has news value.

One memorable experience that underscores the security issue occurred during the Bush Administration. One of my senior bosses at Radio New Zealand and his wife were my guests at the White House. This was at the height of the ANZUS tension, but I still managed to get them cleared through the guards, once their passports had been carefully examined. I ushered them into the menagerie that was the press room, where they found themselves among hundreds of grungy American reporters. I was serving as the White House "pool" reporter that day substituting for a friend. I try not to do that too often, because it means spending long hours at the White House on days when I may want to be free to cover other stories. It also means travelling with the President, and no one picks up my expenses for those trips.

As soon as I deposited my friends, I was called into a pool event. I never thought to warn them that they must stay in the press room. After a half-hour, there was an angry announcement over the loudspeaker system: "Connie Lawn, come to the press room immediately!" It turned out that my friends were under arrest by the White House guards. They had ventured off on their own, and ended up in the Oval Office. To make matters worse, a Cabinet meeting was in session, so all the top U.S. Government officials were nearby, as well as the President and Vice President. When they were picked up, my guests proudly presented their passports as identification. The Secret Service agents took one look and exclaimed, "My God - you're spies from New Zealand!" The two were held for several hours. Finally, they were released and escorted outside the iron bars of the White House. I ran after them and did an interview though the bars (I was afraid to go outside at that point, concerned I wouldn't be readmitted). My boss, concerned about his reputation, pleaded with me not to broadcast the interview on Radio New Zealand. But I explained that all the international press knew about it, and I would be fired if I didn't do the story. My news director, Ray Lilley, insisted in his boldest and coarsest language that I go ahead with the story. I didn't use my friends' names the first time, but they became public in short order. In the end, there was no harm done, and the incident became funny in retrospect. But it was a long time before I invited guests to the White House again. And when I did, I was careful to instruct them to stay put!

Kidnapped in Lebanon

Several months after I returned from the South Pacific, I was again settled back into the routine of covering and filing stories and caring for my family. These everyday activities filled up 18 hours of the day. But it was a problem readjusting to daily life, after the highs of my trip Down Under. Soon, however, events halfway around the world would take my mind off my own personal frustration.

By mid-1982, the tense situation between Israel and the Palestinians had been deteriorating, and Israel became the victim of accelerated terrorist attacks from Lebanese territory. Israeli officials tried repeatedly to get the Lebanese authorities to stop the attacks, but Lebanon itself was fractured and powerless. Finally, in June 1982, Israel invaded Lebanon. The express goal was to rout out the terrorists and provide a buffer zone between Israel's northern residents and the constant barrage of rocket attacks and terrorist raids. But the Israeli troops advanced further and further north, until they reached the Beirut strongholds of the Palestinian Liberation Organization. At some point, the Israeli Government decided to press all the way to Beirut, where the ensuing bombardment was massive and excruciatingly costly to all sides.

The invasion provoked bitter controversy in Israel, and nearly 600 Israeli soldiers ultimately died in the Lebanon conflict that dragged on for over three years. The Israeli occupation of Southern Lebanon continued until the year 2000, with sporadic troubles and deaths on all sides. The invasion caused as much concern and anguish among Jews all over the world as it did in Israel. In an effort to counter this groundswell of negative sentiment, the Israeli Government took the extraordinary step of inviting hundreds of outside Jewish leaders and journalists from all religions and publications to come to Lebanon. Several of my colleagues went, even though it was a war zone, and returned with disparate interpretations of the war. Some, pointing to reports of thousands of tons of Soviet-made weapons Israel had captured from Palestinian strongholds, thought Israel was absolutely justified in its invasion. Others branded the Israelis as ruthless and barbaric, saying they had forever lost their image of the defenseless but righteous David of the Mideast, and had now become the bully Goliath.

My own feelings were mixed. I was well aware that throughout the centuries millions of Jews had perished as a result of Arab attacks, the Spanish Inquisition, Russian pogroms, Nazi concentration camps, and other less publicized campaigns. But it was harder for me - as well as for millions of others - to accept the role of Jews as the aggressors in this drama. I knew that many in Israel had long coveted part of southern Lebanon, to hold as a security buffer or to actually incorporate into Israel. I remembered a visit I had made to the Israeli-Lebanese border many years before. Some of the border towns and Kibbutzim (communal farms) overlooking the rugged hills were the most picturesque areas I had ever seen. The residents wanted to live in security and tranquility, and felt they could do so if they could gain the land up to the Litani River. That small stream and the ancient crusader fortress guarding part of it were clearly visible with binoculars from the Israeli town of Mettulah. The Israelis in the north also recalled that for more than twenty years, theirs was the most peaceful border. They had lived in relative harmony with the Lebanese until the terrorist attacks by some Palestinian groups began. Even in the years leading up to the invasion, the so-called "peace fence" was open, so Lebanese citizens could cross into Israel to trade products or receive medical treatment. A similar type of commerce also goes on across the Egyptian and Jordanian borders with Israel.

Torn and confused by the invasion, I felt I had to go to the region myself, in an attempt to gain some understanding of the situation. I was told I could apply for a journalist trip, sponsored by the Israeli Government, but I wasn't sure I could get in. Moreover, there was only a small window of time I could conveniently leave the country in August and not miss too many major stories. Washington is usually quiet in August, and it is a good time to expand my horizons. So I decided to underwrite the journey myself, as I had done with numerous other business trips in the past. My husband, mother-in-law, and a baby-sitter agreed to care for the children while I went off to study war at close range.

I booked a cheap charter flight to Israel on a plane so small it could hardly make it to Ireland from New York before refueling. A far cry from the luxurious El Al or Air New Zealand, this plane was stuffy and overcrowded. Sleep was impossible, as people constantly shuffled up and down the aisle. One Jewish architect - who planned to study rebuilding possibilities in Lebanon - complained that it was like attending an Orthodox Synagogue, where people are forever walking back and forth and no one listens to the prayers or sermons up front.

Typically of charters, the plane arrived several hours late. But my good friend and editor, Mark Lavie, greeted me at the airport. He advised me against changing too much American money at the airport, since the Israeli sheckel had been dropping in value each day as the U.S. dollar rose. At that time, the situation was bad enough for the Israelis, with inflation running at 200 percent.

Mark took me to his beautiful old home, with its two-foot-thick walls constructed of Biblical Jerusalem stone. There, we sat in his back yard, under his vines and fig tree, as we quietly ate and drank. The peaceful setting belied all the years of turmoil and war. In fact, during those few weeks, all of the Jerusalem area seemed more tranquil and peaceful than I had ever known. For a while, I could almost believe the Israeli propagandists, who had dubbed the Lebanese operation "Peace for Galilee." On the surface, it *had* brought to Israel peace, and a decrease in terrorist attacks. But the calm was deceptive. Throughout the society, public sentiment over the invasion became more deeply divided each day. Many of my friends had lost relatives or friends in Lebanon. Of course, hundreds of Arabs also died in the conflict - those added to the bloody toll of over 10,000 Lebanese who had lost their lives in the Civil War that had raged for more than a decade.

In tiny Israel and Lebanon, funerals were common. Young Israeli soldiers home on leave attended numerous memorials to honor their fallen comrades. Some of my editors, who had sons in elite Army units, told me they spent countless sleepless nights over the welfare of their children. Fathers also had to spend time in Lebanon, to fulfill their obligations to the military reserves. Their absence from work involved more than participation in a dangerous undertaking; it represented both personal and professional hardships. At the same time, it afforded some of them the opportunity to intermittently monitor their sons who were on active duty.

I visited my editors in the century-old fortress that was then the Kol Yisrael studio. It is a stunning stone building, hidden on a narrow, winding street. Once it was the home of a Turkish Pasha. My soul is always uplifted when I return to those studios. The architecture has changed little in hundreds of years, and to see it is to step back into Biblical times.

From the roof and walkways of the studio, there is an unobstructed vista of ancient Jerusalem. In fine weather, parts of Jordan are also visible. The interior of the building has been colonized by strange electronic equipment needed to transmit signals all across the Mideast, and around the world on short-wave frequencies. Most of it was installed when the British ruled Palestine. But the setup has been accomplished with taste, and is not immediately visible from the street outside. In fact, some of the equipment appears to be as ancient as the building. In my twenty-plus years with the station, the tape recorder has broken down hundreds of times as I've tried to file a story in the middle of the night. I clearly recall the feelings of frustration - not to mention sore throats generated by nocturnal shouting at editors and operators. They have since moved to modern headquarters, which are more efficient and less fun.

I sometimes think that I've probably spent more hours with my friends and colleagues in Jerusalem than I have with my own family, although most of those relationships have been conducted by telephone. It's little wonder I feel so close to them, or that I am so renewed and fulfilled when I visit them. Some things in life are far more important than sophisticated equipment and lavish expense accounts. Despite the hardships they must cope with regularly, my friends at Israeli Radio put out a highly professional product. Some of my colleagues who covered the Iranian Revolution once told me that they often listened to Kol Yisrael at the time, rather than the BBC or the Voice of America, because they believed the English Division offered the best coverage of the Mideast. Many diplomats and English-speaking reporters all over the region also chose us first.

They also rewrote us, which is a common practice in this business. Sometimes, I would broadcast a story on the seven a.m. newscast. An hour or so later, I would hear the same story broadcast in the United States, prefaced with: "Israeli Radio has reported ..."

Even my own speculation gets picked up. Once, I reported that the logical point for retaliation would be to attack Syrian-backed forces in the Bekaa Valley. The headline on that item, two hours later, was: "Washington sources report Israel is about to attack Syrian forces in the Bekaa Valley." Another time, following the hijacking of the cruise ship *Achilles Loro*, I predicted that the United States would focus its anger and pressure on Lybia. That, too, was lifted - and events bore me out. For months afterward, Reagan Administration pressure on Lybia was intense. That culminated in the American bombing raid on Lybia on April 15, 1986.

The superb operation maintained by the English Division is all the more remarkable because my friends run it with a tiny staff and a minuscule budget. Most often, no more than two or three people are responsible for an entire newscast. Sometimes it's only one. No wonder my frenzied editors are ready to take my head off, when I try to phone in a story at four in the morning, as they are struggling to put together a newscast, take in reports, and translate the wires or other news reports from Hebrew into English.

My editors do show a great deal of concern and compassion for me during the quiet times, and have been generous with me during my life's major milestones of marriage, childbirth, sickness, and family tragedies. I am always happy to welcome them to my home when they are in Washington, and their visits certainly offer a new perspective regarding my sons' education. But most of my editors were born in a British Commonwealth country, and thus they present a slightly distorted picture of Israel. This became very evident when my son David once announced, "Israelis are just like Americans, but they speak with a British accent."

While visiting with my editors and taking care of business, I prepared to go to Lebanon. I went to the Military Escorts office in the Press Center, where I arranged for an Israeli soldier to meet me at a border kibbutz in the north. We would spend the nights in the guesthouse of the well-established Kibbutz Gesher Haziz, and tour Lebanon during the day. Next, I set about getting together with a group of other Americans who were also keen to go to Lebanon. But the group I was thrown in with didn't seem to be the most stable. One American wanted to go there to "kill as many of the PLO as I can." A New York man - obviously an incredibly quick study - announced that he intended to spend two days in the region, become an expert, and write the definitive novel of the Invasion of Lebanon.

My own plans were not nearly as grandiose. I just felt compelled to see things for myself. And I did not want to have any military officers pushing me around and telling me what I could or could not see. At the time, I was unaware that, depending on the military escort officer assigned to you, a person was not necessarily subject to a barrage of propaganda; reporters could speak with whomever they pleased, if they didn't mind the risk of being shot by one of the many factional fighters.

I approached my wonderful boss at Kol Yisrael, at whose Jerusalem home I was staying. Zvi wrote a letter to the authorities in Hebrew, explaining that I was their Washington correspondent and asking for their assistance. Next, I hitched a ride to Lebanon with the reporter from our station who was assigned to cover "the incursion" that week. But I had no clearance to enter the country, and there was no guarantee

I would be allowed to cross the border once we got to the northern edge of Israel.

We left Jerusalem in mid afternoon, which meant we had to hurry to reach the comparative safety of the Israeli troops in Beirut before dark. I was not informed in advance, but soon learned there was great risk in passing through the coastal towns of Tyre, Sidon, and Damour. That danger intensified at night. The towns had been relatively secure during the brief time the Lebanese Soldiers had been in control, but the main body of the Army had moved north to Beirut, and the PLO had infiltrated back to the towns they had largely controlled for the past ten years. The several thousand United Nations soldiers now in the area seemed unable or unwilling to prevent their return. Ambushes on Israeli vehicles and soldiers were intensifying, and more deaths were reported each day.

My colleague, Danny, and I arrived at the border kibbutz toward five, after speeding past Tel Aviv, Haifa, and the rich farms of the northern section. At the kibbutz, the soldiers gave me a bureaucratic runaround, informing me that it was impossible to get an escort at night. I would have to hang around for a few days, and try to join a group on the way up. Even if I could join one, I still did not have their permission to enter Lebanon.

As Danny and I left the kibbutz, I decided that I would have to smuggle myself across the border. Fortunately, a friend of Danny's, the military affairs correspondent of the Hebrew Division, whizzed by. Danny flagged down his car, and asked if I could travel with him. Schmuel was the quintessential war correspondent. He thrived on danger and high excitement, and nothing seemed to frighten him. He was certain he could talk me across the border. "I'm so persuasive," he assured me confidently, "I could talk the veil off a Moslem fundamentalist."

I climbed into his car, not knowing I was entrusting myself to the fastest, craziest driver in all of the Middle East - an area not known for caution or restraint.

We left Danny far behind in our dust, and made it to the border in a matter of minutes. Schmuel, true to his word, had no trouble convincing the border guard that I was on assignment with him. They were on good terms, treating each other like a pair of American "good old boys." The only thing they asked me was whether I had life insurance, to verify that the State of Israel would not have to pay to ship back my remains or compensate my family. I replied that my husband had a policy - in fact had doubled it before I left the States.

Thus we were waved on past the checkpoint. Within a few seconds, I realized that the dark warnings about the perils of the trip were no idle chatter. If the Lebanese didn't get me, Schmuel's driving certainly would. He drove like a maniac, flying across the terrain at over a hundred miles an hour. We dodged enormous potholes and craters that had appeared overnight, the result of a late round of shelling. We zoomed up and down the Coast Road that winds along the splendid, rugged Mediterranean coast. The road was meant for speeds of thirty miles and hour in the best of times; in fact, it appeared far better suited to quadruped traffic than to vehicles.

Towns I had once hoped to explore and investigate in leisure sped by in a blur. At one point, a convoy of Arab trucks crossed in front of us, threatening to slow us down. When Schmuel couldn't stop them, he changed sides of the street, careening down the lanes in the wrong direction. He leaned on his horn without stopping, forcing panic-stricken Arabs to dive for cover on the sidewalks. Another time, an Israeli military convoy loomed ahead. Undeterred, Schmuel drove onto a median strip that divided both sides of the street. He dodged streetlights like a ski racer traveling at the speed of a passenger train. Resentful Arabs glared at our car in hatred and disbelief. I was beginning to think, however, that their guns and rocket-propelled grenades post less risk than my chauffeur's driving style.

"Don't worry," Schmuel said, patting my white-knuckled hand. "I've had good training. I learned all my tricks driving on the Los Angeles freeway." Clearly this was supposed to reassure me, but I found myself screaming at him, begging him to slow down - cries that fell on deaf ears. It made me appreciate my husband's driving, which now seemed tame by comparison.

Behind us, Danny struggled to keep up, but it was difficult. He wasn't as skillful or as daring a driver as Schmuel. At times our car actually stopped, until we could verify that Danny was all right. Schmuel waved away my desire to switch cars, insisting that he was a safer driver because he had more experience. The sun was setting, creating beautiful pink streaks as we wound down the Coast Road. We reached the outskirts of Beirut at dusk. Schmuel took a shortcut up a dark, dusty road that had been cut out of the cliff. This was a semi-secret road intended to expedite passage of Israeli tanks. Lacking streetlights and buildings, it was also a perfect spot for ambushers, who could operate unseen in the shadows.

We sped up the road, leaving in our wake a tremendous cloud of dust that choked Danny's motor. His car sputtered to a halt, leaving him stranded in the dark in one of the most dangerous parts of Beirut. But we didn't realize what had happened until we reached the Israeli troops stationed in the hills of the beautiful suburb of Baabda. Schmuel left me in the care of about five thousand soldiers while he went back and searched for Danny. Fortunately for all of us, he found Danny - shaken and angry, but still alive.

Meanwhile, the soldiers at the base were treating me well. They were fascinated to learn that I was up there unescorted, couldn't speak Hebrew, had no flak jacket, and had no notion of how to handle a machine gun. One of them handed me his Uzi, but its 16-pound weight seemed like a hundred to me. Some of the officers invited me to share their barracks, pointing to an empty mattress on the floor, but when Schmuel and Danny returned, we proceeded further up the hill, to an encampment in a lush woods of pine and cedars of Lebanon. Below us, the lights of East Beirut sparkled at our feet. But the magical aura of the place vanished as the evening barrage of rockets and bombing began. From our vantage point, it was like looking at firecrackers. I felt safe and distanced from the fray, until a Katusha rocket came crashing through a stone wall a few feet away.

Many of the Lebanese, even though they were victims of the bombs, regarded the clashes as entertainment. Hundreds made their way into the hills at night to watch the nocturnal firework display. They would play games, engaging in lively contests to be the first to identify an aircraft and its bombs. Next, they tried to guess who was doing the firing from the ground positions, and attempted to determine the targets being fired upon. Often, the shooting was as random as the victims were.

Our encampment in the hills consisted of several brown-green Army tents, a radio truck that transmitted our broadcasts back to Israel, and another brightly colored van that looked like a sidewalk vendor for refreshments and souvenirs. Instead, it was sponsored by ultra-Orthodox Jews who helped lead the religious in prayer and wrap their holy garments around them. A small but steady stream of soldiers frequented the van, which was manned by Hasidic Jews in their long black coats and black hats. Towering above all of this strange mosaic was a church that belonged to the college whose grounds we were occupying.

I divided my time in Beirut between the encampment and a battered hotel in East Beirut, the Alexandre, catching a few hours of sleep whenever and wherever I could. The first night we shared supper with some Israeli soldiers and reporters. Like a band of hoboes, we built a campfire in the middle of a clearing. The food was basic "C" rations, courtesy of the Israeli Army. It wasn't bad. Some of the Israelis had been born in Arab countries, and were conversant in the use of exotic spices. They took some herbs and leaves from their pockets, and mixed them into the pot. The result was hot, spicy, and superb.

Weeks later, when the U.S. Marines arrived in Beirut, they subsisted on their field rations, usually eaten cold. In fact, one American radio station felt sorry for them and flew in a special treat of fast-food hamburgers, which were heated then shuttled by helicopter from their Amphibious Ready Group stationed offshore. Even the Italian and French members of the Multinational Force had brought in their own chefs, and sated themselves with rich meals of Continental food, pasta, and wine. At first I couldn't understand why the Marines didn't stop to build a fire and at least heat their food. Someone explained that the French and Italians suffered a high rate of dysentery. So the Americans "toughed it out," and stayed comparatively healthy . . unless they had the misfortune to step in the path of a bomb or bullet.

At one point during my first night, we decided to leave the encampment and head for East Beirut. The rocket bombardment was becoming rather intense, and some of the more ambitious reporters thought they'd better have a look to determine who was doing the shooting and why. I had just overcome my fear of being in the midst of a rocket attack by convincing myself that it was little more than a Fourth of July fireworks display. But I saw this Beirut adventure as a means of testing myself in a wartime situation, and decided that now was the time to confront the situation head-on.

Driving into the city was made more difficult because the streets didn't offer a clear path to town. Various militias would suddenly close off a street and reroute traffic, or simply turn it away. Barricades appeared where none had been the night before. I hadn't a clue where we were going and left it all in Danny's hands. But it was a difficult situation for him as well. He'd been in Beirut at least three times in the past, covering the invasion. Still, he often got lost because of rerouting. Sometimes we would be halfway down a road only to find it had disappeared, having been blown away by a mortar or bomb.

The streets also were totally dark because the lights had been blown out. We often found ourselves doubling back, trying to find another route. Fortunately we were guided by the benign presence of Bashir Geymail. He was running for President of Lebanon, his smiling visage applied to posters which hung from nearly every building or wall still standing in Christian East Beirut. As long as we could see his picture, we felt reasonably safe. But when his pictures stopped popping up and those of Moslem candidates appeared, we knew we had inadvertently come close to the "Green Line" into the West. Various Moslem militiamen, including the PLO, the Morabatum, and other factions guarded the major crossings over that line. For the two of us, who carried American or Israeli press credentials, it might have meant death if we accidentally crossed that line on a dark, unguarded street.

The troops in West Beirut had short tempers, and played rough with reporters from the East. There were many horror stories of correspondents having been roughed up, beaten, and kidnapped and, in at least two cases, murdered by PLO forces. During my short stay, a French reporter was tricked into showing his Christian Phalange credentials when he crossed the line to do a story on the other side. He was pulled out of his car by a PLO guard, thrown to the ground, and pummeled savagely. The Palestinian even held a Russian machine gun to his head and threatened to use it. Finally, the terrorist appeared to change his mind, and took the reporter to the PLO information center. There, the PLO "officials" apologized profusely, and told the severely beaten reporter it had all been an unfortunate mistake. He was free to proceed - if he was able to walk.

Luckily, none of this happened to us, but my time was soon to come. We finally made it to the Alexandre Hotel, which was home base for the reporters covering the eastern sector of the city. On the other side, reporters could stay in the slightly more luxurious and more efficient Commodore Hotel. But both had their problems. One room of the Commodore suffered a direct rocket hit and burned up. Fortunately, the correspondent in residence had gone down to the bar for a drink when the attack occurred. In that case, the drink saved his life.

The Alexandre, on the other hand, had suffered a bomb attack in the parking lot. The bomb exploded with such force, it destroyed numerous cars and knocked out most of the hotel's windows. The maintenance staff couldn't keep up with the cleaning. Even when I arrived about a week later, huge shards of glass jutted up from each window. Piles of razor-sharp crystals also littered the floor of many of the rooms. But most of the rooms were so filthy and bug-infested that a bit of glass scarcely made a difference, and the windows were unnecessary since it was August.

Experts theorized that that 1982 bomb was planted as a warning to the Americans and the Israeli soldiers who frequented the restaurant and the lobby of the Alexandre. It also turned out to be a grim precursor of more terrible bombings to come. These were the truck bombing of the

American Embassy in Beirut in April 1983, which killed sixty people; and the suicide truck bombing of the Marine barracks in October 1983, which claimed the lives of 279 young men who lay in their beds sleeping.

In August 1982, not all reporters considered themselves fortunate to be ensconced in the Alexandre. It had all the trappings of a miniature media event, with "star" reporters clamoring for top billing. For a few days, a society reporter from the *Washington Post* came to call, presumably to report on the swinging nightlife in a city engaged in urban warfare. She hated her room, which was half submerged in filth and sawdust. The reporter threw a tantrum in the lobby, shouting, "What a dump! I'm going to find another place to live!" She was unaware, of course, that the Alexandre was one of the few hotels still standing in Beirut.

I was less fussy than she, however, I was feeling pretty grungy by that time. My skin had acquired a tinge of ashy grey, thanks to the last dusty road we had traveled getting to the top of Beirut. By this time, I was sharing a room with no shower with four other reporters, the bombing having made it impossible to return to Baabda.

In the restaurant, I bumped into several of my reporter friends, whose mouths dropped open in surprise at seeing me there. I'd known they were around, since I'd heard their reports back in Washington. They in turn had been listening to me daily on Israeli Radio, telling them what was happening, as reported by the State Department and the White House - thus putting the various elements of the story together in one neat package.

I inquired as to the whereabouts of one of my favorite reporters, Bill Drummond of National Public Radio. He had been in Beirut throughout the heaviest bombardment of the summer. Back home, we'd shared a tiny booth at the State Department, so I felt it was only natural to share his shower as well. I made my way up to his fifth-floor room, knocked on his door in the middle of the night, and announced, "This is Connie Lawn. May I use your shower?" Bill was startled, but most obliging. I cleaned up while Bill, his producer, and a radio technician tried to wrangle a line from Washington to file a story. They were well used to that five-hour, daily ordeal, but habit didn't make it any less frustrating. It was nearly impossible to get a line out of Lebanon, but the NPR team had arranged to have their editors phone them each night.

Bill and his crew completed their broadcast just as I finished my shower in one of the few bathrooms still functioning in the city. Since they now had a line to Washington, I asked them to call my husband and tell him where I was staying, in case he needed to contact me. Several hours later, toward dawn, the phone awakened my roommates and me. My frustrated husband had stayed awake all night to call me. He was madder than hell when I told him I was fine and was merely touching base. Steve thought the call was an emergency, and expected to find me hovering near death and in need of urgent transport home.

The reporters at the hotel had maintained their macabre sense of humor, even though they all had their horror stories of being caught in crossfire or in the midst of massive air bombardment. Bill himself provided some of the most hair-raising tales that emerged from that time. He told of the time his team had visited a hospital in Beirut, where they tried to communicate to a radio audience the sounds of people dying from burns, loss of blood, or torn limbs.

But in lighter moments, he and the other reporters had perfected the Lebanese skill of merchandising. They found a friendly Lebanese shirt maker, who printed up cotton tee-shirts saying, "National Public Radio - Siege of Beirut, 1982." They sold the shirts for $5 apiece, and I bought several for friends back home at the State Department and White House. The other networks had their own shirts. One said "Audio Militia." Another read, "The Begin Jets," a reference to the warplanes being sent over Beirut by Israeli Prime Minister Menachem Begin. Still another shirt could be easily converted into a flag of surrender, should the reporter find himself confronted by an unfriendly assailant. But the sickest shirt of all belonged to one of the newspapers. It instructed the authorities to send his remains back to the editor in his home state.

The free-enterprise character of the hotel reflected the laissez-faire nature of Lebanon itself. Behind every sandbag on the street was a black market, thriving unlike any I had ever seen before. Lebanon was in a state of near-total anarchy, and had been for several years. But it was a state of affairs which made many very rich - and most reluctant to leave despite the dangers of prolonged civil war.

For example, it was easy to buy any commodity in Lebanon. Bottles of the finest Scotch could be had for about $2 American. These were frequently brought across the border to Israel by returning soldiers and visitors. When the airport was open, the same liquor made its way to prohibitionist countries like Saudi Arabia, Iran, and Iraq, at great risk (not to mention huge profits) to the person transporting it. Some companies conducted weekly shuttle flights to Lebanon from their fundamentalist Moslem countries so they could stock up on these supplies. Brand-new videotape machines were a big higher - they sold for about $50 American. The choices regarding diesel Mercedes were a bit more limited. Everywhere on the streets one could see bombed-out hulks - which no one wanted - and brand-new ones, freshly stolen from Europe. These could be bought in any color or model. I saw very few old or slightly used cars in Lebanon.

The practice of stealing cars is nothing new in the Middle East. It has been widely reported that thousands of German and British luxury cars were stolen, transported through Israel, and buried in the sands of the Sinai desert. When that area was finally returned to the Egyptians, the cars were resurrected and cleaned off. By that time, the heat - as well as the sand - was off the cars and they could be sold, at a handsome profit.

The state of anarchy extended throughout most of Lebanon. It was a country where, by and large, no one had received a traffic ticket for years. The few streetlights still functioning silently implied, "We can't force you, but would you be so kind as to stop at the next red light?" Most drivers ignored them, and sped through in their inimitable aggressive manner. Murder was an even less serious crime than a traffic violation. In a country where thousands had died in the Civil War - even before the PLO, Syrian, and Israeli forces took over parts of that divided nation - it was nearly impossible to prosecute someone for murder. At this writing, no one has been jailed for the bombings which caused the death of Bashir Geymail, or for the bombings of the American and French facilities in Lebanon.

Bashir Geymail did, of course, live long enough to be elected President in the chaotic Parliamentary elections. It was a risky business for the Lebanese to even vote in those elections. The pervasive rumor was that every Member of Parliament was paid a million dollars to venture to the building and cast his ballot. Indeed, in the days following, some of the MPs were shot at or had their houses firebombed.

Bashir's election evoked jubilation in Israel. Many analysts contend that the real reason for the invasion was to get Bashir into office. He was considered favorably disposed toward Israel, and, some felt, he might conclude a peace treaty such as the one between Israel and Egypt. Such a pact, the Israelis hoped, would lead to normal relations, thus curbing the PLO terrorist acts against them in south Lebanon.

A few days before his election, some Western and Israeli reporters were ushered into Bashir's Phalange headquarters for a briefing. I was impressed with the education level and composure of his suave French-speaking officials. We received a thorough briefing on his party's hopes for unifying the country, and ending the terrorism (for which each side held the other responsible). The building in which we sat was modern, solid and comfortable. There were numerous armed troops around, and piles of sandbags in front. The amount of tight security was comforting, and I never believed there was any danger. But several weeks later, a group of prominent Jewish American fundraisers were in that same building, also meeting with Bashir Geymail following his election as President. Twenty minutes after the group left, a terrorist bomb destroyed the building. Bashir and many of his top staffers were killed. Even some young Lebanese girls, in the building for a visit, died in the blast. Such was the precipice on which the country teetered.

I had my own brushes with terror and death during my short stay in Lebanon. The first time, I was taking an elevator to visit a friend on the top floor of the Hotel Alexandre. No one had warned me that the elevators often stopped during fighting. A heavy rocket barrage began, and the electrical power went off, jolting the elevator to a stop between the fifth and sixth floors. There was no alarm bell, and I was all alone. I sank to my knees in the dark and prayed according to every religion I knew (it never hurts to cover all the bases). I could hear bombs dropping and rockets exploding in the distance. Almost afraid to breathe, I waited for the elevator cable to snap - a fear that never materialized. After some very long hours, the bombing stopped and the lights came back on in the elevator cab. Slowly it began to move and let me out on my destination floor. I was a mass of filth and sweat by the time I exited. No one had missed me, of course - they'd feared for their own skins during the assault. After that experience, I never took another elevator in Beirut.

The next incident was far more dangerous although, perversely, not quite as terrifying. The day before the PLO was to be evacuated from Beirut, we were ordered to report to the Lebanese Army headquarters for credentials. This army was scheduled to supervise the evacuation the following day. But the fragmented Christian and Moslem Lebanese Army had often been accused of cowardice, and stayed in their comparatively safe barracks during much of the civil war and invasion. Nevertheless, the word was out: we had to secure our credentials at the Army headquarters. Israeli reporters, however, were excluded.

I decided to stay on alone in Beirut to cover for Kol Yisrael's English Division. Danny had to return to Israel, to prepare for another tour of military duty the next day. My boss asked me to return with him, but I explained that I could not leave now, and miss the liberation of some Israeli prisoners who had been held captive. After the prisoner exchange took place, the evacuation of the PLO was to begin. My boss was nervous for me but grateful I wanted to stay, for he would not have got permission to send another reporter up there in time to cover those events. By that time, I was sufficiently able to communicate with the troops and radio engineers to function as well as to transmit a broadcast using our special van.

To cover the two events, I went by car to the headquarters of the Lebanese Army. A large statue of an angry, bearded man on horseback dominates the front of the structure. He brandished a sword, looking every bit like the fanatical Ayatollah Khomeini of Iran. My driver left me off, when the French-speaking guard at the gate assured me there were hundreds of reporters inside applying for credentials. When my Israeli colleagues were turned away by the guard as they also tried to get in, I told them I would be fine, and would meet them later at the press headquarters set up by the Israeli Defense Forces, or IDF. This was a headquarters staffed by Israelis and young Christian Lebanese who were happy to be interviewed on the many terrorist operations they had been involved in against the PLO.

I walked up a long winding driveway to another guard's booth. He phoned inside the headquarters and seemed to argue about something in Arabic. When he hung up, he let me through, and I hiked up another hundred yards. There, at the doorway to the Defense Ministry, some officers greeted me. There were no other reporters in sight, and my welcoming committee professed to have no idea what I was talking about. We argued in French for a few minutes, but I reluctantly decided that being obnoxious would get me nowhere, outnumbered as I was by several hundred Lebanese troops. I was bitterly disappointed, convinced I would not be able to cover the PLO evacuation. This situation wasn't like Washington, where I could always cover a major event from television if I couldn't get inside myself. I had promised my editors - and myself - that I would cover this story. Now, I would have to admit failure.

Dejected, I'd trudged halfway down the road when an Army jeep drove up beside me. The driver asked me where I was going. When I said the IDF press center, he motioned me to get in, promising me to take me there. In the States, of course, I would never dream of taking a ride with a strange soldier, or with any other stranger, for that matter. But this was a war, and all bets were off. I'd become used to accepting rides with various soldiers in Lebanon.

Another thing prompted me to accept his offer of transportation. I momentarily confused him with the Phalange- backed Lebanese Forces, whose soldiers had once said to me, "We and Israel, we are like one." Their uniforms are actually made in Israel, and are the same as those of the Israeli soldiers, save for some Arabic writing above their pockets. This Lebanese Army soldier's uniform was quite different, but I was too preoccupied to notice it at the time. I climbed into his Jeep, and he took me out of the compound. But instead of turning to the left and onto the main Beirut-Damascus Highway, he turned right, and soon veered onto a small road that wound through the dense woods. It took me only a few seconds to realize I was in trouble. Three times, as we stopped at Lebanese Army checkpoints, I tried to jump out, but he held me back. The other soldiers, aware of what was happening, merely laughed and waved him on. Some even congratulated him on his coup.

As we climbed deeper and deeper into the woods, I began to plead with him in French. Even in my panic, I thought how proud my high school French teacher would be to hear me beg, in grammatically correct French, "Don't hurt me! Don't kill me!" Desperately I tried to appeal to his sense of family. I explained that I had two small sons at home, and a wonderful husband. When he pressed me to tell him about my husband, I blurted, "Il est tres fort; il est Israelien." (*He is very strong; he is an Israeli* - which is quite far from the truth.) The soldier asked me where my husband was, and I said, "La bas," meaning he was right there, calmly waiting for me in the deep woods. The soldier just laughed at me, knowing full well that I was bluffing, and drove even further.

Finally, as we reached one of the most desolate parts of the woods, a small miracle occurred. An Israeli armored personnel carrier came down the other side of the road from over the top of the mountain. It blocked most of the road, forcing my soldier to slow down. I swung around in the jeep, and hit him hard in the mouth and nose with my heavy "Air New Zealand" flight bag. The weight of the bag was increased with my tape recorder and other items inside. I believe I may have broken the nose and some teeth of the soldier, and blood was gushing from his face as I jumped from his jeep. I ran towards the Israelis screaming, "Shalom," which is Hebrew for hello, or peace. This was really one of the few Israeli words I knew. Fortunately, the Israelis didn't fire on me but stopped their vehicle and took me in. My kidnapper, meanwhile, sped away over the mountain. I wonder how he explained his wild "night on the town" to his colleagues.

The Israelis, for their part, showed admirable restraint. They would have been justified in shooting me. Think about it: here was a crazy redhead, running towards them at full speed, having just jumped out of a Lebanese Army jeep. Moreover, I was carrying a great deal of equipment, including an Air New Zealand travel bag. The Israelis would have been forgiven for thinking I was a terrorist toting explosives. Frequently, the most dangerous assaults were carried out by young teenagers - often women - who rushed toward the trucks and tanks, laden with explosives or rocket-propelled grenades. These so-called RPG kids, who were responsible for many deaths in the Mideast, would die in their suicide missions, but believed they would earn a front seat in heaven in the process.

To their credit - and my eternal relief - the Israeli soldiers didn't follow the dictates of their training; rather, they hesitated until I could explain the situation. Shaken and in near hysterics, I showed them my credentials and babbled away in English, which they understood. Then they drove me down the mountain and took me to the IDF press headquarters. There, my colleagues treated me like something of a hero. Meanwhile, a search party was sent out after the Lebanese soldier, but we didn't have his license plate number so I doubt he was ever found. Days later, when I related the harrowing incident to my husband, he reminded me how lucky I was. In his words, "One more dead body in Lebanon wouldn't surprise anyone."

Years after the event, when I returned to Washington, I learned more details about my supposedly chance "kidnapping." I had the privilege of meeting Major Jack Farmer, who was the Operations Officer of the 2000 strong 32nd Marine Amphibious Unit (and later the 22nd Marine Amphibious Unit) at the time of the incident. He was well versed in the ways of the Mideast, as well as in many other hot spots of the world. Although his primary mission was to secure the port and evacuate the remaining 6600 PLO (including Yasser Arafat), Jack was additionally told to keep an eye on some of the American civilians who remained there following the evacuation of some U.S. citizens and U.S. Embassy staff by his Marines that summer. Given the fact that the situation was in no way stable, certainly no Westerner (especially American) could be safe and were likely to get into trouble. Appropriate contingency plans were made covering this eventuality. He, therefore, had been following my exploits in Lebanon. His sources indicated to him that I was set up by elements of the Israeli command, in the first place. The events bear credence in retrospect, but the ultimate truth is difficult to discern.

I understood the Israelis' mode of operations in other well-publicized incidents around the world when they were in a difficult situation. I was sent to places they could not go. That may be why the Israelis drove me to the Military Base, even though they could not get in. They could have wanted to find out what I was able to see or learn (which was very little; I was only inside for a few minutes). But, they may have also followed me in the jeep, and contacted patrols up ahead. For that reason, the armored personal carrier was in a position to rescue me, when the danger appeared too great. If the situation deteriorated they had a viable option to attempt to get me out, which would have provided them much desired "good press" in the United States, given the rising antiwar sentiment toward Israel in the U.S. and in Israel itself. Their alternative option was that if they were not successful or did not believe it could be accomplished within acceptable risk and I succumbed to my fate, well, after all, I was only an American free-lance journalist who should have known better. If this scenario is true, it put me in a terribly dangerous position. But, we all managed to survive, so I am not angered by it.

At least my exploits were benign. They were nothing compared to the tragedy that Major Farmer and his Marines suffered, when their barracks was bombed the following year. 241 well-trained, disciplined, and dedicated Marines were slaughtered. One of Jack's tasks was to plan and coordinate identification of the mutilated bodies of his fellow Marines, escort them home, and try to console their grieving families back in the USA. The tragedy was even more poignant and unnecessary, since the Marines knew they were sitting ducks in their position at the

Beirut International Airport. After the successful evacuation of the PLO from Beirut, the Marines were once more ordered to land in Lebanon on a peacekeeping mission. This was in response to the massacres of unarmed Palestinian men, women and children in the villages of Shabra and Shatila by Phalange militia supported by Israeli troops.

The original landing plan was for the 32nd Marine Amphibious Unit, reinforced with an additional Battalion Landing Team of 1000 Marines, to occupy positions in the area beyond the airport, establishing an in-depth defensive perimeter for the airport. However, because this would place the Old Sidon Road internal to the Marines defensive lines, it would have given the perception that the U.S. was assisting Israel in defense of the Israeli main supply route to the Bekaa Valley in the north. This would have immediately made the Marines a target for concentrated artillery and rocket fire from Syrian and Palestinian positions, and hindered any chance for a swift Israeli withdrawal and the ultimate goal of a viable cease-fire agreement. A strategic decision was made at the highest levels of the national command authority to reach accommodation with the diplomats and politicians, so the Marines were restricted to the confined area around the airport.

As a result, the Marines were assigned to an untenable position, but held it, because that is what their country asked them to do. Their professionalism was evident throughout their ranks, exemplified by the seriousness with which they performed every task. This legacy is written innumerable times in over two centuries of their history.

Chaos Reigns: The Evacuation of the PLO

That night, I shared a room with a platonic friend, a longtime war correspondent for CBS. Larry Pintak was stationed in Beirut for several years, but occasionally took side trips to cover some of the incredible slaughter along the Iran-Iraq border. And, as I was to discover, he had a unique method of shutting out the warfare around him. At night, he slept with music blaring as loud as his radio would go. This drowned out the sounds of the bombardment outside. It also prevented him from knowing whether the rocket barrage was outgoing or incoming since, after so many years in the Mideast, he had become a fatalist. Larry also learned another important technique. Since his room was one of the few with windows intact, he always kept the blinds down. Thus if a rocket struck, there was a somewhat reduced possibility of being hit by shards of glass crashing onto his bed.

Very early the next morning, all the reporters prepared to cover the evacuation of the first wave of the PLO at the Port. First, they followed their daily routine of listening to the BBC and to Israeli Radio, to get the morning news. The Lebanese broadcasts, for the most part, were in Arabic, which few Western reporters could understand. And since each factional broadcast represented a biased point of view, it was hard to distill the truth.

For my part, it was odd to listen to my Australian friend in Washington broadcast the stories I would ordinarily do for Kol Yisrael. He was my substitute while I was away. His were the lead stories each morning and evening, and they tied the events together. I was jealous that he was getting the air time I was used to, but it made me realize the importance of my job from Washington. The State Department had even announced what units of the PLO would be evacuated first, and when they would leave. Amid the chaos in Lebanon, it was often hard for those of us at the scene to get such information. There I was, risking life and limb in Beirut, when I could have been sitting comfortably in the State Department or White House briefing room, getting most of the facts I needed. But the sights, sounds, and impressions of the story were lacking in Washington, and I couldn't spend my whole life subsisting on press handouts, even if we did try to elicit the truth through tough questions.

In war ravaged Beirut, after we finished the morning broadcasts, we went downstairs for breakfast at the Alexandre restaurant. This was a chaotic affair, which reflected the general situation in Beirut. There were no front windows in the restaurant, since they had been blown out in a car bomb explosion. So wanderers from the street simply stepped across the flowerpots and walked right into the dining room. There, they helped themselves to the buffet, gorging themselves on cheese, croissants, and oily hummus and olives left over from the night before. Coffee consisted of hot water and little jars of instant Nescafe, with colorful Arabic handwriting on the outside. Many of us loaded up on the jars and cheese, to share with our friends outside. At the end of the meal, most people did not pay; they just stepped through the nonexistent windows and disappeared. There were few waiters around to demand payment, and the few who were there didn't seem to care.

This morning, however, I ate much less than usual. My stomach and bowels were churning, and I found myself making emergency trips to the bathroom. I knew I was in trouble when I couldn't even drink the coffee. Seeking medical attention was out of the question. The cars were leaving for the Port, and I had to grab a ride if I wanted to try to cover the story, even without Lebanese Army credentials. I flagged down some Israeli reporters, and we sped through the bombed-out streets. We got lost several times in the maze of streets leading nowhere.

Finally, we found a Phalange soldier on a motor scooter who offered to lead us. I was afraid he was a decoy to lure us into PLO-controlled territory. But he assured us he was our friend, and we had little choice but to follow. After twenty minutes of twisting down streets and doubling back and forth over the same area, we finally found the entrance to the port, next to the tall wall that formed the dividing line. Across the way, in the Palestinian section, the PLO were shooting their machine guns into the air. It was a phony celebration, intended to convey that they were leaving in victory when they were actually being forced out. Nonetheless, the bullets struck a number of targets during the rampage. At least fifty people were wounded and two killed on both sides of the line during the barrage. As we got to the Port, a bullet came crashing through the back window of a taxi carrying a Swedish correspondent. Both reporter and driver were injured and narrowly escaped death.

As the evacuation began, Israeli and Phalange soldiers were all around, but there was no sign of the Lebanese Army. True to their reputation, they stayed in their barracks, because there was too much shooting to suit them. I realized that all the risks I'd taken to secure their press credentials were not necessary after all. And all the Officials' delicate negotiations, which resulted in an agreement for them to supervise the evacuation, also were meaningless. In the end, the U.S. Marines, the Israelis and Phalange soldiers of the Lebanese Forces took charge. Those of us holding any of these credentials had no trouble getting into the Port.

To one Israeli reporter, mere access was not enough. Ron Ben-Yishai, then of Israeli Television, wanted to see what was happening in the West. He and an Israeli television crew crossed the line, claiming they were Italian television reporters. There, he interviewed members of the Morabatum, who were Lebanese militants closely aligned with the PLO. He got a major scoop by getting Morabatum leaders to acknowledge they were receiving heavy military arms from the departing PLO, even though this was in violation of the withdrawal agreement.

It was a great story, but it entailed a tremendous risk for Ron. After all, he was a visible presence, and his face was a familiar sight on Israeli television almost every night. Ron later became one of the first reporters to visit the gruesome Sabra and Shatila refugee camps after the massacre there in September. He also broke that story, and phoned Israeli Defense Minister Ariel Sharon at home to question him about it. But Ron was used to taking extraordinary risks. There's a maxim in this business: "You are only as good as your last story." Ron had the courage to live by this principle, and never rested on the laurels of his past successes.

Ron safely crossed back over the line, and told us about his exploits. We all met at the Israeli Radio broadcasting truck, which had been moved down from the hilltop and was parked up against the dividing wall. It was a dangerous place to broadcast from, since bullets and rockets were pouring over the fence. Our editors in Haifa could barely hear us over all the rocket fire. But the sound was, to say the least, graphic. The shooting also drowned out another sound - that of me vomiting violently at the side of the truck.

By that time, "Beirut Belly" had hit me hard. I later learned it strikes most visitors after a few days in the area. Conventional wisdom has it that if the food doesn't attack your system, the water will. I was so sick I had no time to think of physical danger; I was much more concerned about agony and pain. I finally gathered the strength to stagger across the street to a half-bombed cafe. My colleagues shouted at me to keep low, and try to avoid the bullets and bombs, but I failed to do even that.

In front of the cafe, four Arab men were sitting at rusty tables, sucking long water pipes. I asked them in French where to find a toilet, and they motioned me upstairs. I climbed a partially bombed cement stairway and found myself on the second floor. There was nothing there but one bare room, with a crater hole in the center. I assumed this was the "ladies room." I squatted and relieved myself, well aware that the contents of my digestive tract were gushing through to the first floor and might hid the head of some hapless customer sitting below. I felt bad about it, but this was Beirut after all, where all's fair in love, war, and gastric disorders.

Still sick, and very embarrassed, I descended the stairs and walked out of the cafe as casually as possible, without even offering to leave a tip. I ran across the street. By then, the shooting had become so intense that all other activity had come to a halt. One of the Israeli soldiers shoved me into a doorway, where I huddled with other reporters and soldiers. I was happy to be with them, and sought out the handsomest soldier. I joked that if I were to die then, I wanted to be surrounded by good-looking men.

There was some dispute about what we should do. Some felt we would be safer out on the street. That way, it was reasoned, we wouldn't be crushed by the rubble if the building took a direct hit and collapsed around us, as had so many of the other structures. But the rockets were indiscriminate, and most of those killed had been in the West, not the Eastern sector where we huddled. The PLO barrage had actually killed more of their own, as they made their final farewell.

Finally, the shooting died down somewhat and the slow evacuation process began. In the East, the PLO fighters were loaded onto open trucks that would form a convoy to take them into the Port. At about the same time, ships rolled in from the Mediterranean, depositing members of what would become the Multinational Force. Members of the French Foreign Legion had arrived a few hours earlier, to take up positions on some of the streets of Beirut. But this last contingent was assigned to the Port, where they would help shepherd the PLO on board the Greek ferry that was poised to take them to Cyprus.

I ran up to meet the French Foreign Legion and do an interview with the captain of the Greek ship, who was assuring reporters that he would take the arms away from the PLO members before they boarded his ship. As I ran to them, I was assaulted by another surprise attack of Beirut Belly. This time, I just ducked behind the partially bombed wall of a building. Here I was, at a truly historic moment, with the PLO about to be forced out of Beirut, and I was squatting unceremoniously over a pile of rubble, praying I wouldn't be bitten by a rat or devoured by fleas. At the time, the bullets above my head were only of minor concern.

When I was able, I went back to the ship to complete my interview. After speaking with the Greek captain, a handsome member of the French

Foreign Legion rushed up to me saying, "Hi, Mate," in a booming, confident New Zealand voice. He had seen my Air New Zealand travel bag, and the New Zealand flag pasted on the back of my tape recorder. I was proud to be thought of as his countryman and told him I shared his love for that nation, even if I was actually a loyal American. We had a nice chat, and I conducted a brief interview with him. But with his commander glaring at him, the Kiwi was circumspect. Hours later, when I was able to get a phone line to New Zealand, I filed the interview.

My report was starkly graphic, with the sounds of gunfire all around us. I was really proud of the story and thought it would certainly bring the situation home to a New Zealand audience. I was crushed when, months later, I learned that it hadn't been used. One reason related to ethics. To its credit, Radio New Zealand was very loyal at that time (that changed in later years), and it had contracted to get its Lebanon stories from the BBC. Since I'd left my territory of Washington and the United States, I couldn't file to them. A second problem was the fact that, despite his indisputable New Zealand accent, the soldier had not given his real name and hometown in New Zealand. He couldn't, as I pointed out to my editors, since Legionnaires were obliged to remain anonymous, and all had Gallic names like Jacques, Henri, or Charles.

I spent the next few hours in the Port, watching the PLO being loaded onto ships bound for Cyprus and other scattered points around the Mideast. In many ways, the departure was tragic. Although the PLO had terrorized the Lebanese and Israelis for years, they were still being forced to abandon a home they had known for a time, leaving their families largely unprotected. Their fears about their relatives were tragically borne out the following month, when the world learned of the shocking wholesale slaughter in the Sabra and Shatila refugee camps. Phalange soldiers seeking revenge, according to the age-old Lebanese tribal rites of retribution, slaughtered hundreds of Palestinian women and children.

I was skeptical that the removal of the PLO forces would resolve the area's problems. I believed it would only spread the cancer around the Mideast. I also feel the Palestinians are justified in their desire to have a home of their own; they have suffered greatly to achieve that end. Perhaps a Palestinian State will lead to peace, and the Palestinians will no longer be someone else's political pawns, or covet lands in Lebanon, Israel or Jordan.

Personally, I often attributed many of the stories about Palestinian terror at least partly to propaganda efforts. But the huge caches of Soviet-made weapons uncovered in Lebanon revealed that the PLO was certainly receiving substantial assistance from other governments and organizations throughout the world. I also saw the effects they had on the Lebanese population. One day in Lebanon, I visited one of the spectacular beaches near Beirut. I talked with some of the women on the beach, and asked them how many months of the year they were able to swim in the beautiful, clear Mediterranean. They looked at me in surprise, and explained in French that they had not been to these beaches in seven years, for they and their daughters were in danger of being raped and beaten by the PLO.

****

After the first wave of PLO troops left on the Greek ferry, we were told Israeli Defense Minister Ariel Sharon would meet with us in an undisclosed location. Sharon was the highly controversial official who was responsible for the Lebanon invasion. With so many enemies, he had to take elaborate pains to protect himself. Only a few of us were invited, to minimize the danger to him.

I was instructed to go to a certain parking lot, where I would be picked up for a news conference. An Israeli liaison official drove me to the Petroleum Building, a high-rise with a commanding view of Beirut and most of the coast. The official promised to take me back to the Press Center, so I foolishly left my Air New Zealand travel bag in his car. I didn't want to take such a large bag inside, out of fear that it would make the soldiers guarding Sharon jumpy. That turned out to be a serious mistake. Most of my personal notes, overnight equipment, and airline tickets home were in that bag. I lost track of the Israeli official and the bag for several days, and became obsessed with finding it, so I could leave the Mideast.

While my bag sat in the locked car, we were thoroughly searched and then sent up to the top floor of the high-rise. Now alert to the idiosyncratic nature of Lebanese elevators, I labored up the twelve flights of stairs. The building was crawling with Israeli soldiers, which made me nervous. I knew the structure was a perfect target for rockets or terrorist attacks, but the view of Beirut almost made the risk worthwhile. From there, I could assess the damage inflicted on the city by the invasion and the ten-year civil war. Surprisingly, many of the apartments and office buildings were standing, although most had sustained some damage. Most of the luxury hotels along the Mediterranean had been destroyed. In some cases, steel rafters remained up, affording good vantage points for fighters of all stripes.

For a moment we watched the PLO ship sail into the Mediterranean toward Cyprus. Then General Sharon came out to give us a news conference and a situation report. I was the only woman among hundreds of men. They sat me in the front row, where I fought an internal struggle with Beirut Belly, anxious not to embarrass myself any further. (A week later, I was back in Washington, where I rushed home to cover a visit by Sharon. At one appearance at the National Press Club, he greeted me with a big bear hug and said, "You looked so angry at me last week. Why were you so mad?" I tried to explain it was nausea that accounted for my expression, not anger, although I was far from supportive of his policies.)

Before the news conference began in Beirut, I ran into Morris Draper, the American official who was in charge of Lebanon policy that month. I had covered him throughout many Congressional hearings, and was very fond of his wife, Roberta. We greeted each other with a very warm embrace - two Americans in a war-ravaged city, far from home. Home was but a ten-hour plane ride away, once the airport was opened, but meeting a countryman in those circumstances holds special meaning. Several months later, when the American Embassy in Beirut was bombed, Draper rushed back from a meeting to make sure his wife was unharmed. One of the more poignant pictures from that episode depicted them embracing in relief and gratitude.

When the Sharon news conference ended, Morris and I made our way downstairs and returned to the Israeli broadcasting facilities. I had lost the Israeli official who had my bag, but assumed he would turn up later at press headquarters. He didn't. In the meantime, I had reams of material on the evacuation to file to my editors: the interviews conducted at the Port with the Greek captain and the Lebanese Forces soldiers, and the Sharon news conference. Earlier, I'd filed stories on the transfer of Israeli prisoners and the bodies of some Israeli soldiers. My editors said they were very pleased with the material. Without it, they would have had to play Israeli music to fill up most of the Saturday magazine program. Their gratitude did not reflect itself in payments as their funds were limited. I certainly had not gone there to realize a profit; that can best be done from home. Appreciation often means far more than money in this business. After my Beirut adventure ended, Zvi's wife wrote me a short note saying how much she enjoyed my broadcasts from Beirut. For many years I carried that tattered note in my purse.

Before I left Beirut, I was invited to celebrate Friday night Sabbath service with my five thousand soldiers. A chance to preside as the only woman was an opportunity not to be missed. Three separate "services" were held at long tables, set outside in the campsite in Baabda. One table, further down the hill, was for the Hasidic and other devoutly religious men. As a woman, I would not be invited to participate in their group. At the other extreme, a special dinner was held without prayers, for those who did not observe. The men celebrated by watching Lebanese television as they ate. A set was rigged up at one end of the table, and the men watched reruns of American television series, complete with Arabic subtitles.

Our service bridged the two groups. Several thousand men said the centuries-old Shabbat prayers of gratitude. Then we had a traditional meal of challah (rounded and twisted bread), wine, fish, and chicken. As we sat high in the hills, praying and eating, the lights came on in Beirut beneath us. Soon afterward, the nightly barrage of rockets began. This time, there was no bombing from Israeli planes. A few times the rockets came close to our positions. But no one bothered to duck or take shelter. Perhaps we felt invulnerable - after all, this was a very special night.

I left Beirut with a new understanding of the soldiers. I discovered there is often a vast difference between the conduct of the young soldiers who are serving in the military for the first time and that of the older reservists who are called back to active duty. Deep down, both shared the same terror and abhorrence of war. But the younger ones often masked that fear with bravado and, sometimes, by committing acts of cruelty. More frequently, the older ones were less eager to pull the trigger. They were often kinder to the civilian population and to dependent soul like me than were the younger ones. None of them wanted to be in a war situation; they would much rather be home, practicing their law, dentistry, journalism, or teaching, in peace. Many of the younger men also hated the fighting but understood that for the time being, this was their profession. In other societies, they may have had the luxury of continuing their studies, traveling at leisure, or even experiencing an off-the-wall lifestyle. But as Israelis, they were responsible for trying to preserve a country and culture which was threatened from many sides. All the soldiers rose to this challenge in individual ways, but some did so in a more humane manner than others.

After a few more days and nights in Lebanon, it was time to return to Israel and catch my charter flight back to America. I was still quite sick, although heavy doses of Lomotil scavenged for me by fellow reporters helped alleviate my symptoms. Nevertheless, I relished the thought of returning to a more sanitary environment.

I caught a ride back to Jerusalem with two other reporters. I made arrangements to have my Air New Zealand bag returned to Israel, once it was finally located. I believed it shouldn't be too hard to find, even in a war zone. After all, how many green Air New Zealand flight bags could be floating around Lebanon?

The three of us returned safely to Israel, after a long overnight drive. We stopped for dinner at the border kibbutz, where officials and residents were anxious to learn as much as they could about the evacuation of the PLO. One Israeli reporter was especially bitter about my escapades in Lebanon. "Well," he sneered, "I guess it's a good break from your dull routine as a suburban housewife."

In Jerusalem, I awakened my poor boss at two o'clock in the morning and took refuge in his son's room, which I'd been occupying while the son was on permanent military duty in Lebanon. The next day, amid tours of the old city of Jerusalem and the modern Israeli towns in the West Bank, I made dozens of phone calls, trying to locate my flight bag. Understandably, the Lebanese people were trying to survive a war, and Israel was torn apart by the invasion, so I suppose it was rather arrogant of me, in the midst of all this, to try to locate one piece of luggage. But the Air New Zealand bag contained some very special memories for me and, damn it, I wanted it back!

Finally the bag was located and a car brought it down from Lebanon to the border kibbutz. But the officials there were afraid it might be booby-trapped, so they sent it back to the Israeli press headquarters in Beirut. After blistering the phone lines with much cursing and screaming, I arranged to have it sent down again. This time, the kibbutz sent it as far south as the Hilton Hotel in Tel Aviv, where I'd made arrangements with the morning manager to pick it up from his desk. Unfortunately, the afternoon manager was on duty when the bag arrived. He was also afraid of bombs, and returned it north to the kibbutz, several hours away. I learned this when I arrived at his desk a few hours before my flight was due to depart the Tel Aviv airport. I was so frustrated, I broke down and started to cry. As fate would have it, an Australian couple recognized my voice and said, "Oh, you're Connie Lawn! We listen to you all the time on the radio in Canberra." I was so embarrassed to be recognized at a time like this. The hotel manager was feeling quite guilty by this time, and agreed to send a taxi up to the kibbutz to try to recover the bag. He even paid the $90 cost himself, although I wasn't a guest at the hotel.

By now it was sunset, and the Australian couple offered to drive me to the airport. There, new tickets were issued, and I settled down to wait for the plane, which by this time was over fourteen hours late leaving Israel.

Finally, we prepared to board the plane. I had reluctantly given up on my precious bag. As we started to undergo our security check, my name came over the loudspeaker. The taxi driver had arrived barely in time, after a breakneck drive down the Israeli coast. Remarkably, my bag was intact, and still contained my camera and souvenirs from Lebanon, including two little coffee jars from the Hotel Alexandre. I suggested that the guards inspect it carefully, explaining it had been floating around Lebanon and Israel on its own for four days. But no bombs or illegal drugs were found, and I happily boarded the plane with my well-traveled Air New Zealand bag which by now had seen a good deal of the Mideast.

I returned to Washington more appreciative than ever of my home and family. I'd had the incomparable experience of seeing people struggling to survive in the face of anarchy, civil war, and invasion.

But even back home, life was far from routine. In addition to doing about fifteen radio reports a day, I discovered there was a great deal of interest in my Lebanon trip. I soon found myself on the lecture circuit. This was a most rewarding experience that also helped to focus my thoughts on the situation in that troubled country. I became very outspoken over my opposition to the presence of American forces in Lebanon. I felt they were sitting ducks, sent there on a useless mission. Every time another Marine was killed, I walked into the State Department with tears streaming down my cheeks. The diplomats, however, continued to express confidence that limited American military power - backed up by heavy battleships off the Mediterranean coast - could fuse Lebanon into a viable country with a strong central government. But by this time, Bashir Gemayel had been assassinated and his brother Amin "elected" President more or less by default. Most of the reporters who had spent any amount of time in the region felt the Lebanese had had more than enough years to accomplish cohesion as one country. The factions had been feuding on and off for hundreds of years. The only hope we saw for peace was some sort of partition among the factions, although they might be able to unite into a federation.

Sadly, Lebanon still claimed its share of headlines. As the troops pulled out, the terrorists rampaged against civilians. Kidnapping journalists and college professors became the preoccupation of choice. Frustration over his inability to free the Western hostages in Lebanon apparently led President Reagan into his ill-conceived arms-for-hostages deals with Iran, even though Iran may have been the authority behind the brutal destruction of the Marine barracks which killed 279 Americans, along with the 241 Marines. Lebanese and Palestinians were also slaughtered in the Shabra and Shatilia refugee camps, and other areas of the county.

In 2002, the seeds of the hatred fueled in Lebanon bore bitter fruit. Ariel Sharon and Yasser Arafat continued their intense hatred and fighting, as a new war gripped Israel and the territories. Suicide bombers killed innocent Israelis, where they tried to gather at restaurants, markets, or in the streets. Israelis killed Palestinians in retaliation in the territories. One can only wonder if the situation would have been different, if Ariel Sharon had not survived to become Prime Minister of Israel, and if Yasser Arafat had not lived to become head of the Palestinian Authority. Towards the end of the Clinton Administration, the Palestinians were granted 97% of what they wanted, in attempts to form a Palestinian State, next to Israel. A sharing arrangement could have been accomplished regarding Jerusalem, and the question of the Palestinian right to return might have been resolved. But, hard line Palestinians, and Israelis, could not accept the compromise. Palestinians began deadly suicide attacks, and the long-festering war and hatred resumed. Like many blood feuds between ethnic and religious groups, this one may never end. Some Israelis and Arabs appear doomed to fight to the finish.

Encore: Paradise Revisited

After three more years of very hard work in Washington, my hunger to revisit the South Pacific became overwhelming. There had been many changes in the region, especially since the election of the new Labor Government in New Zealand and the dispute over their resistance to the presence of American nuclear ships and weapons. There were also rumblings of growing anti-American sentiment there and in Australia. I vowed to return and observe the situation for myself.

I also wanted to convey to the people that despite the disputes our politicians may be having, I am simply a siphon of the news. My job is not to represent or defend anyone's point of view, but I am concerned primarily that the people I cover be honest and accessible to me. I have often said I could give a fair press to Hitler or Genghis Khan if they were straight with me. Moralists, of course, may not see things this way, but the reporter's sole mission is to report. If the person I'm covering is arrogant, evil, or crazy, he will dig his own grave. The public is more perceptive than most people think. The average listener can distill truths just by listening to a taped voice on the radio or watching someone on television.

True to form, I discovered that any anti-Americanism which might exist was philosophical, and not personal. The people in New Zealand and Australia can be very passionate in their beliefs, and this comes through in dramatic and sometimes violent confrontations, as occurred during the anti-Springboks rugby riots. But on a personal level, the people were as warm, open, and generous to me as before. In fact, this time they even surpassed themselves.

On this trip, Air New Zealand graciously agreed to fly me down. Before crossing the Pacific, they delivered me to the Boeing plant in Seattle, Washington. There, I covered the "roll-out" of Air New Zealand's new 767s. It was an impressive event. As the shimmering aircraft was rolled onto the tarmac, New Zealand Maoris welcomed it with their traditional war challenge, greeting, and ceremonial songs. To those of us in the audience with close ties to New Zealand, it was a very emotional occasion.

I was also impressed with Air New Zealand's commitment to quality control and attention to detail. They had flown their own people up to repeat the inspection of the new craft already performed many times by the Boeing engineers and technicians. One New Zealander even went over 48,000 bolts by hand, and complained if he found any to be misshapen or minutely out of place. For white-knuckled flyers like me, this extra care and precision was most reassuring. I'd fly anywhere with them.

After Seattle, I enjoyed another very luxurious flight to New Zealand. This time, I was determined to travel straight through. As much as I would have liked to linger in the Pacific paradises of Hawaii, Fiji, and Tahiti, I wanted to focus as much on business as possible in three short weeks.

The flight was smooth, wonderful, and uneventful. As on most long flights, we were fed very well indeed. We arrived in New Zealand to a rainy and dismal Sunday morning. I was gratified to discover that two people had come to the airport to greet me. One was an Air New Zealand official, whose thoughtfulness went far above and beyond the call of duty. The other was a very dear friend, the wife of a Member of Parliament. She had unselfishly forsaken her own plans to welcome me at the airport.

My friend and I arrived at her beautiful home, just as the weather was clearing. All around me were magnificent, scenic vistas. I was surrounded by rolling lush green hills, turquoise bays, and fields of grazing cattle, horses, and, of course, sheep. I decided to go for a run, to loosen up my muscles from the long flight. In the distance, a girl came riding up the dirt road on a fine thoroughbred horse. As she approached me, I admired it. She asked, "Would you like a ride?" I jumped at the opportunity, and had an invigorating canter down the dirt road. Surely there are very few other places where a person would offer an expensive thoroughbred to a total stranger. She didn't even ask whether I knew how to ride.

This second visit was even busier than the first. My days began at five a.m., with either phone calls or visits to the Radio New Zealand studios to observe the "Morning Report." Often I was put on the air live while in the studio. Sometimes, when a big story broke from Washington, I tried to cover or comment on it from Wellington. These experiments were generally not too successful. Often, I was unable to get crucial tape or an official discussing the ANZUS crisis, which was heating up at the time. ANZUS - the defense treaty between Australia, New Zealand, and the United States - was threatening to unravel because of a serious disagreement over port access to nuclear ships. Sometimes I phoned Washington to speak with an official about something which had been said. But I seldom got everything I needed, and sometimes missed an important nuance, thus invalidating my story. This reinforced to me how important it is to really be on the spot in order to offer full and accurate coverage of an event.

This trip also entailed plenty of running around, and visits with bosses, old friends, and Members of Parliament. I had more time to just "hang around" Broadcast House and the Parliament this time, and got a better feel for the way the system works. In fact, I practically became a fixture, and was either taken for granted or got in everyone's way.

In addition to seeing many dear friends, this visit was special in two ways. First, I was delighted to come face to face with a four-legged "Connie Lawn," a thoroughbred racehorse whimsically named after me by the Ruddenklau family of Dipton, on the South Island. Certainly this was one of the greatest honors of my life. I will never forget the night Henry Ruddenklau's daughter, Mary Ann, called me from New Zealand. I was in the kitchen in my Virginia home, engaged in an argument with Steve. When she asked me whether her father could name a horse after me, I thought it was a joke, in the tradition of Alpine Golf. Surprised and amused, I agreed. Inevitably I began to laugh, and so did my husband, this piece of comic relief thus defusing our marital disagreement.

I met the Ruddenklaus during the second week of my visit. They had trucked "Connie" and another horse up to the racetrack in Christchurch. I have such memories of my meeting with the family. They are rugged, honest, salt-of-the-earth folks, whom I felt I had known forever. Even though they lived ten thousand miles from me, they were very similar to my husband and his fellow horse racing fanatics. My meeting with my namesake, however, was somewhat less successful than the time I spent with her family. Connie was wild, fit, and beautiful. I was a bit wary of her, and she clearly was unimpressed with me. She refused even to accept my carrots. Still, it was thrilling to see her gallop around a Christchurch racetrack, and I was proud and honored to share my name with this magnificant creature. I also scoured the newspapers for memorable horse headlines, such as "Connie Lawn Shines in Workout," or "Connie Beats Juveniles."

Some marvelous radio interviews also emerged from my meeting with the Ruddenklaus. A Radio New Zealand reporter from Christchurch came to the motel where Henry Ruddenklau was staying. She asked him to describe the horse and me.

"They are both bay and both fit and both spunky," he intoned in his best South Island accent. His trainer, Rex Cochrane, was also there, and revealed why they had decided to name the filly after me. Rex is one of over a million adult New Zealanders who listen to "Morning Report" as they are caring for their animals or getting dressed. He was listening to one of my reports one day and said afterward, "That Connie Lawn is dead right. I'd like a horse like that." Since he is by far one of the top trainers in the country, with several thousand wins under his belt, I was flattered that he felt that way. Later, I heard they were considering naming one of their other fillies "Dolly Parton." Perhaps the horse is well endowed or maybe it just has a beautiful whinny!

After the visit to Christchurch I had one of the most memorable experiences of my life. Mary Ann drove me further south, through the rugged, primitive, and awe-inspiring mountains of the South Island. With typical New Zealand understatement, she remarked casually that we would spend the night at her cousins' farm. The "farm" turned out to be an immense High Country sheep station stretching over 22 miles. In fact, it was almost that far from the front gate to the manor house. To reach the house, we traveled down a frozen dirt road which passed a pond filled with ducks, geese, and swans. Jagged mountains stood like sentinels over snowy fields, where cattle and sheep were abundant.

The night I spent at the sheep station was filled with warmth, cheer, good friendship, and delicious food. It was thrilling to be part of this New Zealand adventure.

The next day, Mary Ann and I left the splendid High Country paradise and drove to the resort of Queenstown. It was still as beautiful as ever, but considerably built up since my last visit three years earlier. And, after the sheep station, the thriving, crowded metropolis felt constricting by comparison.

It was a joy to again visit the beautiful Davis home, where I was reunited with them and my good friend Warren Cooper. I stayed there overnight, but during the day I met with playwright Roger Hall and his friend, artist Graham Sidney. We had two days of superb skiing in the majestic Coronet Peak ski area, which towers over Queenstown and the surrounding countryside. There is certainly no finer skiing anywhere, even in the European Alps or the American Rockies. And conditions were excellent at Coronet, with tons of light, powdery snow and a choice of dozens of open peaks and bowls to ski. For a resident of the Northern Hemisphere, it was invigorating to be snow skiing in the summer, when I knew it would be a hundred humid degrees back home. But it was far from cold in New Zealand. The sun glistened, and the weather was warm enough to ski in a light shirt. I was flattered to be described in a newspaper article about the excursion as a "slim mother of two." In northern climes I am often so bundled up that people ask, "Sir, is this the way to the bottom of the mountain?"

From Queenstown I drove with Roger Hall to his home in Dunedin. There I had the chance to meet an extraordinary lady, Mollie Lawn Kershaw. She, her cousin, Lois Lawn, and I spent hours together, reading old news clippings about the Lawns of New Zealand and Australia. We poured over old chronicles and journals, and I became more convinced than ever that we were linked by ties of blood, as well as affection. I left with an exquisite oil painting Mollie had made of the blue New Zealand mountains, spiking upward through the white and gray clouds. My head was spinning with the excitement of far-flung and long-lost families who had been brought together through the magic of radio.

Back in Christchurch, I had the good fortune to stay with another Member of Parliament and his family. We went our separate ways during the day, but at night we all sat together in our pajamas, discussing life and politics into the wee hours. Such encounters are what really fleshed out my visit.

In Wellington I spent hours observing the Parliament, which was engaged in a heated debate about sex education. It was enlightening to see mild-mannered MPs, whom I had known for years as good and close friends, transformed into tigers on the debating floor. The pit became a virtual Coliseum, where they attacked and parried with each other like the Romans of old. I venture no judgments here as to who were the Christians and who the lions. I will say, however, that the spirited session was far more interesting than our coma-inducing Congressional debates in the States.

I shared with some of the men and women debating on the floor irreplaceable memories - like the time I'd brought my sons to the New Zealand Embassy to interview Prime Minister Lange, then a leader of the Labor Party. I'd sent the boys out into the cold, snowy afternoon to sleigh ride with the Ambassador's grandchildren. Then there was the former Prime Minister, Sir Robert Muldoon, whom I had often covered in Washington and who had once called President Jimmy Carter "that peanut farmer." We'd conducted many interviews together, but the highlight had to be the time I shared a telephone booth with him.

Sir Robert was attending a bankers' convention in the Mayflower Hotel, and I caught him for a brief chat during a five-minute break in the proceedings. It was difficult to find a quiet place to talk, and there was no time to go up to his room. So we squeezed into a phone booth, which was barely large enough for my tape recorder and us. Both of us had rather large stomachs, which protruded against each other. My breasts dangled over his shoulders! But somehow, an interesting and human interview emerged from this odd setting. I asked him if he was bitter about losing the election, and whom he felt had knifed him in the back. I also suggested that he might be his own worst enemy - the man they love to hate in New Zealand. In some cases, his answers were probably more honest and sincere than many he gave to other reporters back home.

Also on the floor of Parliament, I spied another old friend with whom I'd shared some "tight squeezes" of a different nature. That was Michael Cox, who once was the Opposition Finance Spokesman. He'd arrived in Washington at the time of two formal Washington dinners. I managed to get him an invitation to both, but he was required to wear a black tie to the ritzy and exclusive White House Correspondents' Dinner. The problem was that he'd come to Washington without a black tie and tuxedo. The girls in charge of the White House dinner allowed me to bring him in at the last minute, after taking one look at him and breathing, "He's gorgeous." Managing to secure that invitation alone was quite a feat. Reservations for the event are made several months in advance, and a security check is usually performed, since the President and most of his Cabinet, as well as most of the Congress, attend the function.

And so Mike and I found ourselves wandering around the Washington Hilton, with an hour to go before the dinner. There were no shops open to rent tuxedos. Suddenly I spotted a nearby restaurant where the waiters wore tuxes. The problem was that most of them, recent immigrants from South America or Asia, were smaller in stature. Mike is a brawny Kiwi, standing at least six feet, four inches. We bribed a waiter, who found us several tuxedo jackets and black bow ties from the back. As we stood in front of the restaurant, trying to squeeze his huge frame into them, several customers came by. They asked Mike about the dinner menu, and he did a very professional job of making one up for them. As he put on each jacket, a splitting sound betrayed the fabric giving way. Finally, we gave up and took our $10 bow tie downstairs. The authorities allowed Mike through, and we had a thoroughly enjoyable dinner. Mike even met most of the top American officials, who didn't appear to notice that he was the only man there not sporting a penguin getup.

Another picture which stays in my mind from Wellington is that of thousands of Japanese sailors walking into and out of the many shops, carrying enormous bags of sheepskin rugs and other fine New Zealand products. Their destroyer was in port, and the sailors seemed intent on buying out the city. The sight of the Japanese destroyer and the sailors in the streets reinforced to me that the present trade relationship with Japan is much more important than the fact that American soldiers and sailors helped New Zealand fight off the Japanese during the Second World War. The ANZUS defense treaty came into effect as a result of that war. But, as Prime Minister Lange often pointed out, many of the younger New Zealanders don't remember that America helped keep them free of Japanese domination; rather, they remember America as the country that dragged them into the disastrous and divisive Vietnam War. That makes Japan the victor, and America the loser, in the eyes of a good many New Zealanders.

It was also easier to understand New Zealand's preoccupation with nuclear matters, after visiting the exquisite country. New Zealand is a rather isolated gem in the South Pacific. Many of its citizens, especially the younger ones, believe they are not threatened by invasion from any outside power. But they do believe America's nuclear defenses would somehow drag them into a nuclear exchange, just as they felt dragged into the Vietnam conflict. Their position was that they were unlikely to be the target of a nuclear attack if they eschewed all nuclear weapons and nuclear power.

Another member of Parliament invited me to stay in their home, where I met their friends and neighbors and got a better feel for their point of view at an elegant dinner party. The next day they took me to a fantastic North Island farm, which had been in their family for generations. This one was as splendid as the High Country sheep station I'd visited, but the scenery was much different. Here, there were no stark, snow-covered mountains. Instead, the hills were rounded, green, and lush. Even in mid-winter, the fields were verdant, and some of the native bush looked tropical to my eyes. Huge wild lemons grew on bushes around the house, and a jungle of colorful flowers exploded everywhere. The owner caught two horses from his fields, and we galloped over the mountains, dodging herds of friendly sheep and spirited horses, insistent on following us. Back from our ride, he took me to the shearing shed, where he attempted to teach me to use a shearing knife. Although it was electric-powered, I found it heavy and awkward, and could manage only a few seconds. A few meager pieces of fluff later, I turned the job back over to a professional.

As is often the case, appearances can be deceiving. One might assume that families who farm these magnificent stretches of land would be comfortable and well off indeed. But I learned that New Zealand farmers, like their counterparts in the United States, are struggling through hard times. To meet their debts and try to create a secure life for themselves, they have resorted to typical Kiwi ingenuity. They have diversified into other crops, notably berries and kiwifruit. Venison herds, which are raised for sale in country and for export overseas, are also emerging on many New Zealand farms.

I returned briefly to Auckland, where I met with an attorney and some business associates before boarding a plane for the three-hour flight across the Tasman to Australia. In Sydney, my past came together with my present, and the small, incestuous nature of the radio business was again brought home to me. My friend Geoffrey Whitehead, the former Director General of Radio New Zealand, was then the Director of the Australian Broadcasting Commission. Charged with reorganizing the chaotic ABC, Geoffrey was making thousands of enemies, as would anyone in that position; but the fact that he was an Englishman, brought in from New Zealand, did not add to his popularity in Australia, where he was referred to as a "whinging Kiwi Pom."

The day I arrived, a group of Australian elder statesmen had written a letter, excoriating the changes made at the ABC. Geoffrey decided to go public, and lash back. By coincidence, I phoned him from my client's office. His secretary said he was in the midst of a news conference. No, she told me, he was not about to resign, although there certainly was pressure on him to do so. When my editors learned he was having a news conference and hadn't invited them, they complained publicly. I was able, however, to facilitate an interview between them and the besieged Geoffrey, who handled himself very well despite tough, aggressive questioning.

Also in Sydney, I connected with a former colleague who had left the radio business after suffering "reporter's burnout," an occupational hazard of the profession that sometimes crops up when one has spent too much time covering too many tragedies. The most logical preventive measure, reporting upbeat or inspiring stories, doesn't work well, unfortunately, because "happy news" isn't really considered news.

Interestingly, I have observed that men seem to burn out faster than women do. Perhaps this is because men are more accustomed to being in a dominant role; they get frustrated running around or waiting for people to show up or for events to break. They are typically more concerned than women about establishing themselves in their own right, not merely passing along what some Senator, scientist, or criminal is doing. Women, for better or for worse, have been conditioned by society and the culture to be patient and subservient. But on the plus side, fewer women than men in this business are felled by problems of overdrinking or drugs. And now, with plastic surgery, we can last a lot longer on television.

Certainly such was not the problem in my Australian friend's case. He had chosen to go out while on top, rather than on the bottom. This was a marked contrast to many of my American friends who were fired from their jobs in their mid forties or fifties, to be replaced by younger, more ambitious and more aggressive reporters. Often, I would see my displaced colleagues in an alcoholic haze, clustered around a Washington bar. Far better to go out, like my vibrant, sane, and healthy Australian, during a high point, than to fade away like a passing season.

When I returned to Auckland a few days later to prepare for a television appearance with Cathy Saunders, I relied heavily on my friend Eileen Fredriksen, a fellow Virginian who was visiting her family in New Zealand. Not only is Eileen one of the most beautiful women I know, she is also smart, chic, and honest. I could always depend on her for an honest appraisal of my clothes, makeup and performance. She also gave me sound advice on what was and was not acceptable in New Zealand. Moreover, she even loaned me her shoes to wear on the show.

She helped coach me as I sat through countless hours of makeup and hair styling. She was as surprised as I was about how tightly scripted the show was, though I later understood when I saw how intricate the show was. Major segments were shuffled about and interspersed with entertainment features. Eileen and I spent hours with the producer, going over the questions I would ask Opposition Leader Jim McLay, and rehearsing what I would say on the show and when I would say it. We also tried to get Prime Minister Lange on the show, but he was too busy. I knew he would make verbal mincemeat of me in an interview, but I still looked forward to a spirited question-and-answer session with him on TV.

McLay also handled himself well. He was sharp and quick on his feet, and I exhausted my scripted questions before our time was up; this enabled me to revert to my usual practice of "winging it," which was a much more natural format for me.

When at last it was time to return home to the States, I chose a flight with a brief stopover in Tahiti at sunrise. The island - and my memories of my short stay there - are magical. We were greeted at the airport by a small group of Polynesian musicians and singers. The sun was just coming up over the green rugged mountains and the turquoise sea.

We were ushered upstairs to the Air New Zealand lounge, where native hostesses serving fresh orange juice, croissants, papaya, and French coffee welcomed us. My two hours in Tahiti offered a taste of paradise.

As we began the next leg of our journey, I persuaded the crew to allow me into the cockpit for the takeoff. Tahiti and Bora Bora faded into the distance as we flew over a vast coral reef that led to the great expanse of the Pacific. The joyous prospect of seeing my family again was tempered only by my reluctance to leave the South Pacific. It was as if I was torn between two homelands - one of my birth, the other of my heart.

My Eastern flight from Los Angeles left at two a.m., following an eight-hour layover which was far less luxurious than the time I'd spent on Air New Zealand. In addition, our journey progressed during a ferocious thunderstorm which whitened the knuckles of even the most stalwart passengers before we landed perilously indeed in Kansas City. This, it turned out, would be the year in which nearly two thousand people died in plane accidents.

My terrifying experiences flying across the country that day gave me pause to consider the trips I'd taken on Air New Zealand and Qantas. Somehow, I did not believe they would have risked the lives of passengers and crew by landing in such dangerous conditions just to meet a time schedule and have a jump on the competition. My own feeling is that most American carriers make far too many compromises in safety because of the fierce competition and the sheer volume of traffic in the United States.

A final thought struck me as I searched the crowds in the U.S. airports and gazed down at the jumble of houses in metropolises such as Los Angeles and Washington. That thought was that people seem to be more valuable in New Zealand and Australia than in the overcrowded USA, and it may be easier to discover your own worth in those South Pacific countries. Perhaps Richard Nixon was right when he said, "The Twenty-First Century belongs to Australia," and I would add New Zealand as well.

****

There have now been more trips to New Zealand and Australia - seven in all at this writing. And, since I am an independent and can work out my own job and travel schedule, I am certain there will be many others. My life is now deeply intertwined with this exquisite part of the world.

Each trip was busier than the one before. One trip culminated with the plans to publish this book. There were several offers, but I had the best rapport with the editor at "Harper - Collins, New Zealand," Mark Bathurst, so I went with them. Ten months later, I returned to New Zealand for the book promotion tour. That was a heady experience; to do about 10 radio, TV., or newspaper interviews a day, plus give several speeches. I was treated like visiting royalty, and did not have to scrounge for myself as I did on other trips. The book sold well, and made it to the best seller list. We had some tough competition at that time, with books by Jeffrey Archer and Allen Dunn also on the list, so I am deeply humbled by it. Of course, they sold in the thousands, or perhaps millions, and made big money. My earnings were very modest, but it was a heady experience for a first book.

Other trips to New Zealand and Australia were not as pleasant. In 1996, as the radio industry began to consolidate and fire people, I lost my job at Radio New Zealand, after twenty years of hard work. I was not the only one "terminated" but that did not make it any easier. The way it occurred was especially painful; with a terse fax from manager Lynn Snowden saying "my services were no longer required." Months later she did the same to other colleagues. Since the same trends were occurring around the world, I also lost my major stations in Australia, Israel, and South Africa at about the same time. I was devastated. This all took place about a year after Steve and I divorced, and both boys were in college. I had nightmares about becoming a "bag lady," losing everything, not being able to support my boys, and having to live on the street.

Fortunately, at about this time a listener in Perth, Australia bought me a first class, round-the-world ticket. He did so because he liked my voice!

I made it a very hard working trip, visiting 21 cities in 31 days. Those cities extended from London, to Johannesburg, South Africa (where I was terrified by the exploding crime rate), to Perth, all across Australia, and then several major cities in New Zealand. I managed to reestablish myself with commercial stations, and recaptured some of my listeners. But, I will probably never again make the kind of money I made while working with the nationally - supported stations. On the other hand, I no longer have to work seven days a week, for 10 to 16 hours a day. Everything has its season, and its compensation.

The next trip to New Zealand, in 1999, proved to be one of the most exciting ones so far. It was a fitting way to end the millennium. I sent myself on this trip, because APEC was holding its convention in Auckland. President Clinton was going, as were many of my colleagues in the White House press corps (those who could afford the very expensive trips; even the wealthy news organizations are cutting down on travel). President Clinton planned to stay on for an Official Visit; making him the first American President since Lyndon Johnson to visit New Zealand. In addition, 20 other heads of states, and their senior advisors and press, were attending the conference. I felt I would have lost all credibility with my American and New Zealand colleagues if I had not attended.

The trip was fascinating. I began in my beloved Queenstown, where I was honored to again stay with my dear friends, Warren and Lorraine Cooper. Warren had left national politics, having been both Foreign and Defense Minister, and was again serving as Mayor of Queenstown. This couple, along with their friends, John and Trish Davis, have done so much to make Queenstown one of the most magnificent resorts in the world.

The Coopers arranged speeches, radio interviews, and of course, skiing for me at Coronet Peak. I donated my speech to charity, and was pleased we raised several thousand dollars. From the window of the Coopers home, we could look out over the marvelous Lake Wakatipu, (one of the deepest and most majestic in the world), the snow-covered "Remarkable" Mountains, view the cable car, and see Kiwis and their intrepid tourists undertake the New Zealand form of two person hang - gliding. It looked peaceful, exhilarating in the clear mountain air, and terrifying. I believe I might have had a heart attack if I tried that, bungee jumping, the luge ride, or some of the other more death-defying sports in Queenstown. As it was, skiing and horseback riding were challenges enough. But many of my colleagues from the White House took the death-defying bungee jumping plunge, hurtling 150 feet down towards the river, only to be jerked up again at the last minute by the cord. This happened several times until they lost momentum, and remained there, head-first, "dangling in the wind," until rescued by boat. Several of my friends said my graphic descriptions of New Zealand, and the photos I showed them, encouraged them to visit Queenstown and risk their lives!

My Queenstown trip lasted for six days; then up to Christchurch to visit my "NewsTalk" station, do some live interviews, and visit with several members of the Lawn clan. Next stop, a terrifying flight in a small plane, over the mountains, to Nelson. Even my Kiwi friends are nervous about these small planes, which must constantly buck winds and turbulence. In Nelson, I stayed with my dear friend Lorraine MacIntosh, a smashing blonde scientist who was, at the time, President of the Chamber of Commerce. We did more speeches, radio tours and interviews, ended up on the front page of the newspaper, and even had a helicopter ride, which was breathtaking, and less frightening than the planes. We missed the chance to ski together again, since the spring conditions were too sloshy. In addition, the crises in East Timor was heating up, with hundreds of residents being brutally slaughtered because they had voted for independence. The world leaders coming to Auckland would be engulfed in that, and I was anxious to get up there and start reporting. I convinced Lorraine to travel up to Auckland with me; she got press credentials, and was on her way.

Auckland was superbly run. Even with 21 Heads of State, and thousands of visitors, Auckland performed flawlessly. Most of the policemen and women in New Zealand had been sent up to help, and planning had been underway for three years. There were several demonstrations, but they were peacefully contained on street corners. The only time there was a slight problem was a week later, in Christchurch, when the

Chinese President did not like a protest against him, and he delayed his VIP dinner by 90 minutes. But, in Auckland, all was tolerant and smooth.

We worked frantically, day and night, but it was worth it. The first night, I broadcast until 2:00 in the morning, and got thrown into press conferences immediately with my old friends, the Prime Minister, Foreign Minister, and Trade Minister. At 6 in the morning, we staggered into press breakfasts with them. In the interim, on the first night, I slept on the desks, or on couches in the vast Aotea Centre, which had been converted into a giant media and briefing facility. I decided not to stay with my dear friends, Lesley and Robert Max, because they were too far from the center of town. The inner city was sealed off to all but official cars, and many of us were in the same predicament. By the second night, Lorraine had found a college dorm room I could stay in at Auckland University. It was only one block away - straight up the hill - and was the warmest place I stayed in in New Zealand. I always suffer from the lack of central heating - being a real American wimp! It was wonderful to be in a small room where I could blast the space heater, and recreate a sauna effect!

As for Lorraine, she had her own happy ending to the trip. She met a Spanish Yachtsman, who was competing in trials for the America's Cup race. Although from two very different backgrounds, sparks ignited, and it was love at first sight! They married 3 years later, and divide their time between New Zealand and Spain. I am so happy I invited Lorraine to go to Auckland with me!

The trip to Auckland was extremely gratifying professionally and personally. I was especially touched by the policemen, who remembered me, and had me pose for photos with them. A tea lady claimed meeting me was "the greatest thing that ever happened to her in her life!" Even the young journalism students came up to meet me and pose with me. I said, I didn't think anyone in New Zealand heard me much anymore, since I no longer had dominant media outlets. They surprised me by saying, they all read my book as part of their classes! I am gratified. I always said, I wrote the book for the ages of 15 to 25, which I remembered as an especially painful time of adjustment in life. If I can inspire and guide the young adults, I will have fulfilled a major goal in my life!

The APEC meetings went well, with key decisions made regarding trade and the defense of the decimated region of East Timor. Once again, New Zealand and American troops were working together, even if they were still not official "allies." But, the deep and wonderful friendship had been enhanced.

From Auckland, there was the quick return by Clinton and the White House press corps to Queenstown, where my friends risked their necks in adventure sports. Then, back up to Christchurch, for the "State Visit" part of the trip.

My wonderful relatives, Helen and Ross Lawn, picked me up at the airport, drove me around, and offered me generous hospitality at their beautiful home. Christchurch is truly the "garden city," and I have never seen more impeccable gardens in my life. It was wonderful to once again have reunions with the Lawn Clan in Christchurch; this time I really felt a part of their family.

President Clinton performed well in Christchurch. The people appeared to love him; unlike their reception for the visiting Chinese President in the city at the same time. He was picketed by protestors; President Clinton got out of his motorcade and pressed the flesh. At one point, he held a news conference in a 1918 roadhouse called "The Sign of the Takahe." Reporters and White House staff stood out in the cold for nearly an hour before it began. But, it proved to be a marvelous reunion for me with many of my New Zealand friends, including Don McKinnon, former Prime Minister Bolger, and other Ministers and top diplomats. Now that the intense, and successful APEC meeting was over, they had time to relax; let down their hair, and talk about personal matters. On the American side, the economic advisors and others discussed their feat of bungee jumping. They said they felt stronger by submitting to the ordeal, but remained afraid of heights.

After the press conference, our bus traveled down the road in the Presidential motorcade, as the residents poured out onto the streets to meet Clinton. It was such a thrill to see how excited the people of my beloved New Zealand were about my President. Truly an historic moment, and I was proud to be there, "up close and personal."

From Christchurch, I few up to one of my favorite places, Wanganui. There, my dear, creative friend Jean Stewart took care of me, arranged speeches, and let me stay in her magnificent home on a hill overlooking her ornate gardens and the lake below. I was thrilled to engage in two other gallops along the black, volcanic Castlecliff beach, on horses provided by my friend Jenna Nicholson. For a northerner in tame Washington D.C., it is an adventure beyond belief! We gallop along the Tasman Sea, jump over logs that have washed ashore in the rough surf, and see the Mt. Ruapehu Volcano in the distance. It was not erupting at the time, as it did with great force in 1995. This was the same volcano I had once skied on with my young sons.

This time the horse rides were more dramatic, since I was riding a steed which had been rescued from the wild, and saved from slaughter by those who thought the herds of Kaimanawa horses needed to be culled. "Darkie" was a wonderful black horse, but had enough of me on the second ride. He managed to throw me on the beach. One minute we were galloping together; the next I was flying though the air without him. I lay there, covered with sand, four hours before my plane was to leave for the U.S. I shook off thoughts of spending weeks in a hospital, so I staggered up, traded horses with my colleague, and galloped back.

At the Wanganui airport, Jean and two wonderful Maori friends saw me off; presenting me with soulful Maori gifts and prayers. In Auckland airport, I met with my good friend and editor, Mark Bathurst, and his partner, Susan. Then off to California. This time, I had good things to look forward to on my way home. The flights were long, but delightful. I left, confident I will visit New Zealand many times in the future; my life will always be bound up with the good people of that wonderful country. Whether I return as US Ambassador; a journalist; or a tourist, I will return!

The First Bush Presidency

When George Bush Sr. became President in January 1989, he inherited most of the problems of the Reagan Administration. The massive debt continued to burgeon to the $1 trillion level. It has been said that when the United States sneezes, other countries catch pneumonia, and it is certainly true that the fiscal struggles in the States exacerbated those in New Zealand, Australia, and other nations.

President Bush was far brighter and more experienced than his predecessor and former boss, Ronald Reagan, but his confusing speech patterns and eccentric mannerisms unfortunately overshadowed Bush's strengths. Bush, whom the camera treated harshly, extemporized more, and his ad lib remarks were often garbled and difficult for reporters and commentators to understand, much less distill into a 30-second radio report or even shorter sound bite.

Reagan, on the other hand, was a former actor who relied on his Washington "scriptwriters" to produce the beautiful prose which he was known to deliver in classic Hollywood style. He could easily galvanize many segments of the public, while Bush too often confused them or turned them off. Compared with Reagan, as someone wryly observed, "Bush looks like something that came out of a microwave oven."

From a reporter's point of view, Bush was a pleasure to cover. He assigned some extremely capable staff to deal with the media. In the White House, bald, portly, funny Marlin Fitzwater stayed on as press secretary. When he announced Fitzwater's appointment, Bush was asked why, having promised new faces in the government, he had named a holdover from the Reagan Administration. The ever self-deprecating Marlin said, "I'd love to have a new face." Throughout his years serving the Bush White House, Fitzwater tried to streamline his physical appearance through diet and exercise. But world crises intervened, and 20-hour days made sensible eating - and the sleek new body he longed for - an impossible dream. Alas, the special coconut candies I would buy him on trips to Florida and the myriad confections other reporters brought him didn't make his task any easier.

The general press staff included some fine professionals. Among them was Sean Walsh, who was open, friendly, and as handsome as a California movie star. He was nice to all reporters, from the high and mighty to the lowly, and his fair and democratic style helped smooth relations with the media. Of course, President Bush himself set the tone, by making himself far more accessible than Ronald Reagan had. While Reagan had held only a handful of well-orchestrated news conferences during his eight years in office, President Bush would speak to reporters at a moment's notice. He was not afraid of public burnout, even though he made little news with some of his appearances.

The press staffs at the State Department and Pentagon were also extremely helpful and professional. Margaret Tutwiler, spokeswoman for Secretary of State James Baker, was often criticized for her Alabama cadence and style, which foreign listeners sometimes found offensive. Nonetheless, she earned the respect of the press on her first day on the job, when she admitted she knew little about foreign affairs but vowed to work hard to get us honest answers for our questions. This she did, by and large, although the responses she produced were sometimes off the record or "on background." Tutwiler also made it clear to the press that she spoke with authority. She informed us, "I know this President and this Secretary of State very well, and will have full access to them." Indeed, she had known both of them on a personal basis for many years, and had been a key political adviser to them. That shared history and her access proved far more valuable than the raw foreign policy experience she lacked.

Likewise, Pentagon spokesman Pete Williams proved a model of strength, warmth, efficiency, and competence. To reporters like me, those attributes were invaluable during the Persian Gulf War, when both press and public were clamoring for every scrap of information they could get. By fostering good relationships with the press, Williams established loyalties which served him well during delicate high-pressure times. Stories began to circulate about his personal life, rumors sown by his adversaries in hopes that he might lose his job. But most reporters found the stories irrelevant and scurrilous, and Defense Dick Cheney staunchly supported him as well. Thus the efforts to discredit a loyal and popular civil servant fizzled.

Bad Economic Times and the United 811 Tragedy

When President Bush became President in 1988, he inherited a miserable and faltering economy, and he did little to improve it. One of the many consequences of the fiscal crisis, which affected people all around the globe, was the decline in the standards of U.S. airlines. Many of the carriers were crippled by the deregulation promulgated during the Reagan years. The air traffic control system was rickety, in the wake of Reagan's firing of thousands of skilled controllers during their strike. The weaker airlines, even those which had been giants in their day, collapsed. These included Pan American and Eastern. Even the mighty United Airlines suffered setbacks in quality in some areas. This situation led to a tragedy which directly affected New Zealand.

On February 25, 1989, on a United jet bound from Honolulu to Auckland, catastrophe struck Flight 811, when the cargo door of flight 811 blew open. Nine passengers were sucked from the plane to a terrifying death over the Pacific Ocean. One of them was 24-year-old Lee Campbell from Wellington. He died because, according to The Wall Street Journal, a $3,027 repair job had not been made on the cargo door. Today experts are uncertain whether the exact cause of the tragedy was the faulty door or an electrical problem. It is all too clear, however, that whatever the cause, nine people died needlessly, and the rest of the passengers suffered unimaginable horrors as the plane limped back to Hawaii, where the pilot made a miraculous landing.

A tragedy like this is one of the most difficult stories for a reporter to cover. I learned of the accident at 9 a.m., Washington time. I immediately called Radio New Zealand and informed them that we had a major news emergency on our hands. Fortunately, from the standpoint of news, an energetic and alert editor was on duty. It was only 3:00 Saturday morning in New Zealand when the news broke, and we had the story on the air by 3:15. That is rare for a Saturday, when most radio stations are short-staffed. Moreover, on weekends the emphasis is on sports, and few radio stations are geared up for hard news stories. But Radio New Zealand rose to the occasion and was far ahead of anyone else in its coverage.

As one might guess, covering of a human tragedy is a two-edged sword. It is news, of course, but it can also be the source of great grief to the victims' survivors, or intense joy to those who learn their loved ones have lived through the ordeal. I did not know until a year after the United flight 811 tragedy that my news report had fueled an eerie premonition on the part of Lee Campbell's mother. Susan Campbell told the *Wall Street Journal* that she had awakened before dawn on that February morning. She felt a strange sense of foreboding, and beheld a clear picture of her son Lee in front of her. A few hours later, she awoke again, this time to a radio report on the accident involving flight 811. Presumably she was listening to a Radio New Zealand report, since we dominated the market and had more news than the other media at that hour. This is the kind of information that a reporter hates to bring home to a family. As a human being, and as a mother, I find it the hardest news of all to broadcast. Tragedies like this are the stuff of nightmares for years afterwards, and I share the grief of the families. Often, I cry after I broadcast, or read about, an especially poignant news story. My former husband found it odd that I should cry for strangers; but reporters do possess compassionate streaks, even as they strive for the sensational.

The United story continued to unfold after we broke the first bulletin. The horror intensified, as more families in New Zealand awoke and heard the somber news. Frantically they tried to phone the airport, or United, to learn the fate of their loved ones. Reporters were seeking information as well. United, overcautious in its response, refused to give much information until every name was accounted for. That policy needlessly prolonged the grief of families who could have learned good news an hour earlier. In desperation, some of the families telephoned me from New Zealand, to see if I could tell them about their relatives, but I was as much in the dark as they were. The story has now long since evaporated from the headlines; but for the families, the tragic repercussions will linger forever.

****

When George Bush moved into the Oval Office, I predicted he would launch a series of military actions. He did so, partly because he believed they were necessary and partly, I believe, because he felt it necessary to prove his manhood. He was still burdened by the "wimp" tag which had stuck to him throughout the bitter presidential campaign of 1988. In reality, he had performed bravely and boldly throughout his business and diplomatic career; nevertheless, he was unable effectively to communicate decisiveness to his constituents, the American public. Bush never fully mastered modern technology; the camera was not kind to him as it had been to his predecessor, the former movie actor, and thus he often appeared weak when he needed to convey strength.

Soon after he assumed office, Bush launched military strikes against Manuel Noriega of Panama. The President was determined to rid the Central American nation of its ruthless dictator, and disprove a recurring theory that during his term as Director of the CIA, Bush had been cozy with Noriega. Noriega and other unsavory characters often claimed they had been paid agents of the CIA, and that drug deals actually had been engineered to assist the United States.

The military action against Panama lasted only a few days, resulting in Noriega's arrest; his conviction followed several years later. But hundreds of Panamanians and some American soldiers died in the invasion. At this writing, there is democracy in Panama, and the population appears to have greater liberty. The downside is that families in Panama remain homeless in the wake of the invasion. The U.S. action in Panama did little to alleviate the crime, corruption, and drug problems there, and massive infusions of smuggled drugs whether from Panama or from other nations - continue to flow into the United States.

President Bush's biggest military operation, of course, was the Operation Desert Storm, the action launched against Iraqi dictator Saddam Hussein. Unquestionably the military operation in the Persian Gulf and the forging of a vast allied coalition were a brilliant success. But the sweet taste of Allied victory was marred by one bitter fact: despite the routing of the Iraqi troops, Saddam remained in power. He went on to terrorize the Kurds, driving them from their homes, and to punish the Shiite Moslems in the south. Thousands of men, women, and children died after the cease-fire went into effect.

Many military specialists still argue that Saddam could have been driven from power, if the war had gone beyond the first 100 hours of the ground assault. The Iraqi Republican Guards appeared to have been cut off and eventually may have surrendered, as did thousands of Iraqi troops in the desert. Without his loyal Guards, Saddam could not have survived.

I think my father analyzed Bush correctly when he said, "Bush thinks in increments of 100." He sometimes gave Congress deadlines of 100 days to pass crucial legislation (which was wishful thinking). Bush appeared to want to end the war at a tidy 100 hours, leaving many experts and soldiers flabbergasted and dismayed. The massive military buildup and counter invasion ended abruptly with a nighttime announcement of cease-fire coming from the White House - thousands of miles away from the scene of the action.

Coverage of the Gulf War was unlike that of any previous war, or any prior major news event. The Persian Gulf War was truly a CNN event. For the first time, nearly the entire civilized world was linked together by the Cable News Network, which I had long speculated would change the face of news reporting. This is why my advice to any young reporter starting out in the business is: Sell your soul to a cable news organization, if you can get in on the ground floor in any of the network's stations around the world. Unfortunately, I was too old - and too involved in raising my family by that point - to take the step myself when CNN began to take shape. (Now, of course, reporters can turn to Fox, MSNBC, or a number of all news organizations in this country or overseas).

Because of CNN, all the major military briefings were broadcast live around the world. All of my clients, as well as anyone else who had the cable service, could see the endless briefings from the military in Saudi Arabia, at the Pentagon, and occasionally from the White House or the State Department. There really was little need for stations to spend a small fortune to send a correspondent to Saudi Arabia, where he or she would spend most of the time holed up in a hotel, watching the same briefings viewed around the world. That was an extremely frustrating experience for reporters in the region, and many of them risked their lives to break away from the managed news and get to the scene of the action. Some of the correspondents, such as Bob Simon from CBS, were even captured in the process, and spent weeks in fear, deprivation, and horror at the hands of the Iraqis.

The whole Persian Gulf period was a frustrating and demanding one for me as well. Years earlier, I would have been on one of the first planes to Saudi Arabia. Now, however, there was no need to spend my limited funds to undertake such an expedition. Like millions of others around the globe, I remained glued to my television set. Fortunately, the Gulf War presented the enterprising journalist opportunities here at home. My editors began to rely on me to produce 25-second summaries of long and complicated briefings. I did not use any sound from a briefing itself, unless I attended it personally. Even then, I rarely fed tape, because my clients already had it; they all paid to subscribe to CNN, ABC, AP Radio, or any of the other services which provided live coverage.

Still, it was exciting to be able to supply my own analysis to put the story into focus for those listeners who had relied on me for many years. At least once a day I would go downtown to attend a White House briefing. Most of these were not broadcast; if they were, background segments in Marlin Fitzwater's office were held without tape, videos, or attribution. This gave us the chance to add some more flesh or insight to the story. But with or without the live international television coverage, informing the public of Iraq's invasion of Kuwait, the vast international mobilization, and the war itself were a grueling experience for journalists. It meant over a year of 18-hour workdays. That kind of intensity burns out many reporters, and a number of them drifted into quieter, less demanding fields after the war. Many, however, did not go voluntarily. Newsrooms all over the world, strapped financially after spending too much money to monitor the unfolding story in the Persian Gulf, were forced to cut back their staffs after the war. First, travel was cut sharply for White House and State Department reporters, who were accustomed to traveling around the world at a moment's notice. Then, some of the major news organizations closed their Washington bureaus completely as more efficient technologies evolved. The world was linked together electronically to a greater degree than ever before and, as in many other fields, the human element was becoming less essential. Those who survived were truly the best, smartest, most glamorous - or most ruthless - in their field.

The Hillary Morgan Story

Despite the trend toward international media, there are still some stories that an individual reporter can break and nurture. Again, they often infringe on the right of privacy and are a two-edge sword. The case of Dr. Elizabeth Morgan and her young daughter, Hillary, is a case in point. This was one of the most celebrated, publicized, and perhaps destructive child custody cases of the century. I tried carefully to avoid taking sides in the dispute and attempted not to judge one parent over the other. But I was very concerned about the welfare of the child, and was pleased and gratified when New Zealand took the same attitude.

The case had received a great deal of publicity in the United States and Britain for several years. Dr. Morgan, a brilliant plastic surgeon, accused her ex-husband and his father of molesting Hillary. She did not want him to have unsupervised custody of the child, as was ordered by a judge in Washington, D.C. Dr. Eric Foretich, an equally gifted oral surgeon, swore he had never molested Hillary or her older stepsister, as was charged by others involved in the cases.

The arguments between the family became more vicious, and Elizabeth became increasingly certain that her suspicions were well founded. Finally, she asked her parents to spirit the child away. Since the parents were British citizens, they first took her into hiding in England. Then they took her to Christchurch, New Zealand. Since Elizabeth failed to produce the child for visits with her ex-husband, she was sent to jail. Regardless of whether her allegations of child sexual abuse were accurate, it was an extraordinary sacrifice for a woman of her background to spend several years in one of the roughest prisons in the United States.

There she witnessed the savage rapes of other inmates, and was forced to live in one of the most brutal societies in the country. It took an act of Congress to gain her release from jail, but she still was under court order to produce Hillary. Fortunately, while she was still in prison, she fell in love with a federal U.S. judge and married him immediately upon her release. At some point she made her way to New Zealand, and that is where the saga began for me.

February 23, 1990, was the morning before my older son David's Bar Mitzvah. This is a major event in the life of every young Jewish man and woman, and signals their acceptance into the adult community of Judaism. The ceremony involves years of study and preparation. It is also the occasion of a massive family reunion and, in many cases, parties the night before and the day after the Bar Mitzvah. As David's mother, I had responsibility of preparing for the social festivities and ensuring that my son practice his own role in the ceremony. The intensive study was a combined effort involving David, the rest of the family, the rabbis, and tutors.

At about ten o'clock in the morning, before the first night of the Bar Mitzvah, I received a call from a woman who said she represented the "Friends of Elizabeth Morgan." She had a big story for me, if I agreed to use it right away. My first response was, "Do I have to?" I was just about to go to a family business meeting which my father had arranged, since all family members and lawyers were in Washington at the same time. The voice at the other end of the line said she would be quite happy to give it to another reporter, if I was too busy to use it. That was an offer I couldn't refuse. She told me that Elizabeth, Hillary, and the grandparents were "somewhere in New Zealand, and had been there for several months." Eric Foretich had apparently tracked them down through a private detective, and was about to reveal their location. My caller wanted me to do so first, so I could give the people of New Zealand the entire story. Of course, they wanted me to slant it to Dr. Morgan's perspective, but I played it straight, which was dramatic enough.

Again, it was early Saturday morning when I broadcast the story, and only one hapless editor was on duty. Fortunately, she was one of the best we could have. I asked Lee Pearson whether she had heard of the case, or whether it had broken in New Zealand. She said she was unaware of the Morgan-Foretich battle, and I filled her in, explaining that it had been a major ongoing saga here in the States for several years. I did the straight story, and then, a few hours later, learned that the family was in Christchurch. I filed a follow-up item, and then suggested to Lee that we copyright it and offer it to the wire services. At the same time, I released it to my American station, USA Radio News, which had nearly 900 stations in this country. They released it promptly and gained credit for it in the United States.

Then I left the house and began my errands. Shortly after the story ran, all hell broke loose! The U.S. stations traced the story to me, and the phone began ringing off the hook. By the time I got home several hours later, there had been over 200 phone calls from all the major U.S. television and radio networks, the local newspapers, *The New York Times*, and countless others. The reporters frantically needed a live body to talk to and couldn't reach anyone else - all the other principals to the story were either out of the country or refused to identify themselves. The reporters begged me to come in for interviews, but I told them I had to be in Temple in a few hours for the first part of my son's ceremony. (In our temple, the rite begins on Friday night, when the father passes the holy Torah to his son. Then it continues with the major part of the ceremony the next morning.)

Our house was a scene of utter confusion, and my son David was in tears. This was supposed to be the biggest night of his life; he was justifiably nervous, and his mother was stealing his thunder. I tried to apologize and help him understand my dilemma. I could not ignore my colleagues, either, at a time like this. I tried to explain that I might have had a similar problem if I were a doctor and had a patient who was dying. But of course, David still felt shunted aside at a crucial juncture in his life. Finally we agreed to a compromise: I would give the local TV. stations interviews, if they could bring their satellite trucks to my house. And we would have our exchanges outside, since David was too distraught to have them inside and there was so much chaotic activity in the house.

An hour before we had to leave for the temple, trucks for three of the stations pulled up in front of our house. We were on a busy street, and our neighbors were wondering if a murder had been committed. We stood in front of the house, and I did each interview live. The February winds were blowing and the light was bad. When I saw myself on reruns later, I looked like Quasimodo with a bad hairstyle. The interviewers asked what would become of Hillary Morgan. I could not predict the outcome with any authority, of course, but I ventured to say that the people of New Zealand were very fair, and usually put the interest of children first. I believed that would happen in this case. Indeed, my assessment was borne out two years later, when the courts in New Zealand ruled that Hillary and her family could remain in that country.

After the first set of interviews, a fourth local television station called. I told them it was simply too late to do an interview for their early news, but gave them directions to the temple. I said I could come out front and meet them after the service, so we could do an interview for their late news. We ended up doing just that in the midst of a hailstorm! I knew our rabbi would not allow them to bring their cameras into the temple and destroy the solemnity of the occasion; so we met out front, where we discussed young Hillary, a girl torn apart in a fierce custody battle. The temple made a strange backdrop for the interview, but inside, David performed like a pro and his Bar Mitzvah went off smoothly. By that time, many of the members of the congregation had seen me on TV. before they arrived, so they understood about the pressure we were under.

As for the Hillary Morgan case, it dragged on for years. It was still a big story for me several months later, as I bounced back and forth between interviews with the Morgan camp and the Foretich supporters. But the story had been broken, and now was the domain of a million reporters. At my suggestion, some American reporters went to New Zealand for several months, but they managed to create bad relations with the good people of Christchurch. That was unexpected, but I should have anticipated it. You see, many of the people in that wonderful city had known about Hillary for months, and kept the situation quiet out of respect for her privacy. I wish I could have done the same, and know many people dislike me for having broken the story. In my own defense, I will say that it was not something I sought out, and I was doing only what was requested of me. This goes with the territory - that often-symbiotic relationship between the media and the public, each of whom uses the other.

There was an interesting postscript to the story, years later. Elizabeth and Hillary – now called Ellen – were able to return to the United States with help from the US Congress. Steve and I had divorced in 1994. In the year 2000, I was blessed to marry another fantastic man, and one whose tastes are closer to mine; Charles Sneiderman. Our wedding was performed on top of the Kennedy Center by Judge Paul Michel, the second husband of Elizabeth Morgan. We had become good friends in the aftermath of the ordeal. So life goes on in strange, complicated, but fulfilling ways.

Years of Blood and Terror

As this book draws near its end, the reporting and the learning process go on. There has been a flood of major events in the past years that reflect a world wracked with violence. There have been deadly plane crashes, including the Soviets' downing of a Korean Airlines jet; another major air crash in Japan; and the crash of an American military jet in Newfoundland which took the lives of nearly three hundred servicemen and women who were returning from dangerous duty in the Sinai desert. There was also a fatal plane crash in Detroit, in which the only survivor was a four-year-old girl whose family, like many others, perished in the crash. There was the terrorist downing of Pan Am Flight 103 over Lockerbie Scotland; one of the most horrific acts of terrorism against innocent travelers ever; until the hijacking and terrorist attacks of 9/11/2001. There were also crashes of other American and Egyptian flights, as well as disasters in other parts of the world. I never forget the horror of those events, and think of the terror the passengers and crews experienced as they hurled towards their deaths. In the midst of these large-scale accidents, there was also the crash of John F. Kennedy Junior's private plane off the waters of New England. While talented and intelligent people died in all the crashes, this was so horrific and unnecessary, and happened to a man, his wife, and sister in law; three young adults who might have been anything in the world. In Kennedy's case, he may have even become President. In France, there was also the senseless car crash of Britain's Princess Diana and her lover. Again, a loss to the world which cannot be replaced. All these tragedies I had to report on, while trying to be as respectful, dignified, and unsensational as possible – usually an impossible task to achieve.

The world has seen a vast increase in terrorism, especially in the Middle East and Europe, and now in this country. Witness the massacres at the Rome and Vienna airports, where innocent passengers were slaughtered as they awaited planes during the Christmas and New Year holidays. There was the bombing of the Federal Building in Oklahoma City – an act of terror against Americans by some deranged and hate-filled Americans. And who could forget the hijacking of the TWA and the Egyptian jets, and the Achilles Lauro passenger liner? In those cases, too, innocent passengers were killed, and some were brutally tortured first. But, all of these cases were eclipsed in scope a few years later, by the attacks against the World Trade Center and the Pentagon. Few people in this nation ever thought they would live to see the day when office workers had to chose between jumping to their deaths from the upper floors of the gleaming World Trade Center Towers; or face the torture of being burned alive. The passengers in the hijacked planes, or the workers in the Pentagon had no choice – they were taken by the flames or the lack of oxygen. Other attacks continue by deranged terrorists, including the senseless killings of good people in Mumbai, India. Al Qaeda and its followers continue to practice their cults of suicide and murder and wars intensify against them in Iraq, Afghanistan, and other parts of the world.

Among other crises points, the Persian Gulf tension continued, prompting a huge military buildup by America and its Allies in the Gulf. In 1991 and 1992, the Persian Gulf skirmishes and invasion took place. The Coalition drove the Iraqis out of Kuwait, and killed thousands of Iraqi troops (many of whom may have been forced into the battle against their will, and were quick to surrender). The US and allied operation ended prematurely, keeping Saddam Hussein in power and making the world a far more dangerous place. Through all the violence, the basic problems of the Palestinian situation, or the Arab-Israeli conflict, have not been fully resolved. For a brief while, during the Clinton Administration, it looked as though the Israelis and Palestinians would be able to live in peace, with two small nations side by side. But, the attempted settlement ruptured for a variety of reasons. The deadly dance between the two sides continued, with homicide bombings and retaliation. Some sought "martyrdom," while others became martyrs, while they were innocently sitting in a Pizza parlor, dancing in a disco, driving in a vehicle, staying home, or commemorating the Passover Sedar.

Not all the tragedies have been manmade. Brutal natural disasters occurred which killed thousands of innocents, such as the earthquakes in Mexico, Haiti, the Tsunami in Indonesia, and the volcano in Colombia.

Assassinations of great leaders such as Egyptian President Anwar Sadat have hampered the world's endless quest for peace. And, in that same year of 1981, there were attempts on the lives of both Pope John Paul II and President Reagan. Both men miraculously survived those attacks, displaying some of the toughness inherent in leadership. Politics and revolution, such as the ouster of Ferdinand Marcos in the Philippines and President Duvalier in Haiti worked significant changes sometimes. In other cases, the basis country remained the same.

Technology, for all its benefits, has had its share of problems. The Challenger space shuttle exploded two minutes after launch, tragically killing seven gifted scientists and aviators. The long-term coverage of that explosion, with its tasteless dwelling on the recovery of the astronauts' remains, represented in my view, at least a new low in American journalistic standards.

The years 1985 and 1986 were also the years of the ANZUS crisis between New Zealand and Australia, an extremely depressing time for many in two countries which had once been stalwart allies. That crisis consumed much of my energy in addition to the other events. When a major story broke anywhere in the world, I found myself broadcasting for twenty hours at a stretch. Somehow, the Washington perspective - or news flowing into Washington from the crisis area was always in demand.

Before ANZUS, I had been known in Washington bureaucratic circles as "the butter queen" for all the questions I asked about New Zealand dairy imports into this country. Now I became notorious for my ANZUS questions. I even asked President Reagan a question about the issue during one of his formal news conferences, which was seen by about 60 million people. The crisis was just erupting then, and I wasn't certain he would be informed on it. So I phoned spokesman Larry Speakes' office first, to tell him I would pose the question if I was recognized. I asked him to brief the President so neither of us would look foolish. I didn't want Reagan to look at me and say, "Who the heck is ANZUS?"

The President gave a short but satisfactory answer. His response at that time held up, and became the basis for his administration's actions two years later, when it ruptured the defense relationship with New Zealand. That occurred during a meeting in San Francisco, one I had the privilege to cover for New Zealand and Australia. But the question at the news conference to President Reagan set the stage for all this, and I believe it was the first time a President had been asked about New Zealand or Australia matter during a formal, prime-time news conference - but it was not to be the last.

Later, Secretary of State Shultz and other top State Department officials accorded me exclusive interviews on the same topic. Although I report to several areas of the world, it is the South Pacific region which seems to capture the imagination of the Washington officials. It reached the point that, when I raised my hand, the White House or State Department spokesmen would look at me, smile, and say automatically, "Nothing about New Zealand today, Connie." This happened even if I was about to ask about a completely different topic. But I enjoyed the easygoing rapport we had, and after knowing each other for many years we could tease each other unmercifully.

The Clinton White House - A "Wag the Dog" Presidency?

The administration of the populist U.S. President, William J. Clinton, began with a burst of hope and confidence, but this feeling of euphoria was to be short-lived. At the start, I had political respect for the determined young team of Bill Clinton and Al Gore, and their dynamic and very capable wives, Hillary Rodham Clinton and Tipper Gore. While I respected many of their policies and aspirations for the country, I became disgusted by President Clintons sexual encounters, especially the relationship with the then-21 year old intern Monica Lewinsky. The President's reckless behavior, and lies to his family, supporters, and the nation, constituted an abuse of power which cannot be condoned under any circumstances. Fortunately, the full knowledge of the sexual misconduct did not erupt until the final stages of the Clinton-Gore Administration, and they were not completely paralyzed by it. In fact, despite the sex - or maybe because of it, Bill Clinton became an extremely popular President, while rabidly hated by people in some circles. He was the first elected president to be impeached in the House of Representatives. But, it did not stick in the Senate, and he attempted to make light of the entire impeachment process. It showed the wisdom of his earliest strategists, who campaigned on the motto "It's the economy stupid." With the economy booming, nothing stuck to the President. He survived, although the salacious sexual scandals will always be part of his legacy. But his wife, daughter, supporters, and staff members, suffered. Millions of dollars, and thousands of hours were spent defending this man, and keeping him in the presidency. In the process, the world got a view into the sexual life of the president that was shocking and unprecedented. And, young children heard terms such as "oral sex" in the media, and asked their embarrassed parents to explain it. One of the most benign descriptions was, "Oral is different from the written kind!"

From the start, the Clinton - Gore team had many enemies, and had to fight off a raft of legal investigations and accusations over the years. But they persevered and succeed in many important programs. In retrospect, many of the accusations against Bill Clinton appeared to have been justified.

The economy appeared to be strong and robust under Bill Clinton. It did not begin to fall apart until the end of his eight years. It might have been an artificial boom, or may have been part of the ordinary boom and bust cycle, which keeps economies from becoming too overheated. The Clintons lost many of the programs they wanted, especially health care reform. And, the President only succeeded when he became more moderate, and compromised with the Republicans. Right wing Republicans, and left wing Democrats, were the losers in this Administration, but I have to believe the American people were the winners, at least in terms of many moderate programs.

The Clinton Administration's initially sound footing became shaky early on, but this is the rule rather than the exception for new White House regimes. President Clinton was young, arrogant, and had a lot to overcome. The Administration had a very short honeymoon. It didn't take the public and the media long to lash into him and begin to criticize his every move. This phenomenon perhaps was captured best in a brilliant Time magazine cover story titled, "The Incredible Shrinking President." It noted, "With a White House staff shakeup and the lowest four-month approval ratings of any postwar president, many Americans are wondering whether he has what it takes."

But criticism of a president is nothing new, and comes with the territory. Bill Clinton had a long and often rocky road to travel. He was only forty-six years old when he was elected to occupy the Oval Office. He had been Governor of one of the smallest and poorest states in the nation, Arkansas, when he made the leap from the Governor's Mansion in Little Rock to the Washington White House. So perhaps he and his youthful, energetic and idealistic staff members could be forgiven a bit of arrogance when they made it to the center of the free world's political universe.

Clinton had to adjust to a larger scale of leadership. But even during the tense political campaigns he had to fight charges of draft dodging due to his opposition to the Vietnam War. Moreover, he was tagged as a womanizer who had engaged in numerous extramarital affairs. Eventually, the voting public accepted him despite these failings. The allegations did not cost him the nomination - as it did onetime presidential hopeful Gary Hart - or ultimately re-election. But, his political and moral reputation was tarnished, as was John F. Kennedy's following his death, when allegations of numerous affairs surfaced.

The long running lawsuit waged by Paula Jones, followed by the Monica Lewinsky scandal, cost the President millions of dollars in legal fees. Jones alleged Clinton exposed himself to her in a hotel room, and demanded sex. The President denied it, claiming her charges, and legal supporters, were part of a right wing cabal out to destroy him. The public may never know the full truth about this situation, but the graphic charges and alleged descriptions of the Presidents' anatomy demean him and the office. President Clinton eventually settled the lawsuit, reportedly for nearly a million dollars; this in addition to the astronomical legal fees. He was also prevented from practicing law in Arkansas, and before the United States Supreme Court. This was a major blow for any lawyer; especially for a man who had been Governor and President of the United States! Had Clinton settled the lawsuit from the beginning, there might not have been the Ken Starr report, the lying under oath, and the Impeachment proceedings and House vote against him.

The Paula Jones accusations were just one of a string of sexual charges against the President. The Monica Lewinsky case was the most dramatic. In it, he had oral sex, phone sex, and even cigar sex with a daughter of a Democratic supporter, who began her career as a White House intern.

The scandal engulfed many in the White House, and numerous White House employees or supporters had to make the pilgrimage before the Special Prosecutor's Grand Jury. That cost them time, emotional hardship, and thousands of dollars in legal fees, even if they knew nothing at all about the situation. In the White House press corps, we were shocked at Clintons' conduct and lack of honor. We thought he should have at least confessed, and had the decency to resign. But, Clinton was a survivor, and put himself above all others. On a humorous side, the sick jokes proliferated in the White House, as well as around the country. Some of my fellow reporters suggested we should wear knee pads to the briefings, and don rubber gloves when we shook the hands of the President!

In addition to Lewinsky, there were charges made by other women over the years. Jennifer Flowers talked about a 12 year relationship, but Bill Clinton only admitted to one incident. A former Miss America also said there had been a brief tryst in the back seat of Clintons limousine when he was Governor of Arkansas. She expressed remorse, but said they were both consenting adults. The Kathleen Willey accusations continue to be confusing and contradictory - she claims the president came after her sexually, in a room off the Oval Office, when she went to him in a state of depression and financial desperation, pleading for a paying job. Tragically, her husband committed suicide on that day, but his actions were not known at the time of the alleged incident.

****

In the first days of the Presidency, Clinton's staff members - whose brilliance and enthusiasm helped bring him to the White House - created a perception of chaos, as well as bad feelings in the infancy of the administration. The missteps may be forgotten in the long term, but it remains true that Clinton failed to duplicate the accomplishments achieved by Franklin Roosevelt in the historic first hundred days of his administration, or the New Frontier euphoria of Jack Kennedy. Rather, he appeared to resurrect the failed strategies of the Jimmy Carter Administration. (In fact, the Clinton team roster included some of

Carter's former advisers.) History will judge whether Clinton rose above and moved beyond those mistakes, or continued making the same ones.

From the start, the Clintons were hit with problems and negative press blowouts. Some related to a two-hundred-dollar haircut on board Air Force One, the abrupt dismissal of experienced and well-respected White House travel office staff and other matters that kept spin-doctors busy. But the young President, a masterful politician and effective lobbyist, did get some important bills through the Congress, including a major overhaul of the U.S. budget. It was such an ambitious program that it barely squeaked through the Democratic-controlled Senate. The one tie-breaking vote, cast by Vice President Al Gore at three o'clock in the morning, was enough for the President to claim victory.

But that victory was not without cost. Clinton infuriated many of his most ardent supporters by accepting major compromises, such as on the energy tax. In fact, compromise was a lesson he learned the hard way, after enduring several embarrassing defeats on Capitol Hill. Thus he met Congress halfway on issues such as trade with China, allowing more Haitian immigrants into the country, and others. These were often the reverse of his campaign promises - but many voters have long learned the fragility of such vows.

During his tough presidential campaign, candidate Clinton had sworn to achieve reform in the military which would allow gays in the armed services. This earned him the support of an increasingly significant political bloc, the gay and lesbian community. But in the end, the staunch opposition of the military and a majority of the American populace in general proved too strong. He agreed to a "don't ask, don't tell" policy, wherein closet homosexuals could remain in the service provided they did not flaunt their sexual preference and did not admit to it or engage in homosexual acts in public. Meanwhile, many of Clinton's supporters in the military had "come out of the closet" in anticipation of a change in military policy. They faced dismissal from the military because of their candor.

Clinton himself was facing a hostile military hierarchy because of his own refusal to serve in the Vietnam War. One Air Force general was forced to retire, after publicly calling Clinton a "gay-loving, womanizing draft-dodger." Other servicemen called him that - and worse - behind his back, but did not articulate the words in a public forum.

Hostility among the military increased in the early days of the administration. A high-ranking military officer came to the White House for an appointment. He was insulted by one of the young White House staffers - one of many in the so-called "Kiddy Corps" who lacked historical perspective. She told the much-decorated General and war veteran they did not "deal with the military" in the White House. Insulted, General Barry McCaffrey left, and the account made its way into the news media. President Clinton later took the General jogging one morning to smooth things over, and appointed him to head National Drug Control Policy. He became a very effective "drug czar," but the episode did little to improve relations between the White House and the Pentagon.

Many in the military did not forgive Clinton for the debacle in Somalia. He failed to order enough military backup to protect the Americans there, after the mission changed from a humanitarian to a military one. American servicemen were captured, killed, defiled, and dragged through the dusty streets of the country they had gone to assist. This was an unnecessary tragedy, in the minds of the military. As for the other major American intervention - Bosnia and Kosovo - the jury remains out. But there are concerns Americans will remain there for a long time, with no clear exit strategy in sight.

President Clinton began to gain some grudging respect from military after his lightning missile attack of Iraqi intelligence headquarters on Saturday night, June 26, 1993. He accomplished what other presidents before him had failed to do: he carried off the raid without any leaks. All the reporters, and most officials in the Congress and the Executive Branch, were taken by surprise. Though the raid somewhat crippled the Iraqi intelligence headquarters, it did little long-term harm to that country's intelligence-gathering capability, because the President made a conscious decision to conduct the Tomahawk missile attacks in the middle of the night, Iraqi time. Then, only a handful of low-level intelligence workers and cleaning personnel would be in harm's way. About eight people were killed in the attack, including a woman and an infant who lived nearby. Three of the missiles went off course, which is considered a good ratio in such a complicated, high-tech operation.

During an East Room news conference, I asked President Clinton about his rationale for such a decision. I wanted to know why he did not strike during the day, when the intelligence chiefs would be at work. He said he was trying to send a message and destroy facilities - not end up with a large body count. There are many who question the effectiveness of such a strategy. But the President has said he would attack again, if Iraq continued to engage in unacceptable acts. In this case, the ostensible reason for the June 26 raid was to retaliate for Iraq's role in plotting to assassinate former President George Bush and hundreds of others when the Bushes visited Kuwait in April 1993 - a plan which fortunately never reached fruition.

Though administration officials deny it, the raid also may have been conducted for domestic political reasons. Clinton's public approval ratings did go up for a while afterward. And the President may have found a new motto for his Administration: "Don't tread on us" - words he quoted during an Oval Office speech from the dramatic rallying cry of the American Revolution.

The fallout of the incident on the press contingent was highly negative, but that is of little concern to the population as a whole. Most of the regular White House reporters were told they could go home at three-thirty that Saturday afternoon, since there would be no further news that day. Toward six p.m., however, some of them got word from the White House to rush back for a major announcement. The news of the raids came a short while later. Most of the top - and best paid - reporters were caught up short and missed the story completely. UPI's Helen Thomas - the dean of the Washington press corps - was not told until twenty minutes before the general announcement. CNN's Wolf Blitzer, arguably one of the most influential reporters in the world at the time, was having a quiet evening at home with his family when he got the word. He did his first few broadcasts by phone, with a map of Washington, D.C., and a long and embarrassing still photo appearing on the screen. Then Wolf rushed from his suburban home to the White House.

Meanwhile, back in the Oval Office, President Clinton delayed his national prime-time speech by about fifteen minutes. I believe he may have done so in order to assist Wolf and other influential reporters. That way, they could be at the White House in time to introduce the President's speech, analyze it afterward, and attend a "background" briefing on the evidence against Iraq.

For my part, I got word of the event fifteen minutes before seven o'clock on Saturday night in Washington. I was able to get bulletins on Radio New Zealand and USA Radio News. Then I covered the speech and its aftermath for them and my other major stations. I woke my Israeli listeners to the news in their early morning. Because of the story, I spent the entire night broadcasting, but was grateful I was there to do the story. Many of my colleagues could not be reached, and missed the story altogether.

As for my fellow reporters, they were furious. The next time they had access to White House press secretary Dee Dee Myers at a briefing, they excoriated her. It turned out that she and some other top White House staffers had been "out of the loop." They were not even present at crucial National Security Council meetings, where the raid was discussed. The former communications czar, George Stephanopoulos, may have been there, but he was now an advisor, and not designated to talk to the press. Dee Dee was embarrassed and frustrated, and the press was furious. She explained that she had not lied to the press, because she didn't have all the facts herself. She told an angry press corps, "The information you get from this podium is accurate, as far as I know, but not always complete." But she admitted she knew something was up several hours in advance, but did not think to call in the press corps at that time to prepare them for a major announcement. That admission did not endear her to the journalists. Several liked Dee Dee personally;

at the same time, a press secretary must be informed, and must convey that to the media. Other press secretaries over the years have resigned when they found themselves in such an untenable situation.

We journalists understand that sometimes secrets must be kept, and can keep them. I have held many high-level national security issues to myself when asked to do so. But the White House could have recalled the press, told them to prepare for a major announcement, and not given them any details to leak. In addition, secrecy was not of prime importance in this raid. No U.S. jets were at risk, since unmanned Tomahawk missiles were used. No secret rescue attempt would have been put in jeopardy. Even the allied invasion of Iraq was conducted with great fanfare and lack of secrecy (indeed, the bluster and buildup were part of the strategy).

The Clinton Administration considered the mission a success, despite the fallout from their handling of the reporters. No one believed the administration was finished with Saddam Hussein, who could find himself under attack again at the slightest provocation - against the United Nations, the spy flights, the Kurds, or Shiites. Indeed the war of attrition continued throughout the presidency and beyond, with daily patrols over the no fly zones. The American and, sometime, British planes, struck back with powerful missiles and bombs, and probably inflicted some damage to facilities and personnel. But Saddam Hussein hung on, controlling the lives and fortunes of the people in Iraq. It is all part of a terrible legacy which, tragically, might have been terminated during the George Bush Administration, had Operation Desert Storm lasted a bit longer.

The Clinton White House also continued to closely monitor Iran, Libya, India and Pakistan, the Sudan, the rest of Africa, and other Mideast hot spots which might require U.S. or U.N. intervention. The much - celebrated peace treaty in Northern Ireland is still inconclusive, although much progress has been made. In Israel, violence with the Palestinians hit a fever pitch, but the major explosions erupted after Clinton left office. Only the American and UN peace keeping presence forces some degree of a civilized veneer in the former Yugoslavia. But, as soon as the outside troops let up their guard, the ethnic factions continue their fratricide, as they have done for hundreds of years. The rapes, tortures, and massacres are horrible, and the suffering of people cannot be adequately described. But, debate continues over whether Americans need to be part of this. Some believed the American presence was a distraction from other misjudgments President Clinton had made. Other critics believed the President's biggest scandal was campaign contributions he took from Chinese interests, and they may have influenced policy. The White House strongly denied this. But critics saw a "wag the dog" scenario - they accused Clinton of involvement in other parts of the world, to take the focus away from his real dealings with China.

In the midst of all the problems, in 1998 there was another close call with Iraq. The Iraqis closed off certain sensitive sites to the UN team of inspectors, who were trying to locate and destroy Iraq's weapons of mass destruction. Saddam Hussein also tried to oust, or decrease, the number of Americans in the team. Tensions mounted, and the US threatened the use of military force. President Clinton was able to muster some support from allies - especially Britain and, to a smaller extent, Australia and New Zealand. The American forces built up in the area, and many of us made plans to go to the Persian Gulf. I had some very positive experiences, and met some fine diplomats, as I got my journalists visas for Kuwait and Bahrain. But, at the last minute a compromise was brokered by the UN, and the tensions lessened. After several months, the forces were redeployed to other troubled areas of the world. The press corps returned to their focus on domestic issues - such as the sexual scandals. They were distracted briefly by other world crises - notably, the emergence of India and Pakistan as full-fledged nuclear countries, after they both detonated a series of underground nuclear tests. The President also launched a lightning series of Cruise Missile attacks against terrorist bases in Afghanistan and Sudan, and vowed to conduct a full-scale war against terrorists. He did this after terrorists, allegedly financed by Saudi millionaire Osama Bin Laden, may have been involved in the deadly bombing of 2 American embassies in Africa. There is no doubt these are dangerous and tragic times for Americans. But, there is also some suspicion, because President Clinton ordered the strikes, just 3 days after confessing to the nation he did have an illicit affair with Monica Lewinsky. Instead of "Don't Tread on Us," the public wondered if "Wag the Dog" was the operative analogy. That was a reference to a movie, in which a President manufactured a make-believe war, to cover up an unwise sexual affair he was having in the White House.

Eventually, the UN inspectors were ousted from Iraq, amidst charges some had actually been spies for the CIA and other intelligence agencies. The Iraqi problem was far from resolved, but Saddam Hussein could be a convenient whipping boy for President Clinton whenever he needed him. In truth, Saddam also needed Clinton to help unify his people. If they were convinced they were in peril from " the great Satan," they would be reluctant to overthrow Saddam Hussein.

During his presidency, Clinton also embarked on a frenzied series of international travels, to fulfill a goal of visiting every major continent and region before he left the White House. The President hoped the positive economy, and budget, and success in foreign policy would be his legacy for history. They might well be, but the sexual scandals will be there too. And, time will only tell how his wife and daughter react to him after the White House.

****

The last years of the Clinton Administration were met with some successes, more compromises, and the unraveling of promising foreign policy issues. They included the centerpieces of his administration - peace in the Mideast and Bosnia. The Cold War is supposed to be over, with the collapse of the Soviet Union during the Reagan and Bush Administrations. But Russia and its former satellites are in trouble, and bear watching. Fluidity is the hallmark of international affairs and, again, the jury remains out. Inside the building, however, the White House staff improved dramatically, when Leon Panetta and then Erskine Bowles took over as Chief of Staff, and Mike McCurry as press secretary. The White House became kinder, gentler, better organized, and a happier place to work. The improved atmosphere continued as the much beloved McCurry moved on, and Joe Lockhart replaced him. John Podesta moved in as Chief of Staff, and managed to hold the White House team together, despite the immense strains of the impeachment fight. Some of the staff left, expressing bitterness and frustration. Of that group, some had thousands of dollars in legal fees to pay off, because they were hauled into testify before the Grand Jury about the sexual scandals. Others, such as one time wonder boy George Stephanopoulos, broke with the Administration. He wrote a fascinating memoir about the Clinton White House, and reportedly went onto make millions of dollars as a writer, commentator and ABC superstar. Monica Lewinsky also made money, but had enormous legal fees to pay off. No matter whatever else she does in life, the former "valley girl" from Los Angeles will always be remembered for shocking and immoral conduct in the White House - the House that is supposed to be a monument to the highest ideals of the United States.

In 1999, just as the situation appeared to be settling down for Bill Clinton, the United States became involved in a series of other crises. The US, which is the key component of NATO, launched a series of intense bombing campaigns over Yugoslavia. It did so to avenge and end the atrocities committed by Yugoslav leader Milosovich. But, the action also precipitated the tragic exodus or slaughter of thousands of refugees from Kosovo. This may have happened anyway, but the world was at first unprepared for this situation. The refugees' suffering cannot be denied. Nor can that of the ordinary Yugoslav, who faced massive bombing. Mistakes were made, where hospitals, civilian buses, and the Chinese Embassy in Yugoslavia was bombed. Many of the Serbs in Yugoslavia claimed they did not believe the atrocities in Kosovo, and before that, in Bosnia, actually took place. Or, if they did, like the "good Germans" of the Nazi era, they were only following orders.

The air campaign over Yugoslavia ended after 79 days. It was, in general, a brilliant campaign, despite the bombing of the Chinese Embassy and the civilians killed on all sides of the border. Perhaps the bombs went astray, caused "collateral damage," or some targets were intentionally hit. Rumors persist in intelligence circles that some one intentionally caused the Chinese bombing, in hopes of punishing China or driving a wedge between the Clinton Administration and that country. Those charges are unproven, and could be treasonable, if true. But, the war did end, without the need for combat ground troops. Now, American and NATO ground troops are in the region, of course, to keep the bitter antagonists from murdering each other, in the centuries-old stream of reprisals. This continues the American stream of world-wide deployments; not to conquer, but the keep the peace. America continues as the world's policeman and superpower; a role it might not have sought, but now has, as a tribute to the endurance and success of the varied fabric comprising the American people.

Other crises of 1999 included devastating tornadoes in Oklahoma and Kansas - some of the most powerful on record. This gave Bill Clinton occasion to be at his presidential best, offering money and sympathy. The tragic shooting of high school students in Littleton Colorado devastated many in this country. The Clintons used this as an opportunity to try to change the culture of violence in this country. Another crises evolved over Chinese penetration of Americans nuclear labs. China appears to have obtained most of Americas key nuclear secrets from the labs, over a 20 year period, and now reportedly has the secret codes to manufacture the neutron bomb; destructive atomic warheads, or nearly anything else it wants. This unfolding scandal and security lapse could prove to be one of the most important security breaches in American history; one that had gone one for at least twenty years until it was detected. But, there are also indications the investigations were mishandled, and the truth may never be known.

In the final days of the Clinton Administration, the President committed more acts which tarnished his legacy. He delivered a number of very controversial pardons to people who had committed crimes and harmed American society. Some of the pardons were delivered against the recommendation of the Justice Department, or without the knowledge of the Presidents own staff. There were unproven allegations that the President received money and gifts in exchange for the pardons; these were all officially denied. There were also distasteful incidents, in which Bill and Hillary Clinton (later an elected Senator from New York and then Secretary if State), were accused of taking items from the White House which did not belong to them. In the end, much of the furniture and other items were returned. Bill Clinton also tried to squander the taxpayers' money, by renting one of the most imperial and expensive office buildings in New York City. When that became too controversial, he changed to a site in Harlem, where he was welcomed with great fanfare from most neighbors.

Many of the antics left an extremely bad taste in the mouths of the public. Still, the Clintons maintained their popularity in many quarters. Fame and controversy sells. They both received multi-million dollar offers to publish their autobiographies. And, with the thousands of dollars Bill Clinton receives for his lectures, he should be able to pay off his legal fees, and finance the two expensive houses the couple bought in New York and Washington. It remains to be seen whether he will help out his former staff members with their legal fees.

****

Even during the crises, tensions and problems which always exist between the media and the White House staff, there was also good-natured rivalry. While some would argue the press is co-opted, it made the relationship run more smoothly. In addition, Clinton was exciting, sinful, sexy, and immoral. All of that made for good copy, and the reporting careers of most of us covering him soared during the Clinton years. He was incredibly self-destructive – a brilliant and cursed individual. We in the media benefited from those faults.

Despite legal battles and numerous investigations, the Clinton Administration got things accomplished, and we were able to communicate them - warts and all - to the public. That is the way a White House should function. Had they enjoyed an even more open and trusting relationship from the start, they might have experienced greater success, and might have even prevented their loss of the Congress and the Impeachment, without Senate conviction, of President William Jefferson Clinton.

The Thaw Between the U.S. and New Zealand

There is one area of policy where I have been able to have an impact - that of the small country I love, New Zealand. The crises brought on by the impasse over nuclear weapons, and nuclear powered ships, dragged on for over a decade. Most younger people have forgotten about it, and learned to live with the standoff. But, for many of us in the middle of it, it is a silly irritant and something which should be resolved in a mature manner.

Even the most conservative observers believe the Reagan and Bush Administrations were heavy-handed and insensitive in their treatment of New Zealand. The policy set in place in the 1980s severely penalized that country's security relationship with the United States and Australia, because New Zealand would not accept nuclear-armed or -powered ships. The United States was insulted that a small country like New Zealand would have the effrontery to say no to American military power. Making matters worse was anti-American sentiment of some in New Zealand, and the game of one-upsmanship played by politicians in both countries who hoped to score domestic political points over the issue. New Zealand suffered another disadvantage. It did not have a powerful lobby behind it, as did Israel and other small countries, so it was easy for a U.S. administration to run roughshod over it. Nor was there the mutual will to "agree to disagree, and save face," as existed between U.S. and Japan, Scandinavia, and other areas which also resisted port calls by nuclear vessels but were determined to avoid a rupture with the United States.

I have sought to focus the Clinton Administration on this problem, in hopes that a new policy will be set in place. For the first few months of the Clinton regime the officials carried over the policies of the Reagan and Bush Administrations - policies which were highlighted when I asked President Reagan about the dispute during a formal White House news conference when the problem first arose. I had anticipated being called on during that news conference, which is quite an accomplishment during any administration. It is the superstar journalists, those with well-financed news organizations behind them, who get the front-row seats, and are called on in nearly every news conference. Thus, especially among reporters serving the smaller markets, the competition to be recognized is fierce.

It was particularly hard to get a question in during a Reagan news conference, since he held only a handful each year. Moreover, everything was stage-managed, like a Hollywood movie. But I had known his news secretary, Larry Speakes, for a number of years and, as I explained in a previous chapter, I called him to let him know that if recognized, I intended to ask President Reagan a question about ANZUS and New Zealand. "For God's sake," I said, "make sure he knows what I'm talking about." I was called, and Reagan responded with a polished and complete answer. Unfortunately, it had been crafted by the military and foreign policy experts in the Pentagon, State Department, and National Security Council, each of whom had its bones to pick and was determined to stop the anti-nuclear "cancer" from spreading beyond New Zealand - which they clearly believed was expendable.

The policy was hard - line; it reduced New Zealand from a favored ally to a "friend." In that status, New Zealand lost many of the military and security advantages it had enjoyed.

With President Clinton in office, I was determined to put in a pitch for little old New Zealand, and see if we could at least restore the situation from a cold to a warm friendship

I tried to do my part to focus the Clinton people on the problem by posing the question during another formal East Room news conference - the first of the new administration. I had already asked the President about five questions in less formal news conferences; some he was able to answer, some not. But interestingly, the New Zealand one got all the attention and some expected - but unwelcome - laughter. It is difficult to tell exactly what my colleagues are laughing at when I ask such a question; perhaps the reaction goes back to my earlier days as the "butter queen." But no doubt they are also reacting to my effrontery in posing serious questions about such a small and far-away country. They might ask silly and irrelevant questions themselves, but it seems those can be forgiven - as long as they pertain to domestic issues.

I prepared well for my question, and consulted with friends in New Zealand and U.S. agencies before asking it. Some feared that broaching the issue might cause the Clinton Administration to firmly shut the door. But I felt the time was good and the issue relevant, since Prime Minister Bolger had delivered a strong speech to the American Chamber of Commerce in New Zealand, saying it was now time to move beyond the nuclear rift. In addition, I had raised the matter several times during the week with White House Press Secretary Dee Dee Myers, so I was confident the President had been briefed or was at least aware of the issue.

As it turned out, either Clinton or I were done in by poor staff work. I tried to appeal to the President's domestic bias. I said: "Mr. President, I have an easy problem for you, and it's domestic, too. This one's very easy. A lot of Americans are not wildly pro-nuclear and thought the U.S. may have overreacted in past years in its very heavy-handed treatment of New Zealand. Would you consider meeting now with a New Zealand leader and discussing the situation? Isn't there some way that a compromise can be reached so you can agree to disagree, but still restore the political and security relationship?"

An embarrassed President said, "I've given absolutely no thought to that question, and I'm afraid if I give an answer to it, I'll be in more trouble tomorrow than I can figure out." Laughter rippled through the press corps. Later, the Associated Press published an article saying, "Connie Lawn stumps the President." Dee Dee Myers joked that this was the newest White House game. I was embarrassed, and sorry I was not permitted a follow-up question to persuade him to investigate. But allowing follow-ups was not the norm in this Administration. At least I knew I had set a process in motion, and focused the world's attention, if only momentarily, on the fact that the United States had continued to "stiff" New Zealand for the past eight years.

After that press conference, a White House staff member came up to me and asked, "Do you think the people in New Zealand will be offended by his answer?" I responded by saying, "That depends upon what you guys do next."

I also gave the staffer a section of Prime Minister Bolger's speech. Back in the press room the next day, many of my colleagues were not laughing. They asked very serious questions about the standoff, and said they were amazed it was still going on. Many promised to write follow-up articles at the appropriate time. Indeed, The New York Times published a very fine one, headlined, "A Clinton Quip is Just a Quip? Not So, Say New Zealanders." It quoted one New Zealand woman as saying, "This will not play well in New Zealand - this is a major issue, and they're quite touchy." A prominent Australian paper said the answer showed President Clinton had little interest in Australia, as well as New Zealand, if he could kiss off a question like that. But many of my colleagues believe it was better that he gave this answer than fall back on the existing policy. I do believe the incident got the ball rolling.

As for the President, I believe he regretted having to offer a non-answer. As the next formal news conference wound down, the Press Secretary called a halt to questions, but President Clinton looked at me and said, "Let's take one more." That is when I asked about the Iraqi bombing. It was not the appropriate time to ask about New Zealand, and I cannot afford to be thought of as a one-issue reporter. I am far from that, given the number of countries I cover, and the number of U.S. stations which carry my reports on USA Radio News and Radio America.

At the same time, this nuclear issue is a relatively simple one. It is not as complex as the Mideast or Bosnia. Perhaps the high-level security relationship cannot be restored, unless one side backs down on nuclear matters. But a President who invites the heads of China, and numerous other controversial countries to the white house can certainly restore a high-level political relationship with New Zealand, which is a key supporter in other areas and was a member of the U.N. Security Council.

I was proud to have been able to help improve relations in a major way, five months after my first question. The breakthrough came during the APEC conference in Seattle in November, 1993. I had planned in advance to be there, and told Radio New Zealand and my other clients I would pay my own way if I had to. I was confident in my ability to convince President Clinton and Secretary of State Warren Christopher to recognize me at a news conference and to announce new policy, or at least express a change in attitude towards New Zealand, in their response to my question.

In Seattle, I made my way to the enormous press center which had been established for the 3,000 journalists expected at the conference. There were an equal number of delegates and assistants from the 15 Asian and Pacific countries attending, making it the largest and most confusing gathering I have ever covered.

Typical of the confusion was the broadcast I made to one of my Asian countries. It is common practice to ask an official from a foreign country to make a comment or summarize their views on a matter in their own language, and leave it to ones' editor to cut the recording as they wanted. I had worked hard to get one such interview, which I then fed down the telephone line. The editor at the other end snapped to me, "Damn it! You have sent it in Mandarin - I want it in Cantonese!" At least I had no such problem with the New Zealand and Australian dialects, although their form of the language is often very different than the American one.

The huge convention center turned out to be well organized, thanks to the efforts of the USIA and the Foreign Press Center. Briefings and papers were churned out constantly. Some lazy reporters decided to stay in their posh hotel rooms, where all the major activities and developments were fed to them via closed - circuit t.v. There in - room bars were also well stocked and most of them (except me) were on an expense account! It was easy for them to stay in and cover the conference from their room, even from bed. But, I needed to ask questions and conduct interviews, so I barely saw the room I had paid for.

The major breakthrough on the New Zealand front occurred because Jim Bolger found the time to come to Seattle. He was exhausted by the recent general election in New Zealand and the subsequent uncertainty over who would govern the country and how the financial markets would hold up. The fact that he came for three days, however, brought about the first meeting in ten years between an American President and a New Zealand Prime Minister.

The New York Times published a brilliant editorial the day before the leaders met, under the headline, "Time to Warm Up to New Zealand," thus continuing the interest it had already shown in its feature following my question to President Clinton at the East Room news conference. It is hard for a Democratic administration to ignore that type of editorial in the most prominent liberal newspaper of the nation. When I saw it, I raced around the convention center in great excitement, showing it to as many people as I could. I filed a story on it, which went right to air. Shortly afterwards, Warren Christopher held a news conference. He was asked several questions about New Zealand, but I led the onslaught. I drew on the arguments in the editorial, and the Secretary of State gave some positive answers, saying, "New Zealand is not out in the cold, and we would not want them to be there." Such a response is intended to prod the bureaucrats towards drafting a change of policy, but the best was yet to come - President Clinton's own answer to me on cold, windswept Blake Island in Puget Sound, a 45 minute boat ride from Seattle.

It was no picnic getting to the island. Only 100 reporters out of the 3,000 were chosen to go, in a variety of representative groups, known as "pools." I knew I couldn't get into the White House pool, which was reserved for the reporters who travel with the president on a regular basis and spend a fortune doing so. I tried to get into the Australian or New Zealand pool, but they were reserved for the reporters who travel with the prime ministers of those countries, even though, in the end, not everyone eligible used their coveted pool pass. They did not relish getting up at 3:30 in the morning, and freezing on the island for over six hours. I was invited to join the Asian press pools, but felt that was not ethical, since I only did a small amount of work for that part of the world.

Fortunately my friends at the Foreign Press Center, who were running the press operation, found me a place on the International pool. Even then the White House staff challenged me, as I stumbled onto the bus in the predawn cold. This is one of the constant problems of being a free-lancer; you belong to no one, even when you yearn to be part of a team. (I reckon I actually belong to the whole world, which is a pretty good consolation).

After a choppy boat ride to Blake Island, we were in position before the 14 world leaders arrived (There should have been 15, but the Malaysian president was boycotting the conference). This allowed the photographers to snap them as they got off their boat and walked to the Indian lodge where the meetings were to be held. We retreated to a huge tent, where volunteers attempted to keep us warm with tepid coffee and space heaters. Some of the delegations had brought small flags to prop up on their desks in a show of national pride. The South Koreans were the smartest, though. They had boxes of noodle soup to which they added the hot water. The rest of use watched in envy as they enjoyed this filling and flavorsome beverage.

Events on the island made for good camaraderie and good stories to tell back home. As we worked, the wind picked up, the sea grew rougher, and nearby Mount Rainier became obscured by clouds laden with Arctic snow. I began to savor the prospect of being marooned for the night and sharing the lodge with 14 leaders.

In the mid-morning, Dee Dee Myers came into the tent to brief us. I asked whether New Zealand Prime Minister Bolger and President Clinton had actually met and talked, and she confirmed they had done so at least twice, but not before she had snapped, "You're so obsessed with New Zealand!" This sort of reaction hurts, but I turned away and filed my story. I also warned my editors a news conference was coming up and would be carried live on CNN. I informed them I would probably ask a New Zealand question, and urged them to put it on the air right away, just as soon as it had been answered. In this instance, CNN would prove more of a help than a competition, since I wouldn't be able to file the story until the news conference was over and we had taken the long walk back to our windswept press tent. I don't know what the regular Radio New Zealand reporter was doing all this time back in his warm hotel room. Again, he was there at the expense of the company - I had paid my own way, and had gradually taken over the situation.

The news conference was held outside, with a view of Puget Sound behind the assembled leaders. I managed to secure a front row seat, on the side where I knew President Clinton usually looked. I was nervous, being aware of my reputation for "always" asking New Zealand questions, and was glad to have two colleagues from other New Zealand media around me (they had actually made it to the island). I went up to them, and urged them to ask about progress between the US and New Zealand, which they assured me they planned to do.

As the press conference got underway, however, the president didn't look at them; he kept looking at me. I believe he was eager to now answer the question he had been unable to respond to last June. By the time I was called, however, I was so cold I could barely work the buttons on my tape recorder, and taking notes was out of the question. I put it as naturally as I could: "Mr. President, is New Zealand now figuratively out of the cold, if not literally? Have you now restored the political relationship with New Zealand?"

The President, who loves to laugh, responded, "Actually, we're out in the cold today." He added that Jim Bolger and he had a good talk and agreed to at least take a careful look at the relationship and see what else might be done. He noted, "We have an awful lot in common, and a lot of natural instincts towards friendship and cooperation. And I think that both of us are uncomfortable with what has become of our relationship over the last several years."

The President promised me there would be more to say in the upcoming future, and indeed there were statements, policy papers, and that all - important Bolger visit to the White House the following spring.

The President had given me a marvelous answer, and I was grateful for it. Afterwards, I went up to Dee Dee Myers and said I probably wouldn't ask another New Zealand question of the president until a NZ leader visited the White House.

While that did eventually take place, the high level strategic and security relationship was not fully restored. It could not really be while differences over the nuclear issue persisted, and neither side shows any inclination to back down. It now seems an archaic dispute, with the US putting very few nuclear weapons on ships - certainly not on those likely to visit New Zealand. And, American officials could always have an unwritten agreement, that they would not send nuclear powered ships into NZ ports. It looks as though the next American ships headed there will be the yachts that challenge NZ in the Americas Cup Race, and try to win back the majestic silver trophy so gallantly won by the Kiwis. There may be other ships too, carrying tourists to the races. But, there are unlikely to be any military ones, even though many in the military and intelligence community continue to treat each other with respect, and sometimes exchange important information in a quiet, unofficial manner. Despite the unresolved nuclear dispute, trade and tourism continues to boom, and that has greater impact on the average New Zealander in any case.

But those events were yet to come. After our rough boat trip back from the island, we returned to the giant press center, where I conducted a brief interview with U.S. Assistant Secretary of State Winston Lord. I was gratified to be congratulated by some of my Australian and New Zealand colleagues and, since I am the only one among them who consistently succeeds in putting Pacific questions, to be dubbed "the official spokesman for the region." The benefit of my long years in Washington is that I receive the recognition denied visiting correspondents, who are therefore less likely to be called on the I am.

Prime Minister Bolger and the other New Zealand officials were delighted with the President's response, and with the general tenor of their meetings. These events had a positive impact on New Zealand for years to come. But, despite the years of the standoff, it must be stressed that the nuclear issue is a relatively simple one. It is rather cut and dry, compared to the complex and tragic problems faced in Bosnia, the Mideast, Africa, and other areas of the world.

My Quest for the Ambassadorship to New Zealand

It has long been my dream to become the U.S. Ambassador to New Zealand, and in 1997 and 98 it nearly happened. Because I came so close, I am determined to try again and make it, or another Federal appointment happen one day. I would like to serve my country before my working days are over.

I sought the New Zealand post because I have a great love for both countries. I would be so proud to represent the United States in New Zealand, and was confident I could be a bridge in a way that has never happened before. That is because the people of New Zealand know I have so much affection and respect for them, and most of them have displayed those same attitudes towards me.

It is very unusual for a reporter to become an Ambassador, but it is not without precedent. In the few times it has happened before, it took place when that reporter has special ties to the country, as I do with New Zealand. New Zealand is usually considered a "political" posting; a foreign service professional is not generally appointed unless there is a crises (as there was during the ANZUS situation. At that time, one of the best Americans in the Foreign Service, Paul Cleveland, served as a superb US Ambassador, and did what he could to clean up the mess!).

In fact, New Zealand and Australia are considered such plum postings, that the standard joke is, a nominee has to contribute big money to the President to get those counties. At one time, the "going rate" was said to be 10 million dollars for Australia, and 5 million for New Zealand. While those rates are excessive, the traditional appointees have either contributed money to the President, done volunteer work, brought a lot of votes to the President, or done him some other political favors which had to be rewarded. That has been the route in the past and, unfortunately for me, it will probably be the case in the future. That does not, however, mean the person appointed is a bad Ambassador. Some have been disasters, while others have been superb.

In October, 1997, the post for New Zealand Ambassador became open for competition. The position had been offered to the outgoing Mayor of Seattle Washington. He received "agreement" or acceptance from New Zealand, and I broke the story (as I always have in the past) about the name and background of the Ambassadorial nominee (in this case, Norman Rice). For some rather murky reason, the nomination fell apart. He said he was not certain he was under consideration; the White House officially said there was miscommunication. My talk host in Auckland, John Banks of "Radio Pacific" asked me about it on the air, and I said I should now throw my hat in. I have thought about it for years; it would be a culmination of much I had worked for, and would be a fitting tribute to both countries. Shortly after that, I received a number of letters and phone calls from friends and supporters in New Zealand. They urged me to go for it! I spoke to press secretary Mike McCurry, who said bluntly, it would be a great thing, but he doubted it would ever happen. McCurry knew I had been trying to get a job with the Government for several years, because I am anxious to be of genuine service to my country. He told me the steps I would have to take, and the people I needed to talk to. One of the most important was White House Chief of Staff Erskine Bowles, a true professional and a Southern gentleman, liked and admired by all. Fortunately, I ran into him a few days later, and asked if I could discuss a personal matter with him. He was very gracious, and gave me about five minutes of his time. He also surprised me by addressing me by name and saying, "What a good idea - you have done a lot of work with New Zealand." Bowles asked me to send in my papers, and promised they would get to him and receive consideration. I also sent him an audio cassette of my two questions to President Clinton in his news conferences - questions which helped to focus on the nuclear rupture between the two nations, and gave the White House a way to shape a solution (I am so pleased that they resolved it the way I suggested - by isolating the nuclear dispute, and moving on with the relationship in other positive ways, as befits close friends and allies in all other aspects of the relationship).

In the ensuing weeks, I mounted a full - scale attack, and devoted about five hours a day on my efforts to become Ambassador. In some cases, I was told there were no actual rules, so I created them myself, as I have in all other aspects of my life. Erskine Bowles introduced me to his deputy John Podesta, and we had brief talks on a "catch as catch can" basis. I also spoke to National Security Advisor Sandy Berger the same way, and made certain my papers and files got to him. I spent hours on the phone with some fine people in Marsha Scott's personnel office, and they were wonderful to me, although I never had the chance to speak with her directly. Unfortunately poor Marsha had to devote some time being hauled before the grand jury, during the Impeachment scandal, because she has been a long - time friend and confident of the Clintons. That was an added strain on her time and finances, and must have had an emotional impact on her. She can be forgiven, if she could not always devote as much time as she wanted to all of her responsibilities. In addition to White House and diplomatic contacts, I spent hours calling, or writing to anyone who could help me on this issue. Since I had over 30 years of contacts in Washington, I found there were a number of people I could call and turn to.

The most gratifying aspect of the search was the impressive support I received from top Senators and the World Bank President, James Wolfensohn. He is a "good Australian boy" who has done brilliantly in Europe and the United States. Among other things, he is very close to Bill Clinton, and has hosted him in his vacation home. Wolfensohn believed I would be an excellent Ambassador, and spoke personally to President Clinton and others about my appointment. He also wrote me a letter, confirming his assistance, and wishing me the best. I was incredibly gratified by the extent of his assistance. One day, I ran into him as he was about to enter a White House meeting on the Asian financial crises, which was just erupting. This man had some of the major burdens of the world on his shoulders. But, he had time to ask me how it was going, and promised to mention my situation the President. He concluded by promising to "visit me in New Zealand, and go fishing" if I received the posting!

Another Australian gentleman who was extremely helpful was Ambassador Andrew Peacock. He is one of the most astute and polished Ambassadors in Washington, and is enormously well-connected. The Ambassador is close to Secretary of State Albright and to National Security Advisor Sandy Berger. He talked to them about my situation, and offered his support. In this case, Sandy Berger was the key. The Secretary of State could not push for me, even if she wanted to. It is her obligation to support the professional foreign service officers for the position of Ambassador. The State Department does always, in fact, submit a list of suggested names. But, their officials admitted to me in private, they would be "sacrificial lambs," since New Zealand was to be a political posting. Once the Ambassador is named and confirmed, however, they are given a State Department office to work out of; receive a "charm course" of instruction by State, and do answer to the Secretary of State, the President, and the various Assistant Secretaries of State and other officers associated with the Asian and Pacific region. They would also have contact with those same officers in the National Security Council. And, if the Ambassador is smart, he or she would not just focus on the country they are representing. They would keep a close eye on the region, and assess New Zealand's role in unfolding events. That became increasingly crucial in 1999, as the worlds Asian and Pacific leaders (as well as President Clinton and Secretary Albright) prepared to visit New Zealand for the APEC (Asian - Pacific Economic Cooperation) Conference. The World Cup yacht race, and the Millennium, which began in New Zealand, also brought many important and ordinary people to New Zealand. That is why it is so crucial to have an Ambassador who knows and loves the country, and also is known by many on the people on a first name basis. I had been trying to convince the White House I fit that description. A political contributor cannot learn about 20 years worth of personal friendships from reading about them in a briefing sheet, or attending a diplomatic charm school.

In addition to approaching Australians, I of course connected numerous friends in the New Zealand community, both here and in New Zealand. I wrote letters to Foreign Minister Don McKinnon and to Prime Minister Jenny Shipley, both of whom I have known for years. I knew it would not be proper protocol for them to support me at this juncture. But Senator Jesse Helms, the powerful Chairman of the Senate Foreign Relations committee, indicated it would be helpful to him if he knew I had support at the highest levels in New Zealand. I had, by this time, sent a series of faxes to the Senator's offices in North Carolina and in Washington. He and his staff were lovely to me, and appeared gratified I as coming to them at this time, while the nomination process was still underway. They indicated that had not been done before by someone seeking a job in this Administration. But, the Senate's job is to advise, as well as consent. No one can gain any foreign affairs position, which requires Senate confirmation, without his willingness to schedule a hearing, hold a vote in his committee and on the full Senate floor. So, when the Senator suggested I contact the New Zealand officials, I accepted his advice!

Don McKinnons office faxed back, and advised me they could not get involved at this time. Prime Minister Shipley's office wrote a much more helpful letter. In it, an assistant said, "What exciting times for you. ..This is a domestic matter for the United States, and not a matter the Prime Minister can become involved in. Can I wish you every success." The warm tone of the letter was gracious and welcome, and was what I needed to give to Senator Helms. I also sent copies to add to my growing files in the various White House offices. (I have learned to send several copies. There are so many people competing for positions, and for time and attention, it is easy to get overlooked if you don't keep pushing and communicating).

In addition to the support I already cited, I had warm letters of recommendation from my Senator, Charles Robb, a member of the Foreign Relations, Armed Services, and Intelligence Committees. He was very helpful, and made several calls on my behalf. Other Senators and Congressmen also supported me. Their support is crucial, since the

Senate approves appointments, ratifies treaties, and - along with the House of Representatives - votes on the White House programs.

I did not ignore the First Lady, Hillary Clinton. I admire her greatly, and know she has an enormous influence on the President. My file was passed directly to her through Ann Stock, who used to be her very efficient Social Secretary. I also tried to mention my application directly to the President and Mrs. Clinton, during a social occasion. I do not know if it registered, as they had to endure their endless round of hand shakings and formal photos with the guests.

Over the months, I turned to many people to help. Even Washington attorney and Clinton confidant Vernon Jordan said he would call the White House for me, and his secretary later told me he had "taken care of it." This was shortly before the Monica Lewinsky scandal broke, and Vernon was dragged into it, because he went to great lengths to help her. Poor Jordan - a fine and distinguished man, who was hauled before the Grand Jury five times on the Lewinsky matter, and said he answered basically the same questions each time. I believe him to be an honorable gentleman, who has been given many blessings, and seeks to assist others who turn to him. I am grateful he tried to help me, and hope he can soon resume his normal lifestyle, without the glare of publicity and investigation.

I also spoke to Richard Holbrooke, the new U.S. Ambassador to the U.N. He was once the youngest Assistant Secretary of State for Asian and Pacific Affairs, and was instrumental in helping me in my coverage of N.Z. and Australia. Holbrooke used to say at the time I was "the best reporter in Washington" since I was one of the few Americans who cared about that region of the world. Ambassador Holbrooke gave me some tough, practical advice in my quest, which I proceeded to follow.

Others who helped me included ordinary people from New Zealand, who phoned or wrote the White House on my behalf. The strongest of these letters came from my good friend Jean Stewart of Wanganui, who has done so much on my behalf. I will always be grateful to her and others, and hope those letters will continue to come.

I also cannot forget my friends in the White House press corps. Veteran (and star) reporter Sam Donaldson raised the issue during one of the briefings, which is broadcast throughout the nation. He asked spokesman Mike McCurry about the status of the next Ambassador to N.Z. Mike joked he was "in cahoots with me," and others said, "that's Connie's question." At first, there were the usual jokes about sheep. Then Mike looked right at me and talked about "the importance of the bilateral relationship and the work we do in the Pacific region." They also talked about the nuclear issue and ANZUS. And, on sheep, Sam made reference to the expensive sheep he owns on a ranch in New Mexico. Sam said "I want the new US Ambassador to NZ to perhaps destroy by fire all the sheep in that country." Mike said, "Mr.Donaldson is apparently looking for competitive advantage when it comes to the procurement of sheep."

Despite the jokes, there was serious content to the exchange. Afterwards, several reporters asked me about the situation. Since time was running out for Senate confirmation in 1998, and I figured I had little to lose, I told then I was officially under consideration, according to the White House, for U.S. Ambassador. They all agreed I would be perfect for the position. They added, it would set an important precedent, if more White House reporters were named Ambassadors. And, they said they looked forward to visiting me in N.Z. for the APEC meeting and the Americas Cup Yacht Race.

Sometimes, it is difficult to tell how seriously the White House considered me. I got the impression from the foreign affairs side that I was their choice; one top official even told me I had made it as far as number two on the list. On the political side, there are other factors. One man there even told me, quite honestly, "Bill Clinton has 30 years of political favors to pay off. He only has a few years to do so, and must go through that political list first!" Honest statements, even if it's not the best way to chose an Ambassador. In the meantime, I remained on the list. The appointment eventually went to Carol Mosely-Braun, a defeated, African – American Senator from Illinois. It was a nasty, political and controversial appointment. Senator Jesse Helms, and the Senator who defeated her from Illinois, opposed her. But, 98 other

Senators decided, for a variety of political reasons, it was best to support her. Usually politicians stick together in this case. Ex Senators and Congressmen may need support if they become Ambassadors, so they do favors in advance while they still have power to do so. Ms. Mosely – Braun even had the political clout to be sworn in by Vice President Al Gore in the White House office buildings. Usually, Ambassadors are sworn in by the Secretary of State (if they are powerful) at the State Department. Despite the acrimony beforehand, once in New Zealand, I understand she became a fine Ambassador.

For my part, I am happy with the way events unfolded. I did not have to give up my beloved reporting or my private life. I was lucky to be able to marry a great man – Charles Sneiderman. I will continue to serve as the second longest-credentialed White House correspondent, (at this writing) reporting to my listeners around the world. But, my quest to be U.S. Ambassador to New Zealand may resume in the future. If I get it someday I will try to do my best to enhance excellent relations between two of the finest countries, and some of the best people, in the world.

“America, Let’s Roll” President George W. Bush

Was there ever a President in modern history who grew and then shrank so quickly in office, or provoked more passions, as did George W. Bush? It appears unlikely.

The son of President George Bush was first elected to the White House while he was Governor of Texas. He was 54 at the time. The election results were finalized after an agonizing 36 days of ballot counts and recounts in the state of Florida. Finally, the election was determined by the decision of the U.S. Supreme Court, following a series of rulings in the Florida courts.

The results may be argued for years to come. Vice President, and Democratic nominee Al Gore enjoyed many advantages, coming into the election. Gore followed an extremely popular President, Bill Clinton. But, Gore was so upset by Clinton’s moral and ethical lapses (which were numerous) that he put a distance between himself and Clinton. The two former friends had a falling out. Despite the fact the economy appeared to be booming, and the United States was not involved in any major wars, Gore was never able to inspire the American people. There was criticism of his personality, which was cold at times. He had trouble communicating his core beliefs, and there may have been some ethical failings as he helped Bill Clinton in fund raising efforts. There were also difficulties with the way he ran his campaign and his political staff. With all these problems, Al Gore managed a slim victory in the popular vote. But, he lost in the Electoral College, after the messy Florida election was decided. The final decision was made by the Supreme Court, which had many Justices on it appointed by the first President Bush. Al Gore went onto become a respected elder statesman, specializing in matters of climate change. He also became a millionaire and established a private television network. Texas Governor Bush became the second American, after John Quincy Adams, to succeed his father as U.S. President. He then went onto win reelection, four years later, after one of the most bitter and expensive campaigns in modern Presidential history.

I was privileged to cover the elections, and try to make sense of them, for my stations in this country, and for many of the BBC programs. I was also doing part-time news casting for the Voice of America. And I did commentary on a nightly basis (at Midnight and 1:00 am) to two of the most popular, private Morning "drive" shows in South Africa. I also did afternoon White House reports for the Paul Barry radio show on Clear Channel; several shows on Radio America, USA Radio News, and other outlets. This meant a huge number of potential listeners – in the millions at times in this country and around the world. I occasionally contributed to radio and television stations in New Zealand, Australia, and Israel, but it was not like the old days. They received the bulk of their news directly from the world-wide cable television outlets, and had little need (or budget) for my services. I was sad to lose them as regular clients, but was kept extremely busy with commentary and analysis for the others. The clients I had still required broadcasts at all hours of the day and night. Most commentaries I could do from bed, and then go back to sleep. At times, for the BBC, I went into their studio, even if it was 3:00 in the morning here. During the day, of course, I broadcast from the White House. The hardest client was the Voice of America. Many of the shifts were overnight, or entailed getting up at 4:00 am. That was really rugged for me, and for my colleagues around the world, who have endured such eight or ten hour shifts for years. The best shifts for me were the ones that began in the afternoon, and went to midnight. To those who think broadcasting is glamorous – beware. Someone has to work around the clock to bring the news to you!

****

Before George W. Bush came into the White House, there were many of us who underestimated him. Perhaps we were right – only history knows. Before the election, and into his Presidency, his speaking style and wild University days were the topic of many jokes. "Saturday Night Live" did an especially viscous television parody of him, and it stuck in many people's minds, who believed this was the real George W. Bush.

There were many reasons why Bush won the election. The bottom line may have been, he was the better candidate. The pendulum always swings in politics, and the public appeared ready for a religious Conservative, who did not lie, abuse power, and cheat on his wife. Al Gore was also, I believe, a man of honor, but had the Bill Clinton stigma, as well as the other problems.

I began to go to daily briefings at the Transition Headquarters, a few blocks from the White House. Those offices became the White House in waiting, until President Bush took the oath of office on January the 20th, 2001. I developed an instant fondness and respect for Ari Fleischer, the White House spokesman, and the rest of the staff. That included Communications Director Karen Hughes, Deputy Press Secretary Scott McClellan and the other deputies, National Security Advisor Condoleezza Rice, Chief of Staff Andrew Card, and Secretary of State Colin Powell. And, we cannot forget First Lady Laura Bush, who did so much to shape her husband, and forge him into the man who became President. I did not trust Dick Cheney and Donald Rumsfeld, whom I had covered for years.

I had known many of the people before, when they served in previous Administrations. But, that would not have mattered. They treated everyone exceptionally well. I remember walking down the hallway of the Transition Office with Mike Wallace, the no-nonsense host of "60 Minutes." I expressed to him my admiration for most of the new staff. He agreed, and added, "and they are nice too." If a man like Mike Wallace could be won over, the staff was more than doing its job. This does not mean we did not criticize and ask tough questions, when we had to.

At first, a solid foundation of respect and helpfulness was in place, and that was to serve President Bush in good stead, in his difficult first year in office. As the years rolled by, his Administration deteriorated, and he eventually did much to lead the world into needless warfare and economic depression. What a shame he became President – especially one who lasted for two terms.

The War Against Terrorism

President Bush was dealing well, at first, with the many challenges of the Presidency. That was a surprise to many of us.

This transformation did not always last, however. The President fell apart at times, as he was faced with the continuing bloodshed of the Iraqi war; the disastrous hurricanes in the South, and sinking popularity polls. He often rambled, bumbled, and had that "deer in the headlights" look. But, he could still rise to eloquence with a well-written speech. Such was the case with a speech he made before the historic Cathedral and Square in New Orleans, after the hurricane and floods. Great effort was made to bring in generators, light the Cathedral – while the rest of Louisiana was black – and portray the President in the strongest, most majestic terms possible. It worked. But, more on the hurricanes later.

The President was in Florida when the September 11, 2001 attacks began against the World Trade Center, and Pentagon, and perhaps the White House or Capitol – although that attack was averted by the brave passengers who fought the hijackers and crashed the plane into a Pennsylvania field. As they began their counterattack, one of the leaders shouted, "Let's Roll." President Bush later used that as his rallying call, in the war against terrorism.

Everyone remembers where they were during the attacks. I was fortunate enough to still be home, doing my early morning round of stories. I was lucky, because I could continue broadcasting for some 30 hours, without much of a break. Had I been in a building under attack, or on the road, I would not have been able to broadcast without interruption (that is, if I was still alive and not injured). Cell phones were sporadic, and not terrific quality, so that would not have done the job for my clients. Some of my colleagues, who were in Florida with President Bush, were unable to return to Washington for several days, which greatly diminished their output. In the end, many had to spend a day in a bus, to get back home, because all non-military planes (except Air Force One) were grounded. The well-funded network correspondents, such as ABC's Ted Koppel, broadcast where they were. He was in London, so his "Nightline" originated from there for several nights.

One of my sons, Daniel, was home at the time, and became a great assistant. My other son, David, was in law school. My husband was at work at the National Library of Medicine. Like all Federal Buildings, his was eventually evacuated in the emergency, since no one knew the full extent of the dangers.

I have relatives in New York and New Jersey, and promptly called them before all the phone lines became blocked. Luckily for us, my nephew Jeff was not in the World Trade Center. He may well have been, since he does a great deal of work in that area. My dear father once had an office on one of the top floors of the World Trade Center. I am sorry he has passed away, but am relieved he did not live to suffer through that horror, as had so many innocent victims. I also shudder to think how my father – the ultimate businessman – would have coped with the monstrous attack on the Capitalist system which he passionately defended all his life.

To this day, I still have nightmares, when I think of people jumping from the top of the World Trade Center, to escape the intense heat and flames. At least my poor father did not share their terrible fate.

As the attacks were underway, there was shock and disbelief around the world. As I watched the Towers burn and crumble, I remember asking Daniel, "what happened to the Tower? I can't see it." It was like a line from a prophetic John Denver song. It was unbelievable to think of the Towers collapsing. It recalled the great announcer of the crash of the Hindenburg, saying, "the humanity ..oh, the humanity." It is impossible to really feel the terror and pain the victims experienced in the moments before their death. The choices some of them had to make were unimaginable – whether to burn to death, or jump from great heights to a crushing death on the New York concrete. Was it better to jump alone, or link hands with colleagues and try to die together, as many of them did. They perished, in a heap of ashes, and became forever part of the ruins where they once worked. Their pain is over, but their families will suffer and mourn for the rest of their lives.

The passengers on American Airlines Flight 11 and United Airlines Flight 175 also experienced terror before their deaths. They knew they had been hijacked, and indicated in heartbreaking phone calls to loved ones, they expected to die.

The American Airlines flight 77 plane crash into the Pentagon was also horrific, and was heard and witnessed by thousands of people in the region. Again, the poor victims died an excruciating death – through flames or smoke. And, all the passengers who died on the hijacked planes were just as innocent as those who died in their offices. Thankfully, many of them, as well as the ones in New York were able to call loved ones and say goodbye. There is no evidence anyone in the Pentagon had that chance – most of them did not know what hit them, prior to the attack.

No one will ever forget the bravery of the passengers who died in the hijacked plane, United Airlines Flight 93, which crashed in a field in Shanksville, Pennsylvania. That plane appeared destined to strike the White House or the Capitol. The passengers, aware of what was happening from phone calls to loved ones, tried to retake their plane. In doing so, it was forced down, and crashed violently. Their lives ended, but many more were saved. And all those terrified, brave passengers live in history as heroes.

As the attacks occurred, we in the news business tried to communicate to the rest of the shocked world. I spent most of my time doing live broadcasts for USA Radio News and Radio America – two superb networks. I am proud to work for them, especially at a time like this.

I also broadcast to BBC, New Zealand, Australia, and South Africa, when they could get through the lines to me. Broadcasting is like the military – we spend a lot of time waiting for action, or for the phone to ring. Then, when there is a big story, everyone wants you at once.

The September 11th tragedy transformed much of the country. American flags appeared everywhere, along with lapel pins. There were also signs proliferating, proclaiming "God Bless America." The petty political disputes that raged before the attacks receded, but surfaced again during the 2004 political race. In 2001, President Bush made speech after speech, and each one was inspirational. He declared a long term war against terror. This time, there is a sense the country meant it. We learned to take nothing for granted – not life, the beauty of our cities and monuments, and the people and places we love. We also have a new breed of heroes – the soldiers, police and firemen, and the CIA and FBI agents. All of them routinely risk their lives for the rest of us.

The future conflicts will be painful, and last longer than the World Wars, Korea, Vietnam, or the Cold War. If America succeeds in "drying up the swamp," as one expert said, and makes the world inhospitable to terrorists, it will be a boon to humanity. But Americans are no longer naïve – they know hatred of the United States, Israel, Jews and Christians and the democratic, capitalistic way of life, will continue in many quarters. But, no one can let September the 11th go unchallenged. If only the free world had gone after terrorists in the 1970's – when the modern age of terrorism began – there would not have been all the attacks, tragedies, and senseless murders of innocents in many parts of the world. But, the world has now changed. We are finally at war against terrorists. May God help us all.

I believed President Bush was correct to wage the war against Saddam Hussein, whether he possessed weapons of mass destruction or not. It was a benefit to rid the world of that monster and his family. Yet, we should have gotten out of Iraq when he was captured. The longer we stayed, the worse it got, for the entire world. And the war in Iraq took the focus off AlQaeda and the Taliban in Afghanistan, which are far more serious threats to the world.

There are tyrannical despots in many nations, and the United States cannot go after all of them, despite our policy of pre-emptive attacks against those who threaten us and our friends and enemies. Still, how different the world would have been if nations had eliminated Stalin, Hitler, Yasser Arafat, and numerous other killers early in their career. It is a life or death topic, well worth debating.

Parenthetically, I may have had a small role to play in the President's decision to enunciate his major policy shifts. This is one advantage in attending the White House Briefing on a daily basis - an event which is sometimes watched each day by millions of television viewers in this nation and around the world.

Once, when the Bush Administration appeared to be making plans to attack Saddam Hussein in Iraq, I posed a question to Ari Fleisher. I said, with all due respect, could you please explain something. If we were perhaps attacked by Osama Ben Laden and Al Qaeda terrorists from Afghanistan, why are we going after Saddam Hussein in Iraq? Ari Fleischer paused, but could not give me a convincing answer. Soon after that, the Bush Administration announced its policy of Preemptive Attacks, against those who threaten America and American interests. They also believe Saddam Hussein was providing money and support to terrorists, in many countries. That was another reason for the strikes.

Another time I asked an important question concerning the massive numbers of US troops deployed in some nations for over 50 years - including South Korea and Germany. I suggested they would be better utilized in a part of the world of much greater strategic importance to the United States now - the Persian Gulf and the Mideast. To my surprise, and that of many of my colleagues, Ari Fleischer indicated planning for such redeployments was under consideration. The Washington Times picked up the story for its front page. Other papers just did not get its importance at the time. In a matter of weeks, the Pentagon announced formal plans to redeploy troop concentrations from Korea, and Europe, to the Persian Gulf.

It is gratifying when colleagues of mine call me one of the most "thoughtful" of White House reporters. I work hard to ask important questions which have impact. I do not grandstand, or give long speeches, but just ask the question. I had suggested the President try openly to assassinate Saddam Hussein, before launching an invasion. I also suggested we should support breaking Iraq into 3 countries. Those public suggestions got no where, although many agreed with me.

Problems and personal hurts persist. I do not have an assigned seat in the White House press room even though I have covered the Presidency for over 42 years - just a few years shy of the incredible Helen Thomas. My major professional disappointment is that I have not had a big, rich company to pay my way on Presidential trips (again, the usual cost is one and a half times first class air rates!). So, the few trips I go on, I finance myself. Since I cannot spend over a million dollars a year following the President's every move, I do not get an assigned seat up front. I understand that situation, but it is annoying - the more so since many of us do not travel, but still have vast impact. As I have said before, I am grateful to have a broadcast booth in the White House, which is really more important to me than an assigned seat. But, it means I have to scramble to take some ones' assigned seat if that person does not show up (many of my colleagues are in the same boat). If you are not in the coveted first four rows, you do not often get called on. Or, if you do, the major cable networks have stopped carrying the briefing "live." (Thank God for the coverage of CSpan Television and Radio - may that superb outfit endure for ever! It carries everything, although not always "live." CSpan is the electronic media "of record.")

I am fighting to have this and future White House's enforce the "two minute" rule. That is the signal we have to scramble into place for the briefing. I argue, those of us who are seatless should have a chance to occupy an unclaimed seat. As it is now, the assigned owner can take the seat, even if the briefing is underway. This forces the people to trip over others, and disrupt the briefing. It looks awful at best of times - especially in a briefing that is carried on the media across the world. Every Administration, and every press secretary, has their own way of working, and I have hopes the changes will be made, as many of my colleagues and I have recommended. Of course, those who have an assigned seat in the White House Press Room have no intention of giving up their arrangement. What ever happened to Seniority? Until I get a seat, I will keep standing against the wall, or sitting on the floor. It is still a privilege to be part of the real estate in the White House.

Other problems emerged with White House coverage as the Bush Administration progressed. The news conferences became more managed, and President Bush started to call on people from a pre-arranged list. This meant, he favored the big, rich news organizations. The rest of us felt neglected at such crucial times. Even if we had clear eye contact with the President, and he knew us, he did not deviate from the list. Most of the public probably don't care – they don't like reporters very much anyway! But to those of us trying to do our jobs, it is very difficult and frustrating.

Press Trip to Israel

I had the good fortune to be invited on another media trip to Israel, from September 3rd to the 11th, 2004. It was my first return in 13 years, and was marvelous! – uplifting and instructive. It enhanced my prestige and authority in reports I did from the scene – it always helps to be on the spot.

This may have been the most important and useful trip to Israel I have ever taken and I have visited Israel many times, including a few weeks spent picking bananas on a Kibbutz. I also reported to Kol Yisreal English news for 20 years (from Washington), so have quite a familiarity with Israel and Israelis. The other 8 journalists on the trip also had great, in-depth knowledge of Israel and the Arab nations, and all found this trip exceedingly useful. With Israel, one loses touch with the shifting political and social situation very quickly. Because of the timeless nature of the Biblical Holy Land, it is important to return often.

Our trip began with a luxurious flight on Continental Airlines on a Friday night. Everything was smooth, professional, and efficient. Our only disappointment was the fact our sponsor Josh Block could not join us, after all the hard work the press secretary put into arranging the trip. But we were met by a wonderful Israeli-American, David Kreizelman, who did a great job keeping us together, He and our expert guide, Asher Afriat, enhanced the trip. Asher has degrees in law and archeology – we couldn't ask for a better guide.

In Israel we felt remarkably safe. That may have been a rationalization, but security was professional, and we were well guarded most of the time. The presence of the security barrier in many areas helped to keep out the deadly bombers. There were the usual well-trained and well-armed Israeli soldiers in evidence, but security was not as oppressive as I had expected. Much of it was conducted by electronic means and profiling. I felt no fear walking the streets and eating in the wonderful outdoor restaurants. I did not take public busses, and worry about the large number of Israelis who have to rely on them for transportation. We also avoided the areas of greatest tension – Gaza and Ramallah, for example.

It may sound corny but, if one feels nervous in Israel, it is best to visit the Biblical sites – starting with the old city and parts of the destroyed Temple in Jerusalem. You look at thousands of years of history, and know you are a small part of this unfolding story.

Upon arrival Saturday night, we checked into the Inbal Hotel in Jerusalem. Then we had the first of many sumptuous meals in Jerusalem. Our guest lecturer was David Horovitz, who was introduced to us as the Editor in Chief of The Jerusalem Report. Two days later, he was front page news, as it was revealed he was named editor of The Jerusalem Post. In his new position, his stories will receive greater international exposure. At dinner, he talked to us about "Israeli Society and the War on Terror."

Sunday, September the 5th, was a fascinating but grueling day, especially for a group of journalists who had been wide awake most of the night writing stories. Our body clocks were still on American time. But, the first morning we had a moving tour of the Old City. The topic was "Jerusalem: At Historical and Religious Crossroads." The centuries – old Church bells rang, and a poignant Russian and Greek Orthodox ceremony was in progress at the Church of the Holy Sepulcher. Many worshippers were sobbing – some might have had friends and relatives who had just died in the vicious terrorist attack on the school in Beslan, Russia.

After two hours in the Churches and markets of the Old City, we had a fantastic lunch at the Anna Ticho Restaurant. Professor Raphael Israeli of Hebrew University provided us with a Regional Overview – very useful.

Then, on to the American Colony Hotel, where we had a testy session with Dr. Saeb Erekat, the Palestinian Minister for Negotiations. We gave him high marks for showing up and meeting with us. But, we were tough on him, especially when he claimed Bill Clinton lied, when he revealed that he had offered the Palestinians 98% of what they wanted during the exhausting negotiations at the end of the Clinton Presidency. We told Erekat, all other versions differed from his. Erekat also denied there was any corruption among the Palestinians. When I asked him about corruption and violence, and asked where Arafat squandered the millions or billions of dollars he earned from corruption,, he snapped back and said, "a lady does not ask those questions!" I also angered him, when I asked him what would happen when Arafat eventually died (which he did two months later). Clearly, that was an issue he and the other Palestinians did not want to face in public.

The rest of the day was spent in more high level briefings by Israeli officials. Since they were off the record, I will not discuss them, except to say they were eye opening!

Finally, at night – more briefings and more fantastic Mediterranean food, in an outdoor veranda overlooking suburbs of Jerusalem. The restaurant was the Caravan, Abu Gosh. The food was enough to feed us for a week! Our speaker was Ilana Dayan, Producer and Moderator of Uvda. She is a brilliant woman, who pursued legal studies at Yale Law School. She is in sharp disagreement with many Israeli government policies. Her topic was "Democratic Societies in Existential Conflicts."

By the way, there must have been some calculated risk in eating in restaurants open to the outdoors. But, it was wonderful, and none of us wanted to give way to intimidation by terrorists.

Monday, was one of the most important days in many ways. We started with a visit to the Yad Vashem Holocaust Memorial. It is always heartbreaking to witness the history of anti Semitism, and view the memorials to the over 8 million exterminated Jews. But this visit might play an important role in future history. Russian Foreign Minister Sergi Lavrov was there – just days after the series of deadly terrorism attacks in Russia. In them, a grade school in Beslan was attacked, and hundreds of Russians – mostly children and their parents, were killed. There were also attacks in other parts of Russia. He was gracious when I went up to him to offer sympathy. We were told the Foreign Minister was especially moved by the dark, candlelit memorial to the one and a half million slain Jewish children. He related it to the school massacre in Russia. He was also informed of an Israeli saying that, "there is no future without children." We felt this visit may harden Russia's attitude towards terrorists.

It was appropriate that, after Yad Vashem, we went to the Mevasseret Zion immigrant absorption center. The topic was "Integrating Refugees into Israeli Society." We watched and spoke with recent Ethiopian immigrants to Israel. Some could not read or write their own language, but were learning how to write Hebrew and use a computer at the same time. They also learned about modern society – they had come from extremely primitive backgrounds.

Later we had free time, which gave me a chance to catch a swim in the pool. I felt like Miami Beach, until I noticed the handsome,well-armed Israeli soldier next to me. Then, ten of my former colleagues from Kol Yisrael came over for a reunion. I had not seen them for 13 years; but we had spent 20 years in hard work together. It was a wonderful reunion.

We also had another briefing with Oded Granot. the Arab Affairs Analysist for Channel One television. We were also good friends from his days in Washington, and his topic was "The Arab Media Today."

Finally a dinner which we all judged to be one of the most interesting. It was held at Darna, a fantastic Moroccan restaurant. But, the best part was the speaker, Khaled Abu Toameh, a brave Palestinian reporter who risks his life every day, reporting for The Jerusalem Post. He published stories, revealing that PLO functionaries beat up and threatened to kill journalists who reported about corruption and chaos in Ramallah and other areas dominated by Yasser Arafat, who was still alive at the time.

On Tuesday, September 7th, we began with a breakfast meeting at the hotel with Gideon Meir, the Deputy Director General for Media and Public Affairs, at the Ministry of Foreign Affairs. We expected propaganda – instead, it was very interesting. He showed us with graphic clarity, the ways the media is manipulated to insure an anti Israeli attitude. This is true in some of the major news organizations. He also showed us a horribly anti Semitic cartoon, reminiscent of some of the worst anti-Jewish printings of the Nazi era. It won a prize in Europe for the best cartoon. When the creator was interviewed, he asked why there were no similar cartoons against Arab leaders. He said, there is concern about that, because the Arabs put out a "faqua" or death sentence against those they don't like, whereas the Israelis do not do so.

For the next few hours, we toured parts of the West Bank and saw various sections of the Security Barrier. It is controversial, but has reduced bombings and saved many lives. Walls are nothing new – they have protected people since pre-Biblical times. We saw Israeli settlements – some of which are large cities and an instrumental part of Jerusalem. Many of the residents commute to high tech jobs inside of Jerusalem. We also saw Arab settlements – some new, and some old and some in tatters. They gave way to Bedouin encampments nearby. The proximity of the Arab and Jewish villages put them, unfortunately, in close shooting and rocket-firing distance of each other. Maybe someday they can all live in cities, in peace and brotherhood.

After a few hours, we had a luncheon briefing with a former chief of the Mossad, Israel's security service. He is Dr. Ephrain Halevi. His most interesting comments were off the record, and he knew a lot more than he disclosed! Our restaurant, the Taverna, offered a sweeping view of all of Jerusalem. As we talked, about 30 Israeli women soldiers appeared on the balcony, to receive their own history and geography lessons.

In the afternoon, we transferred to a small armored vehicle, and drove south to the outskirts of Ramallah –headquarters of the PLO. Our high level military briefings, at a sensitive Israeli military headquarters, gave us an excellent overview of the anti – terrorism fight. It will be a long one but Israel, the United States, the United Kingdom, Australia, and now Russia are among the nations in it for the long haul.

Our long haul for Tuesday was still not quite over. Again, another fantastic dinner, at Mishkenot Sha'ananim with one of our best and wittiest briefers – retired Colonel Daniel Reisner. He was the former head of the International Law Division of the IDF, or Israeli Defense Force. His topic was Israel in the International Legal Arena. Reisner took part in most major legal discussions, including Camp David negotiations and others. His insights were most instructive, and humorous. We had to travel several thousand miles to find a lawyer with a sense of humor. Some of the points he made included the fact, the US, the EU, or the UN could force Israel to tear down the barrier, if they imposed sanctions. He also said the barrier is useful now but, in the future, suicide bombers would succeed in tunneling under the barrier. Somehow, peace will have to be reached before then.

Wednesday, September the 8th, we were sad to have a final breakfast at the Inbal, and then leave Jerusalem, a city with had an effect on all of us. We took long bus tours through several parts of Israel, including the harsh Judean desert. We had a strategic survey of the Jordan Valley, and a visit to the Bet She 'an archaelogical site. The Graeco-Roman name for the city, baths, and theater was Scythopolis, and settlement began in the fifth millennium BCE. As the only women in our journalists' group, I probably should not have been allowed in the baths – no women were at the time. The men had all the spoils and the women were shunted off to other, less luxurious areas.

Next we traveled North to what many consider to be the most beautiful parts of Israel –around the Galilee, the Golan Heights, and Metulla. The region had a great deal of personal meaning to me. When I was younger, I spent some time picking bananas on Kibbutz Massada in the north. In 1982, Metulla was my last jump off point, before I managed to get into Lebanon, and cover the evacuation of the PLO from Beruit.

The general region was as lush and wonderful as I remembered – in some sections you felt as though you were truly back in Biblical times.

The modern area was not always so lush. Israelis made Herculean efforts to drain the malarial swamps, irrigate the fields, and utilize modern farming methods to produce successful farms. They export fruits and vegetables, but have increasing difficulty in exporting them to areas in Europe. It is hoped those attitudes will change at some point. The North also has many high tech manufacturing centers to supplement the rural exports. And, as always, there are the many sensors in place the try to keep Israel safe from terrorists and other invaders.

In the North we climbed to the steep highlands of the Golan Heights, where some of the sharpest, toughest, and deadliest fighting in Israeli history took place. We explored the tunnels where Syrian fighters attacked Israeli settlers below. From the top peak, we could see the expanse of Damascus, Syria. We were close to the choke off points of two of Israel's main water supplies – the Jordan River and the Sea of Galilee. Those supplies are safe as long as Israel controls the Golan.

On Wednesday night, we had one of the most remarkable experiences of the trip. We ate at the beautiful, modern home of Orna and Lior Weinberg, and their two young sons. Theirs can be described as "the last house in Israel." Beyond their backyard is Lebanon. To the right, in the distance, is Syria. Of greatest concern is the Hezbolllah training camp in Lebanon. From the Weinberg's house, the yellow flag of the camp can be seen. Occasionally shots are fired. There are frightening stories of Iranian mullahs visiting and coordinating assistance and strategy. Recent reports say missiles have come from Iran, across Syria, and into that area. Can you imagine leading a normal life under those circumstances? Still the Weinbergs and their neighbors are trying. They have their bomb shelters ready, but a family of four – plus pets – would not want to spend too much time there. Picking apples from their orchards pose a special risk. The trees grow right up to the border. There have been times when the workers or the soldiers in the orchards have been shot and killed by the Hezbollah shooters.

Finally, after a wonderful evening in Metulla – the most picturesque little city in Israel, we spent a night in the guest house of Kibbutz K'far Blum. A very interesting Kibbutz and one of the oldest in Israel. Too bad there was not more time to explore it, but there was so much to do, and so little time.

On Thursday September the 9th, we departed for a survey of Christian sites, as we made our way south to Tel Aviv. One of our first stops was the beautiful, spiritually uplifting Church of the Beatitudes. From the Church, you look down at the sparkling and important Sea of Galilee. At the spot where Jesus was said to have preached, one member of our group read "The Sermon on the Mount." There are no words to describe the majesty of that experience, provided to us by Jay Nordlinger of the National Review.

We left this region for another important experience at Ceparnahum. There Jesus was believed to have spent from one to three years studying with Peter. One of the phrases carved in stone was "Thou are Peter and upon this rock I will build my Church." We also visited the first century Temple – one of many visited by Jesus. It is now called the "Synagogue of Jesus." Jesus was said to have led prayers and performed miracles in the Synagogue. Hundreds of tourists and Christian pilgrims were in evidence at the site. Everyone I spoke to expressed joy, fulfillment, and peace during their visit to Israel. After three very hard years, Israelis and visitors have recaptured their spirit, determination, and joie do vivre. There is always the sense of possible danger, but that makes life so much more precious and sacred.

From the Biblical and spiritual, we were thrust back into the realities of modern life. We drove South to the Tel Aviv Sheraton. Our first briefing was a lunch meeting with Binyamin Ben Eliezer, a former Minister of Defense and Labor Member of Knesset. This man has been through a lot! His topic was ideological shifts in Israeli politics. He also had some tough words for the developing nuclear situation in Iran.

Finally, onto a very important visit and briefing at the Ichilov Hospital in Tel Aviv. We were given a detailed briefing and tour by Dr. Pinhas

Halperin, director of the emergency room. He explained about the different injuries caused by the various types of terrorist attacks, in buses, markets, and so forth. He also told us his doctors and nurses must treat all equally – even those who were the actual terrorists and survived their attempts at martyrdom. He said personnel would be fired, if they did not give them the best care. Dr. Halperin also said, doctors and nurses go into the scene of any attack, if the SWAT teams and firefighters go in. They do not stay in a triage area and wait for patients to be brought to them.

In the midst of more details about the shrapnel in terrorist bombs, and the dangers of possible nuclear, chemical, or biological attacks, Dr. Halperin provided a nice touch. He gave us apples and honey – the traditional Jewish way to greet the upcoming Jewish New Year of Rosh Hashonah.

In the afternoon, we went to our hotel, where I had another reunion with two of my favorite friends from the days of Kol Yisrael. It is gratifying to know they and their families have survived and thrived all these years. Despite the dangers and hardships, they are still there, carrying out the traditions of Israel and all who love this special country.

In the evening we had a brisk walk along the beach to a sea front hotel in Tel Aviv, call the Manta Ray. After another enormous meal, some of the men in our group sampled the famous music and night life of Tel Aviv. I went back to my room to write and broadcast. But, when I finished and looked down from my balcony at 3:30 in the morning, I could still hear music and see dozens of people walking on the beaches and on the streets!

Friday, September the 10th, was sadly our last day in Israel of this trip. We left Tel Aviv early, and headed south to Masada and the Dead Sea. Masada is always an extremely powerful and fascinating experience. We explored the caves, cisterns, baths, and rooms where about 960 Israelis were said to have survived for 3 years. Then, according to history and legend, they committed suicide, rather than face conquest by the Romans, who had spent years and great effort building a ramp, to scale the steep cliffs and try to conquer them. While that version is generally accepted as fact, other accounts say they Jews went out in fierce fighting, as had fellow Jews in Jerusalem and other areas conquered by the Romans. In any case I was pleased to hear Masada is no longer considered the symbol of modern Israel. Instead, it is other areas where Jews have fought bravely. They died in the end, but did not go like "sheep to the slaughter." Instead of a Masada complex, it can be said modern Jews may have an Alamo complex!

Finally, the fun part to round up our trip. We journied down to the Dead Sea, which we had been viewing from high in Masada. We were guests at the lowest point on Earth! The Dead Sea area has been built up, and there are a variety of spas and luxury hotels. We did the traditional thing – bobbing around on our backs in the salty, yet clear water of the Dead Sea. Since no fish or plants can live in it, the Sea is remarkably clear. It is also believed to cure skin diseases and other ailments, and people come from Europe, America, and Israel – of course – for its medicinal effects. After about an hour in the Sea, we swam and used the Spa (which is in an area that doubles as a bomb shelter with thick protective doors). A dose of reality in the midst of paradise. Finally, north to Tel Aviv again.

We had a final, fabulous Shabat feast – this one in the home of David Kreizelman at Moshav Kfar Bin Nun. He had been in charge of us all week, and done a terrific job. It was all so warm, familial, and normal – there was acknowledgement of the dangers always facing Israel, but it was hard to believe. It is like the dangers facing those of us who live in Washington and New York - we go about life and do not dwell on them.

Finally, we drove to the airport for another luxurious Continental flight back to New York and Washington. Two in our group stayed behind in Israel; others stayed in New York and three of us went home to Washington. As we crossed the Atlantic, the date became September the 11th – three years after the monstrous attacks on the United States. From Newark Airport, we saw a magnificent and defiant sunrise over New York. We saw the empty area where the World Trade Center Towers had stood, and so many lost their lives. As we flew to Washington a few hours later, we were in the air during some of the moments of silence, commemorating the times the hijacked planes hit the World Trade Centers. Then, we flew over the restored Pentagon before landing at National Airport. Our once-close group went our own ways. But, in our minds and souls, we will always have a special bond. And, it all ties together – the terrorism attacks, the incredible trip to Israel, and the will of all people to survive.

Ted Kennedy's State Funeral

Senator Ted Kennedy died in Hyannis Port, Massachusetts on August 26, 2009. The 77 year old "Lion of the Senate" had been battling brain cancer for 15 months. The Funeral for Senator Ted Kennedy was majestic, poignant, emotional, stirring and, at times, very funny. It did not appear to be the end of Camelot. With at least 85 Kennedy relatives, there are many available to play a vital role in the history of this nation and the world.

The Funeral was planned for months. This was the only famous Kennedy son who had time to plan for a funeral. The others were cut down violently and suddenly, in the prime of their lives. But, Ted Kennedy had adequate time to chose the speakers, location, and music. His friends and adversaries had 15 months to praise him, and put history and their own lives in perspective.

The Funeral Mass in Boston was an amazing show of political power. President Obama gave the eulogy. The Obamas, the Clintons, the Carters, the George W Bush family, and many Vice Presidents were there. President and Mrs. George Bush Senior said they were unable to attend. At least 58 present members of the U.S. Senate and 21 former members were in attendance, along with dozens of members of Congress.

The actual Funeral began on the morning of his death. The entire Kennedy family lined up, to offer a dignified and emotional good bye to their leader; the man who had become a substitute father for so many of them. The funeral motorcade from the Hyannis Port Compound to Boston took several hours. Those who were able to line the streets applauded as the procession passed by. Many held signs which said, "thank you Teddy."

The Senator's body lay in repose at the John F. Kennedy Memorial Library in Boston. Ted Kennedy worked hard to build the Library in honor of his brother. Later, he worked for other monuments to honor Bobby Kennedy. Thousands of ordinary citizens stood in line for hours. They filed past his casket, which was draped in an American flag. The flag had recently flown over the U.S. Capitol, where Kennedy served for 47 years.

On Friday night, Boston time, a three hour Irish Wake was held in the Kennedy Library. Senators, other famous people, and Caroline Kennedy said wonderful things about Ted Kennedy. His favorite songs were sung, including "When Irish Eyes are Smiling," "To Dream the Impossible Dream," and "Love Changes Everything." But, there were moments of intense humor, as there are meant to be in any celebration of life. The funniest was a speech by former Senator John Culver of Iowa. He recounted their first sail boat race. The Senator from the land-locked state had never seen a sailboat before, was sea sick, cold, and miserable. Somehow their friendship endured, and they sailed together again for many years.

The next day, Saturday in Boston, had turned cold and rainy. The Senator's casket was now draped in a splendid white cloth. The Mass was held in the Mission Basilica. It is there he prayed each day, while his daughter was fighting to survive lung cancer. So far, his daughter and one son have survived their own battles with cancer. His third son talked about his struggles with asthma, and the special attention he received from his father. Patrick continues to be plagued with substance abuse issues. Of the many speeches delivered, son Teddy Junior's was the most powerful. He talked about his suffering, after losing a leg to cancer when he was twelve. His Father got him through those terrible days, by convincing him he could do anything.

President Obama also gave a powerful final speech, saying, "we cannot know God's plan for us." Musical renditions were also given by cellist Yo -Yo Ma and opera singer Placido Domingo. The Funeral Mass ended with a Recessional to the strains of "America the Beautiful." Then Senator Kennedy's casket was taken by a military honor guard, to be flown to final burial at the Arlington National Cemetery. The American Flag was again draped over it. Senator Kennedy joined his brothers John and Bobby to be buried on sacred ground, near the Eternal Flame. Two of his infant children, and John's wife Jacquline, are also buried at Arlington, and more will follow in the future.

After the Military plane landed at Andrews Air Force Base, from Boston, a long motorcade was formed again. In Washington, thousands of people also lined the streets to honor Teddy. About 4,000 stood for hours on the steps and driveways of the Capitol They honored the man who had served there for nearly 50 years. About 100 of his former staff members were there – Kennedy was known to have the brightest and hardest working staff in Congress. Many of former staffers went onto serve in the White House and Supreme Court.

Prayers were said at the Capitol, and all members of the Kennedy family got out of their buses and greeted those they could . Then the crowd burst into song again – "God Bless America" and "America the Beautiful." It reminded many of the patriotism they felt, after the attacks on America on 9/11/2001.

The motorcade regrouped and made its slow journey down Constitutional Avenue, across the Memorial Bridge, and onto the sacred hillsides of Arlington National Cemetery. About 200 people and a small group of reporters covered the actual burial. Ted Kennedy's grave was marked, at this time, by a simple white cross. The surprise of the ceremony was provided by Cardinal Theodore McCarrick. He read from the letter the Senator had recently sent to the Pope. The letter was delivered by President Obama. In it, Senator Kennedy talked about his intense Catholic faith, despite disagreements. He admitted he had been "an imperfect human being." The Cardinal also read from the Pope's letter, in which he gave Kennedy his blessing.

Then it was all over. Arlington Cemetery and the Kennedy grave sites are open to the public. In the country. the fight goes on over health care reform and other important issues of social welfare and world peace. As more bills are passed, they will carry Ted Kennedy's name. There are already more than 300 he sponsored. Now, other Kennedy's will carry the torch, sail his boats, and carry on the fight without him. There are many who disagree with him, and have intense hatred for the Kennedy's. But, despite his shortcomings and excesses, it must be said, in the words of the King and I, "this is a man who tried."

After his death, the Kennedy magic disappeared, as least as this is written. The Senate seat he held for nearly 47 years was won by a Republican. Many Independent voters said they did not like being taken for granted, opposed the massive and expensive health care bill, and were concerned about the loss of jobs and the trillion dollar deficit. Their votes do not bode well for the Democrats. In politics, the pendulum always swings, and at least one influential Democrat was not around to swing it his way.

Barack Obama is President

Americans truly made history in November, 2008, when they elected Barack Obama to the Presidency. He is a brilliant man, well spoken, energetic, and handsome with a beautiful family. His election was historic, because Americans finally elected an African –American to office. But, I prefer to think of him as biracial. His father was from Kenya, but his Mother and maternal Grandparents were white Americans, from the Mid-West and Hawaii.

The Obamas took much of the nation and world by storm, but he has had a very difficult first year in office. I think it is important to have a man of color as the leader of the United States. It also changes our image in the rest of the world. The population of the nation is changing dramatically, and there will be many more political leaders with mixed colors, ethnic, and religious backgrounds. If they are smart, disciplined, and well educated, it should make America better.

I first spotted Barack Obama during a Democratic convention, when he made a dramatic prime time speech. I predicted then, he could be President. The 2008 Presidential race was brutal, with a large field of qualified candidates. For a while, the conventional wisdom predicted Hillary Clinton would win. I never bought into that. It sorted out very well, with Barack Obama as President, Joe Biden as Vice President, and Hillary Clinton as Secretary of State. Former President Bill Clinton runs around the world, making speeches and supporting good causes. He went to North Korea, and gained the release of two imprisoned American television journalists. But, Bill Clinton has no formal role in the Obama Administration at this time, although he and George W. Bush are raising money for the poor people in Haiti who were devastated by the massive earthquake.

Fortunately, John Edwards did not become the candidate. It was revealed later that he had an affair with a staff member and fathered a daughter, while his wife was (and is) fighting terminal cancer. Edwards repeatedly lied about the affair and the baby, until he was forced to fess up. He reportedly spent over a million dollars trying to cover up the situation, according to his one time friend and top aide. But, it all unraveled. Thank goodness the American voters rejected him, and he did not go on to become part of the Obama Administration. I have seen many sleazy politicians in my time, but this situation has to take the prize. I can only grieve for his family.

President Obama came into office with heavy burdens inherited from the Bush Administration. The economy was at near Depression levels, and the wars in Iraq and Afghanistan intensified. Tension continued in Iran, parts of Africa, and between Israelis and Palestinians.

Domestically, President Obama is having a very rough time, as I am writing this. But, it is early into his Presidency, and no one can predict the future. As President Obama said during the funeral of Ted Kennedy, "No one can predict God's plan for us."

The President is under fire, in some quarters, for the economic stimulus plan and the multi trillion dollar debt. Recession has cut deeply, and millions are out of work in this country and around the world. The debate is fierce over health care reform bills, and lawmakers have faced angry crowds in town hall meetings (although most have been respectful to the President in his meetings. He can still see and hear some angry crowds on the streets, if he is able to witness them). At the end of his first year, a devastating earthquake hit Haiti, causing massive destruction on the suffering island. The Obama Administration handled relief efforts well, as did private citizens, and other countries. The outpouring of assistance shows the positive side of human nature, which should be manifest more often.

There are many who hate Obama because he is Liberal, part – Black, or sponsors programs they do not like. Maybe that will change, and there will be more unity in the nation. But, it is a tough call. His White House staff is still far from perfect, and has a long way to go. In the press room, only the reporters from the top, wealthy news organizations are called on routinely, and can ask numerous questions. The news business is in trouble, and more organizations are cutting back, going under, or unable to go on very expensive trips with the President (over one and a half times First Class Air Fare, on a usual trip). I suppose it is fair they get the best seats in the press room, and are called on the most. But, it is painful for the rest of us.

On a personal note, I am very concerned about the continued military buildup in Afghanistan. My heart breaks for all who are killed and maimed, from America and other countries. I believe Iraq was a mistake in the long term, because it lasted too long and damaged the US. We did not even get an "oil benefit," and Iran became stronger as Iraq descended into turmoil. Afghanistan may live up to its reputation as the "graveyard of Empires." On the other hand, terrorism is on the upswing. A man came close to blowing up a US airliner over Detroit on Christmas Day, 2009. Terrorist attacks against US Embassies were thwarted, but at least 7 CIA experts were blown up in Afghanistan. Al Qaeda and other terrorist groups are expanding in the Mid East, Africa, Asia, and perhaps here at home. Clearly, they need to be fought. But, I would like to see as many attacked with drones and missiles, with fewer soldiers on the ground, if that is possible.

This is not to say we don't honor our servicemen and women. My husband, Dr. Charles Sneiderman and I have gotten very active with Wounded Warrior organizations. We ski with them as much as we can, write stories, and publicize their plight. For us, it is a case of "dislike the wars, love the warriors."

As I have said, this is still a young Presidency, and the future is unknown. But, when we view the violence, brutality, and chaos in much of the world, we must be thankful for the United States and the other countries which live a generally peaceful, civilized, prosperous, and cultured existence, despite the present recession. Let us hope that passes soon, and people can reclaim their lost homes and jobs.

You Can Do it too. The Final Chapter, 2014

As the news business has matured - and I along with it - it has become rougher in many ways. At all the news bureaus, there have been massive cutbacks in expenditures. Many of the major newspapers and magazines have died or on trouble. In the future, they may all exist on line, but not in print. There have been enormous consolidations in the radio industry, and many of the stations are part of billion dollar conglomerates. They cross national lines. News stations in New Zealand and Australia now have owners in Pittsburgh or London. Many of the stations take their "actualities" (or news cuts) from CNN, Fox, Sky, MSNBC, C-Span or other mass news services. In some cases, they are also allowed to use their reporters if they credit them on air. The major role left for many independent reporters is that of a commentator or analyst, and some stations do not want to pay for that. But many of my colleagues - even the network superstars - are in the same boat. Some of them have suffered hefty reductions in salary when their contracts were renewed. If they could not accept, they tried to find jobs in local media, where they became celebrity anchors, or they went into public relations and "consulting." But local newscasts are also in trouble. The major network anchors, however, continue to draw salaries in the millions, the theory being that they bring in the audience and, by extension, advertising revenues.

The Cable News Network, Fox and other cable outlets have hurt me the most, although I had been bracing for that for years. Many of my stations subscribe to cable services, and take their live coverage from them. I am hit the hardest from Washington, because most of the American news emanates from here. But I have been able to cover much breaking news around the world by watching cable, and giving my own analysis. I am grateful for that. So the situation works both ways to everybody's advantage.

Now the Internet poses new challenges and opportunities for the news industry, business, communications, and the entire information system. I am excited about the future; a whole new world lies ahead. I have also joined the ranks of citizen journalists, and write blogs on politics, snow sports, wounded warriors, cultural events, or anything I chose. I think it is wonderful that journalism is now open to everyone, but you do not always get paid for your contribution. You often have to do it as an avocation, and not a vocation. That does not make you less professional in anyway. In fact, it often makes you a better citizen of the world.

I have been extremely fortunate, because I worked for a strong, domestic radio chain – IRN/USA Radio News. I have been blessed to be with them for over 20 years (they merged with Information Radio Network in 2008). But they finally changed in 2014, and many of us left them. BBC is my major international client, and I absolutely love doing "talk back" for them, any hour of the day and night. For a few years I fulfilled a 10 year dream, to contribute my version of Alistair Cooke's "Letters from America." Mine were called, "Postcards from America" and were carried on the BBC's GNS service. They did a series of interviews for BBC stations around the nation. The two or three hour rotation was a bit like Chinese water torture. It took intelligence, glibness, and a strong bladder to survive the rotations, which they fed out at least twice a day.

The White House is my primary "beat," but I can report on any major news stories or features. I have added prestige as the longest serving independent White House correspondent (Helen Thomas was the longest employed correspondent, having beaten me out by a few years! She died in her nineties). Many international stations call me often for analysis and commentary. I have been doing a large amount of such news and talk-back for a variety of BBC radio and television stations around the world, including GNS, The World Service Radio and television, London, Wales, Scotland and Belfast. This is in addition to my traditional stations in this country, Australia, New Zealand, and other nations. At this time, I am contributing a blog, or column to the internet news services Huffingtonpost.com, and Scoop.co.nz in New Zealand. I do snow sports features for "DCSKI.com". Internet sites are the future, and are much more satisfying than radio, in many ways. They have the speed of radio, but the prestige and finality of print. I also do some magazine articles for SnowEast and Washington Life.

In many ways, I prefer the commentary to "hard" news. It means I can express my own analysis and opinions, based on over 47 years of on-the-spot observation from the White House, and other areas of the world. In addition, I have more of a life. Instead of being chained to a studio in my home, or at the White House, I can broadcast from a phone booth or iPhone in the Kennedy Center, or wherever, when I am summoned to do a story. Now I do most of my broadcasting through my computer, or on the versatile and high quality Smart phone. It also means you are on call 24 hours a day. And during crises stories - such as the September 11 attacks, The Clinton sex scandals or the war against terrorism, the broadcasts can last 30 hours at a stretch, all over the world. But, it is wonderful to be in demand, and I wouldn't change it for anything in the world! Of course, it is better to be discussing sex and lust than stories where people are actually dying or being killed.

I had also been very lucky and honored, to be hired as a part time newscaster for the Voice of America. It is a superb organization, with dedicated people, who work extremely hard to deliver unfettered news to the rest of the world. I was there for about 3 years, but left after I remarried and wanted to spend the nights with my husband Charles! Most of the shifts for the new people at VOA were overnight, but that is also prime time in many other areas of the world.

VOA's potential listeners are over a 100 million people a day, in at least 53 countries. But it is impossible to estimate the impact, because the broadcasts also go out on the Internet and television, with streaming audio and video. They work horrendous hours at great pressure and intensity. Many are the nights I have wandered the hallways of the federal building, performing karate kicks and other exercises, in an effort to stay awake and alert during an all night shift. As in the White House, the VOA is also plagued by a rat problem, and the 4-legged creatures seem to be drawn to hallways and parking lots in the middle of the might. They are probably not as dangerous as walking the streets, in a high-crime area of Washington, at that time, but, they are unnerving. Still, the VOA was a fitting fulfillment to a hard-fought career. I have been a miniature VOA all my professional life, and it was fantastic to have the actual organization behind me. In fact, my first book was called "Voice From America."

I feel so strongly about the VOA, that I tried very hard to become its Director during the Bush Administration. I had some excellent support – inside the White House and Congress. My two Senators, and Congressman, wrote especially strong letters on my behalf. But, the terrorist attacks on the 11th of September, changed the role and focus of the VOA. I would still like to serve my country in a federal position, if possible, before my working days are over.

I continue to believe news is the most exciting profession in the world, but you cannot go into it with the thought of making a lot of money. All too often, you may barely scrape by. But you can usually make an honorable living in it. And, you may always hit it big and become one of the major superstars in the business. But, never lose your compass. You enter the business to inform and to expose wrongs, even at the risk of your own life or privacy. Many brave reporters have died gruesome deaths, covering wars or terrorism. To report, you have to have a genuine interest in people, and be concerned about them. If you are dedicated to making people feel, understand, and hopefully lead better lives, than the news business is for you!

There are pitfalls along the way. News is not always a harmonious business. Over the years, as I became more visible, I also made some major enemies. I suppose I was lucky, for I managed to get quite far in the profession before I had to deal with a real crisis. But one such experience occurred which illustrates the pitfalls of success and a high profile.

There is one particular male free-lance reporter in Washington who has been doing essentially the same work as I for over a quarter century. He has a brilliant radio voice, but a domineering, arrogant and nasty personality. For this reason, he has lost many clients over the years. Often those who fired him hired me in his place. This has prompted him to blame me for all his problems.

Early in our relationship, I trusted him and shared my all-important list of clients and their direct contact numbers. He substituted for me when I had to be away. One day, he saw me on television when I was trying out for a position with a television news service (which soon folded in any case). Although I had done TV periodically for years, I would never give up radio - it is my first love, my bread and butter. But this man saw me on television and, without even consulting me, sold my list of free-lance stations to another reporter in California! That was an unheard-of breech of ethics and moral behavior. Later in his career, he sold similar sensitive information to another radio client. He always denied doing it, but the evidence against him was very strong.

I tried my best to stay out of the man's way over the years because I believed he was a very cruel and sick man. But a few years ago, he saw a chance to drive me out of the business and reclaim his place at one of the networks which had fired him. He wrote a series of extremely vicious letters about me and sent them to all the major American networks, as well as the press galleries of the Congress and the White House. All of his charges were false, but the letters were a blatant and brutal attempt to get me out of his way. I was very distressed when the calls began to come in, asking me about the accusations. Fortunately, many of the news executives who called knew me well, and assured me that they had no proof of the allegations. In addition, the original letters were not signed and, as my callers said, "A letter is only as good as the signature on it."

When I told each network about the series of letters, several news directors said, in summary, "Clearly, you are the victim of a vendetta by a sick person who hates you." Most of my friends had a variation on that theme. When the first letters had no effect, my nemesis rewrote them, but signed them with a false name and a phone number in Maryland. When that number was called, this man's voice was clearly on the tape! I recorded that, and played it for all the people concerned. His distinctive radio voice is well known, and they all agreed it was his voice, without a doubt. In addition, the phrases he used about me were characteristic of the way he spoke in daily conversation ("Lawn hangs out at the State Department"; "She is a disgrace to the industry," and so forth). We also matched the typewriter to letters he had written and signed to employers on other topics. Finally, the postmarks all came from the town where he was living. We had a very strong circumstantial case. I went to some topnotch lawyers with the information I had.

In the end, the attorneys told me that a defamation lawsuit of this type could run to $75,000 or more. And although they were positive I would win, there was very little I could collect in damages. He earned limited money and had few assets. In addition, his letters damaged him far more than me. None of the organizations believed him, but they certainly believe he wrote the letters. He continues to deny it but cannot explain how his voice was on that tape. It is a pity I cannot sue, but I have found out through this and other experiences that justice is often a luxury reserved for the wealthy. In another case, I dropped the matter after spending $8,000 on legal fees. At $200 to $300 an hour, it is very expensive indeed to get involved in a complex or protracted legal undertaking. I relate this experience to show how very tough the news business can be when the stakes are high and rivalries are vicious. Fortunately, however, I have found such negative experiences to be few, and more than offset by the many joys and positive memories that a career in journalism can bring.

The man in question strongly denies he wrote the letters, or took any of the other actions. And, in an interesting postscript, we once again become friends. I told him, we are too old, and have been in this business too long, to be distracted by competition in the past. All of the events appeared earth shaking to me at the time. But, they are nothing compared to the wars, terrorism, famine, disease, and terror faced by many people in the world. We must keep our focus on what we are supposed to be covering, and not center on ourselves.

There have been other rough times, but they too have passed. The early days of the Clinton Administration were quite rocky, and the new White House press staff had many a falling-out with reporters. They thought they could go over our heads to the American public, and sell their line directly to the constituencies involved in a particular campaign or issue. It is a technique that worked well for Bill Clinton during his brilliant first presidential campaign. But the staff soon discovered that it needed us too. I was especially hurt when overzealous young White House staffers tried to take away the booth I had waited twenty years to get. I was even sharing it with another organization. But without asking me, the White House gave it to a TV organization, which they deemed more important, although it had been covering the White House only for a few months. When the organization informed the staffers there was a lock on the door (as there are on all the tiny booths), they were told, "Break the goddamn lock off and put in your own." After a great deal of struggle and anguish on my part, we worked out a sharing arrangement and finally formed a radio pool booth, which I had fought for for years. We could have reached such an accommodation in five minutes on our own, if only the White House press staff had not injected itself into the situation. Several of us took turns cramming into the booth which is not much larger than one person. But at least we could broadcast in a controlled environment. When we have to call in our reports from outside the booth, in the general press area, a lot of extraneous background noise - including cursing and expletives - find their way into our newscasts. But, because of overcrowding I have done many broadcasts sitting on the floor, outside the booth. I coexisted with the White House rats and roaches. BBC television even featured a brief segment on me doing my broadcast this way. But, it is better to broadcast from inside the White House, regardless of the circumstances; than to be exiled across the street from the Oval Office. There is a move to do that to us, and we have been fighting it for years.

Despite that rough patch, relations between the White House press corps and the staff improved dramatically in the Clinton years, especially since President Clinton replaced Dee Dee Myers and hired the brilliant and affable Mike McCurry. Mike was well respected and loved by most of the press corps. In fact, he often had us eating out of his hands.

There were many adversarial moments - especially during the tense investigations into Clinton sex scandals, "White Water" investments, or campaign finance violations. But the tension was cleverly alleviated by parties thrown by the White House, to show the press corps they also believe we are human and deserve a bit of respect too. And, Mike would pull a funny trick, like starting the briefing with a paper bag over his head, to honor the helpful "anonymous source" who provides us with even more spin control on a topic, to put it in the best light for the White House. Mike became disillusioned by the sex scandals, and wanted to move out to private life and more time with his family. He was succeeded by Joe Lockhart, who was also professional and cooperative to work with, but lacked the affable humor of McCurry.

The "kiddie corps" which toiled in the Clinton press office also developed a greater respect for us, as they learned about our backgrounds, saw how hard we work, and gained a bit of historical perspective. Besides, they were no longer "kiddies," having matured immensely in their important and demanding jobs. The relations continued to improve, although there was always an adversarial element. After all, our job is to probe, question, and keep them on their toes.

The Clinton White House was followed by the George W. Bush Administration. That entire press organization was superb – headed by Ari Fleischer and Scott McClellan. The press secretaries treated all the members of the press with patience and respect – even those of us who could not spend a million dollars a year on a travel budget. Ari and Scott were especially good about giving me historic answers, which created genuine news, in response to some of my questions. Scott later broke with the Bush Administration, writing a "tell all" book. He should have had the guts to do so before. He was followed to the podium by Tony Snow, a much beloved press secretary, political commentator, and musician. Most of us loved him on a personal level, even if we did not agree with his politics. He died a tragic death from colon cancer. Thousands of us attended his funeral, and even the biggest among us sobbed most of the time. Tony was followed to the podium by his sharp, organized, and beautiful deputy, Dana Perino. She did a remarkable job, and is still around giving speeches and political commentary on Fox TV.

Too bad I could not help change policy, and avert the Iraqi War in the Bush Administration. I did try, by asking several times whether the United States could really afford a guns and butter economy. They assured me it could. In the end, they were wrong and I was right. The world economy is in chaos, terrorism tears apart Iraq and Afghanistan, Iran and North Korea are menacing nuclear states, there is no peace between Israel and the Palestinians, and there is great suffering throughout the world. Terrorists such as the Islamic State and Al Qaeda threaten the world.

The Bush White House press office gave equal time to some of the more controversial and obnoxious reporters, who use the televised briefings to promote their own agendas or causes. That causes great embarrassment in the press corps but, with freedom of speech, we cannot shut them out unless they pose a security hazard.

The infrequent news conferences with President Bush were another story. They were controlled, managed, and elitist. Only the wealthy and powerful reporters were called on a routine bases. If there was time left over President Bush recognized reporters from a particular minority group (women, radio, or ethnic) which he was trying to impress. The President did not realize many of us reach millions of listeners or readers – if we were not with the big traditional groups, we did not count. It did no good to raise hands, call out "Mr. President", or establish eye contact, as I did many times. Those well-established procedures elicited a withering glare, a snide comment, or a total attempt to ignore the reporter.

In addition, many of the news conferences were announced with short notice, causing reporters to risk life and limb to scramble to the White House through rush hour traffic, fight to get a parking space, run blocks to the White House, and then hope to get a seat. After all that, we were not even called in. Most news conferences consisted of two or three taken questions to the White House "pool" at the tail end of another event. Again, they were only to the top of the pack. These practices did not make for warm and fuzzy relations with the press corps, and that disappointment was communicated to readers or listeners. It did not create a residue of good will for the White House to draw on during the many times of crises. Sadly, the Obama Administration has followed many of the same practices. I guess I would do the same if I were President.

For me as well, the learning process continues, but I try my best to curb any tendencies to become arrogant, bored, or overconfident - all of which, regardless of one's profession, can lead to ruin. Besides, with the reductions in the news business, insecurity, rather than assurance, appears to rule the day. This does not help, in a profession that is traditionally dominated by neurotics! I find fulfillment covering the continually shifting diplomatic and political scenes in the United States and in the countries I report to. Occasionally, funny experiences break into the landscape, although some would argue that the whole political process is a joke.

One occasion that stands out in distant memory is the time I rushed to the White House in a teeming rainstorm to cover the brutal Prime Minister of Zimbabwe, Robert Mugabe. (He went onto become a viscous, blood-thirsty despot, who will not be invited to the White House again). I was wearing sandals, which rapidly became drenched in the downpour. At the White House, we were ushered into the East Room for departure speeches, and I found myself in the front row of the press area. I took off my rain-soaked shoes and stood barefoot, right in front of the President, the Secretary of State, the Prime Minister, and other top officials of both nations. Some of the Africans stared at me in confusion, no doubt wondering if they were witnessing a strange American custom which they should follow. They were reassured when President Reagan and Secretary of State Shultz kept their own shoes on.

Another joyous occasion was my meeting with Nelson Mandela, during his first Washington news conference as President of South Africa. When I introduced myself, he came down from the podium, hugged me, and said, "Connie Lawn, I have always wanted to meet you. But, you are not as big as I thought you were!" To widespread laughter, he recounted how he listened to me throughout his hard years in prison.

At that time, he told me, my broadcasts brought hope to him and to his fellow members of the struggle.

All this is by way of illustrating the lesson I hope my readers have learned from these pages - namely, that you too can someday stand barefoot at the White House, if you really want to. You can find a fulfilling and often exciting career in journalism or in any other field, if you work hard enough at it. You may have to go about it in unorthodox ways, but you don't necessarily have to be a superstar, or be employed by a big corporation to do well in this profession. You also have to be flexible and change your style. For me, I am delighted to do more live, interactive "talk-backs" and less static reporting, (although I do love my news stories.)

Reporting lectures down to a radio or TV listener; talk - back shares the microphone with him and her. I remember my children once asking, "Mommy, why do you always sound so angry on the phone when you broadcast? And, my dogs used to leave the room, thinking I was yelling at them. But, that was the old, bossy, big - voice sound of yesteryear, as opposed to the more intimate and friendly sound of today. (Except for the screaming matches on some t.v. and radio shows). The warmer changes suit my personality, where I am often told I sound best when I do not hide the smile in my voice. After all, my nickname was "smiley" as a kid - no point in hiding my personality!

A few words of advice about this profession: first, try to avoid bosses or colleagues who are unscrupulous or exceptionally moody. There seem to be more of them in the creative fields than anywhere else. Such individuals will only cause you grief. You may please them one minute, only to find that they hate you the next. Fire them, before they fire you, and find someplace else to work. Always be true to your principles, and don't take the fall for them!

Remember that everyone is special, and everyone is unique. If you don't find your niche in one place, you'll find it in another. Don't ever give up, and don't get discouraged. The painful moments will soon pass, if you learn how to translate defeat into victory. You might get fired a lot, but that's part of the business, at least in the United States. Even Presidents and Prime Ministers get fired, so if it happens to you, you'll be in good company. If you're a good reporter, you'll probably outlast them all. I have known and covered a lot of very powerful figures in my day, many of whom are now either dead or far from the centers of power they once occupied.

Whatever you do, in any profession, remain aware of your own importance, and keep trying. We are all unique and have the potential to make something special of our lives. It may be necessary to employ unorthodox methods, take risks, and make mistakes. But, we can find our niche, with perseverance and determination.

Also remember that, like me, you'll probably make many mistakes along the way. You are never too old to be naive and to trust someone who is not worthy of your faith and respect. All of us - even the world's leaders - make our share of mistakes. Just keep plugging away, dare to be a bit different from the masses if you can, and, most of all, have fun!

Parkinson Disease and a Queen's Honour

As I write these updates, there have been major changes in my life. At the age of 65 I was diagnosed with Parkinson Disease. It is debilitating, and it robbed me of my radio career. It is hard to broadcast when you sound sick and weak. It is hard to walk, and I get exhausted easily. As the disease gets worse, it becomes difficult to move, swallow, and perform many functions. The pain is intense. I do not know if I can safely ski or drive again. But we all have something. My beloved sister Margo died of cancer at 39 and that is far worse.

As I aged, people were nicer to me and honored me in several ways. I am overwhelmed by New Zealand. I was on the Queen's Honours List, and given a gold medal for service to New Zealand. The titles are honorary, but significant. This is in addition to the Life Time Achievement Award given to me by the National Press Club of New

Zealand, and the champion race horse named "Connie Lawn." Many thanks to a wonderful country!

I hope you enjoyed reading this book. If you want to talk to me about it, phone me, or contact me on the Internet at connielawn@aol.com. Please do so, and tell me if this book helped you in your own career!

Connie Lawn

Washington, D.C.

CPSIA information can be obtained at www.ICGtesting.com
Printed in the USA
BVOW01s1727190315

392473BV00001B/1/P

9 781491 753279